FREE Study Skills DVD Offer

Dear Customer,

Thank you for your purchase from Mometrix! We consider it an honor and privilege that you have purchased our product and want to ensure your satisfaction.

As a way of showing our appreciation and to help us better serve you, we have developed a Study Skills DVD that we would like to give you for FREE. **This DVD covers our "best practices" for studying for your exam, from using our study materials to preparing for the day of the test.**

All that we ask is that you email us your feedback that would describe your experience so far with our product. Good, bad or indifferent, we want to know what you think!

To get your **FREE Study Skills DVD**, email freedvd@mometrix.com with "FREE STUDY SKILLS DVD" in the subject line and the following information in the body of the email:

a. The name of the product you purchased.

b. Your product rating on a scale of 1–5, with 5 being the highest rating.

c. Your feedback. It can be long, short, or anything in-between, just your impressions and experience so far with our product. Good feedback might include how our study material met your needs and will highlight features of the product that you found helpful.

d. Your full name and shipping address where you would like us to send your free DVD.

If you have any questions or concerns, please don't hesitate to contact me directly.

Thanks again!

Sincerely,

Jay Willis
Vice President
jay.willis@mometrix.com
1-800-673-8175

HSPT®

SECRETS

Study Guide

Your Key to Exam Success

HSPT Exam Review for the
High School Placement Test

Published by

Mometrix Test Preparation

HSPT Exam Secrets Test Prep Team

Written and edited by the HSPT Exam Secrets Test Prep Staff

Printed in the United States of America

This paper meets the requirements of ANSI/NISO Z39.48-1992 (Permanence of Paper).

ISBN 13: 978-1-60971-867-1
ISBN 10: 1-60971-867-4

Dear Future Exam Success Story:

Congratulations on your purchase of our study guide. Our goal in writing our study guide was to cover the content on the test, as well as provide insight into typical test taking mistakes and how to overcome them.

Standardized tests are a key component of being successful, which only increases the importance of doing well in the high-pressure high-stakes environment of test day. How well you do on this test will have a significant impact on your future- and we have the research and practical advice to help you execute on test day.

The product you're reading now is designed to exploit weaknesses in the test itself, and help you avoid the most common errors test takers frequently make.

How to use this study guide

We don't want to waste your time. Our study guide is fast-paced and fluff-free. We suggest going through it a number of times, as repetition is an important part of learning new information and concepts.

First, read through the study guide completely to get a feel for the content and organization. Read the general success strategies first, and then proceed to the content sections. Each tip has been carefully selected for its effectiveness.

Second, read through the study guide again, and take notes in the margins and highlight those sections where you may have a particular weakness.

Finally, bring the manual with you on test day and study it before the exam begins.

Your success is our success

We would be delighted to hear about your success. Send us an email and tell us your story. Thanks for your business and we wish you continued success-

Sincerely,

Mometrix Test Preparation Team

Need more help? Check out our flashcards at: http://MometrixFlashcards.com/HSPT

TABLE OF CONTENTS

TOP 20 TEST TAKING TIPS **1**

VERBAL SKILLS TEST **2**

Synonyms and Antonyms 2
Analogies 4
Logic and Verbal Classification 6

READING COMPREHENSION TEST **8**

Comprehension Skills 8
Critical Comprehension 13
Vocabulary 17

LANGUAGE SKILLS TEST **19**

Grammar Review 19
Punctuation 26
Capitalization 31
Improving Sentences and Paragraphs 32
Spelling 45
Paragraph Development 51

MATHEMATICS AND QUANTITATIVE SKILLS TEST **58**

Numbers and Operations 58
Algebra 70
Geometry and Measurement 77
Measurement 89
Statistics and Probability 100

PRACTICE TEST **108**

Verbal 108
Quantitative 116
Reading 126
Mathematics 140
Language 153

ANSWERS AND EXPLANATIONS **165**

Verbal Skills 165
Quantitative Skills 169
Reading Comprehension Skills 175
Mathematics Skills 179
Language 187

SECRET KEY #1 – TIME IS YOUR GREATEST ENEMY **193**

SECRET KEY #2 – GUESSING IS NOT GUESSWORK **195**

Monkeys Take the HSPT 195
Success Strategy #2 196
Specific Guessing Techniques 197
Summary 197

SECRET KEY #3 – PRACTICE SMARTER, NOT HARDER **198**

Success Strategy #3 198

SECRET KEY #4 – PREPARE, DON'T PROCRASTINATE **199**

SECRET KEY #5 – TEST YOURSELF **200**
Success Strategy #5 200
GENERAL STRATEGIES **201**
SPECIAL REPORT: HOW TO OVERCOME TEST ANXIETY **206**
Lack of Preparation 206
Physical Signals 207
Nervousness 207
Study Steps 209
Helpful Techniques 210
ADDITIONAL BONUS MATERIAL **215**

Top 20 Test Taking Tips

1. Carefully follow all the test registration procedures
2. Know the test directions, duration, topics, question types, how many questions
3. Setup a flexible study schedule at least 3-4 weeks before test day
4. Study during the time of day you are most alert, relaxed, and stress free
5. Maximize your learning style; visual learner use visual study aids, auditory learner use auditory study aids
6. Focus on your weakest knowledge base
7. Find a study partner to review with and help clarify questions
8. Practice, practice, practice
9. Get a good night's sleep; don't try to cram the night before the test
10. Eat a well balanced meal
11. Know the exact physical location of the testing site; drive the route to the site prior to test day
12. Bring a set of ear plugs; the testing center could be noisy
13. Wear comfortable, loose fitting, layered clothing to the testing center; prepare for it to be either cold or hot during the test
14. Bring at least 2 current forms of ID to the testing center
15. Arrive to the test early; be prepared to wait and be patient
16. Eliminate the obviously wrong answer choices, then guess the first remaining choice
17. Pace yourself; don't rush, but keep working and move on if you get stuck
18. Maintain a positive attitude even if the test is going poorly
19. Keep your first answer unless you are positive it is wrong
20. Check your work, don't make a careless mistake

Verbal Skills Test

Synonyms and Antonyms

When you understand how words relate to each other, you will discover more in a passage. This is explained by understanding **synonyms** (e.g., words that mean the same thing) and **antonyms** (e.g., words that mean the opposite of one another). As an example, *dry* and *arid* are synonyms, and *dry* and *wet* are antonyms. There are many pairs of words in English that can be considered synonyms, despite having slightly different definitions. For instance, the words *friendly* and *collegial* can both be used to describe a warm interpersonal relationship, and one would be correct to call them synonyms. However, *collegial* (kin to *colleague*) is often used in reference to professional or academic relationships, and *friendly* has no such connotation. If the difference between the two words is too great, then they should not be called synonyms. *Hot* and *warm* are not synonyms because their meanings are too distinct. A good way to determine whether two words are synonyms is to substitute one word for the other word and verify that the meaning of the sentence has not changed. Substituting *warm* for *hot* in a sentence would convey a different meaning. Although warm and hot may seem close in meaning, warm generally means that the temperature is moderate, and hot generally means that the temperature is excessively high.

Antonyms are words with opposite meanings. *Light* and *dark*, *up* and *down*, *right* and *left*, *good* and *bad*: these are all sets of antonyms. Be careful to distinguish between antonyms and pairs of words that are simply different. *Black* and *gray*, for instance, are not antonyms because gray is not the opposite of black. *Black* and *white*, on the other hand, are antonyms. Not every word has an antonym. For instance, many nouns do not: What would be the antonym of chair? During your exam, the questions related to antonyms are more likely to concern adjectives. You will recall that adjectives are words that describe a noun. Some common adjectives include *purple*, *fast*, *skinny*, and *sweet*. From those four adjectives, *purple* is the item that lacks a group of obvious antonyms.

> ➢ **Review Video:** Synonyms and Antonyms
> *Visit* ***mometrix.com/academy*** *and enter* ***Code:*** **105612**

Synonym and Antonym Examples

For this section, you will have one word and four choices for a synonym or antonym of that word. Before you look at the choices, try to think of a few words that could be a synonym or antonym for your question. Then, check the choices for a synonym or antonym of the question. Some words may seem close to the question, but you are looking for the best choice. So, don't let your first reaction be your final decision.

Example 1
Insatiable most nearly means:

A. Compensated
B. Content
C. Fulfilled
D. Unsatisfied

Example 2
Adherent means the opposite of:

A. Antagonist
B. Disciple
C. Piquant
D. Submissive

Example 3
Protrude most nearly means:

A. Contract
B. Evocative
C. Secede
D. Swell

Example 4
Unkempt means the opposite of:

A. Disorder
B. Flaunt
C. Unblemished
D. Volatile

Answers
Example 1: D, Unsatisfied (Synonym)
Example 2: A, Antagonist (Antonym)
Example 3: D, Swell (Synonym)
Example 4: C, Unblemished (Antonym)

Analogies

Determine the Relationship

As you try to decide on how the words in question are connected, don't jump to understand the meaning of the words. Instead, see if you can find the relationship between the two words. To understand the relationship, you can start by creating a sentence that links the two words and puts them into perspective. At first, try to use a simple sentence to find a connection. Then, go through each answer choice and replace the words in the answer choices with the parts of your simple sentence. Depending on the question, you may need to make changes to your sentence to make it more specific.
Example:
Wood is to fire as

Simple Sentence: *Wood* feeds a *fire* as

Wood is to fire as

A. Farmer is to cow
B. Gasoline is to engine

Using the simple sentence, you would state "Farmer feeds a cow" which is correct. Yet, the next answer choice "Gasoline feeds an engine" is also true. So which is the correct answer? With this simple sentence, we need to be more specific.

Specific Sentences: "Wood feeds a fire and is consumed" / "Wood is burned in a fire"

These specific sentences show that answer choice (A) is incorrect and answer choice (B) is clearly correct. With the specific sentences, you have "Gasoline feeds an engine and is consumed" is correct. Also, "Farmer feeds a cow and is consumed" is clearly incorrect. If your simple sentence seems correct with more than one answer choice, then keep making changes until only one answer choice makes sense.

> **Review Video: Determine the Relationship**
> ***Visit mometrix.com/academy and enter Code:* 919115**

Eliminating Similarities

This method works well in the Analogies section and the Synonyms/Antonyms section. You can start by looking over the answer choices and see what clues they provide. If there are any common relationships between the pairs of terms, then those answer choices have to be wrong.
Example:
Tough is to rugged as

A. Soft is to hard
B. Clear is to foggy
C. Inhale is to exhale
D. Rigid is to taut

In this example, tough and rugged are synonyms. Also, the first three answer choices are antonyms. You may not realize that taut and rigid are synonyms. However, it has to be correct. The reason is that you know the other answer choices all had the same relationship of being antonyms.

Word Types

Example:
Gardener is to hedge as
A. Wind is to rock
B. Woodcarver is to stick

In this example, you could start with a simple sentence of "Gardener cuts away at hedges." Now, both answer choices seem correct with this sentence. For choice (A), you can say that "Wind cuts away at rocks" due to erosion. For choice (B), you can say that a "Woodcarver cuts away at sticks." The difference is that a gardener is a person, and a woodcarver is a person. However, the wind is a thing which makes answer choice (B) correct.

Face Value

When you are not sure about an answer, you should try to accept the problem at face value. Don't read too much into it. These problems will not ask you to make impossible comparisons. Truly, the SSAT test writers are not trying to throw you off with cheap tricks. If you have to make a stretch of the question to make a connection between the two terms, then you should start over and find another relationship. Don't make the problem more difficult. These are normal questions with differences in difficulty. Sometimes the terms that go together and their relationships may not be very clear. So, you will want to read over the question and answer choices carefully.
Example:
Odor is to smell as flavor is to
A. believe
B. know
C. feel
D. taste

Would a flavor be "known", "felt", "tasted", or "believed"? The analogy is about a synonym. So, answer choice D which is "taste" is a synonym of flavor and is the best answer.

Read Carefully

To understand the analogies, you need to read the terms and answer choices carefully. You can miss the question because you misread the terms. Each question here has only a few words, so you can spend time reading them carefully. Yet, you cannot forget your time limit of the section. So, don't spend too much time on one question. Just focus on reading carefully and be sure to read all of the choices. You may find an answer choice that seems correct. Yet, when you finish reading over the choices, you may find a better choice.

Logic and Verbal Classification

Logic

These questions will provide you with three statements and then ask you that if the first two are true, what must the third statement be, whether true, false, or uncertain.

Look for the Obvious
Usually the nature of the first two statements will give a clue about what a truthful third statement will look like. Example: John runs faster than Mary. Bob runs faster than John.

Ask yourself what is probably going to be the true statement that you should expect to see as the third statement. It will likely be "Bob runs faster than Mary". Both of the given statements seem to be leading up to that statement.

If you expect that to be the third statement, then you can quickly look at the third statement and see if you are correct. If so, you know the third statement is true. If not, you will have to determine whether or not it is false or uncertain.

Watch for Inversions
Not only does the statement "Bob runs faster than Mary" seem to be a likely possibility, but also the inverse, which is "Mary runs slower than Bob".

Don't get caught off guard and think that your predicted answer isn't the third statement. It's inverse, which is equally true, may be provided.

Example 1: John throws faster pitches than Kyle. Greg throws faster pitches than John. Kyle throws faster pitches than Greg. If the first two statements are true, then the third is:

a. True
b. False
c. Uncertain
d. An opinion

Example 2: Allen sent in his taxes one day after Phil. Phil sent in his taxes before Blake. Blake sent in his taxes after Allen. If the first two statements are true, then the third is:

a. True
b. False
c. Uncertain
d. A contradiction

Answers
Example 1: B: We can diagram the first two sentences as follows: John > Kyle and Greg > John. In other words, Greg throws faster pitches than John and Kyle. If those statements are true, then the third statement is certainly false.

Example 2: C: We can diagram this sentence as follows: Phil > Allen; Phil > Blake. In other words, Phil sent in his taxes before Allen and before Blake. We do not have enough information to determine whether Allen > Blake is true.

Verbal Classification

These questions will give you a list of four words and ask you to determine which does not belong with the others.

Find the Common Ground

The common ground is the characteristics that all of the words have in common. All but one that is. Once you've identified the common characteristic shared by three of the words, you know which is your correct answer, because it does not share that same characteristic.

Example:

a. bass
b. salmon
c. moose
d. tuna

In the example above, answer choices a, b, and d all share one thing in common. They are fish. The lone exception is answer choice c, which is moose and is not a species of fish.

Watch out for Generic Types

Usually the answer choices will provide specific examples of a certain thing. If the more generic name of the common characteristic is given, it is usually wrong.

Example:

a. bass
b. salmon
c. fish
d. tuna

At first glance these all seem the same. They are all fish right? Wrong. Three of them are species of fish. Answer choice c, "fish" is not a species of fish, but is rather the name of the category the other answer choices fall into.

Example:

a. football
b. basketball
c. tennis
d. sports

Notice the similarity in examples. Here again all four answer choices seem similar. The first three are types of sporting activities. The last is the name of the category the others fall into. Choice d does *not* belong.

Comprehension Skills

Context and Literal Comprehension

Learning new words is an important part of comprehending and integrating unfamiliar information. When a reader encounters a new word, he can stop and find it in the dictionary or the glossary of terms but sometimes those reference tools aren't readily available or using them at the moment is impractical (e.g., during a test). Furthermore, most readers are usually not willing to take the time. Another way to determine the meaning of a word is by considering the context in which it is being used. These indirect learning hints are called context clues. They include definitions, descriptions, examples, and restatements. Because most words are learned by listening to conversations, people use this tool all the time even if they do it unconsciously. But to be effective in written text, context clues must be used judiciously because the unfamiliar word may have several subtle variations, and therefore the context clues could be misinterpreted.

Context refers to how a word is used in a sentence. Identifying context can help determine the definition of unknown words. There are different contextual clues such as definition, description, example, comparison, and contrast. The following are examples:

- Definition: the unknown word is clearly defined by the previous words. – "When he was painting, his instrument was a ___." (paintbrush)
- Description: the unknown word is described by the previous words. – "I was hot, tired, and thirsty; I was ___." (dehydrated)
- Example: the unknown word is part of a series of examples. – "Water, soda, and ___ were the offered beverages." (coffee)
- Comparison: the unknown word is compared to another word. – "Barney is agreeable and happy like his ___ parents." (positive)
- Contrast: the unknown word is contrasted with another word. – "I prefer cold weather to ___ conditions." (hot)

> **Review Video: Context**
> *Visit* ***mometrix.com/academy*** *and enter* **Code: 613660**

On standardized tests, as well as in everyday life, you may be faced with words that you are not familiar with. In most cases, the definition of an unknown word can be derived from context clues. The term "context clues" refers to the ways or manner in which a word is used. When reading a passage, students should carefully examine the unfamiliar word and the words and sentences that surround it. The writer may have provided a definition in parentheses following the word, or the writer may have provided a synonym. Synonyms are useful because they offer a common substitute for the unfamiliar word. Also, the author may have provided an antonym, or opposite, for the unfamiliar word. Finally, a context clue might be found in the prior or later restatement of the idea that contained the word, and sometimes the writer may have even provided a detailed explanation of the unfamiliar word.

Literal Comprehension

A reader should always be drawing conclusions from the text. Sometimes conclusions are implied from written information, and other times the information is **stated directly** within the passage. One should always aim to draw conclusions from information stated within a passage, rather than to draw them from mere implications. At times an author may provide some information and then describe a counterargument. Readers should be alert for direct statements that are subsequently rejected or weakened by the author. Furthermore, you should always read through the entire passage before drawing conclusions. Many readers are trained to expect the author's conclusions at either the beginning or the end of the passage, but many texts do not adhere to this format.

Inferential Comprehension

Drawing conclusions from information implied within a passage requires confidence on the part of the reader. **Implications** are things that the author does not state directly, but readers can assume based on what the author does say. Consider the following passage: *I stepped outside and opened my umbrella. By the time I got to work, the cuffs of my pants were soaked.* The author never states that it is raining, but this fact is clearly implied. Conclusions based on implication must be well supported by the text. In order to draw a solid conclusion, readers should have multiple pieces of evidence. If readers have only one piece, they must be assured that there is no other possible explanation than their conclusion. A good reader will be able to draw many conclusions from information implied by the text which will be a great help in the exam.

Readers are often required to understand a text that claims and suggests ideas without stating them directly. An **inference** is a piece of information that is implied but not written outright by the author. For instance, consider the following sentence: *After the final out of the inning, the fans were filled with joy and rushed the field.* From this sentence, a reader can infer that the fans were watching a baseball game and their team won the game. Readers should take great care to avoid using information beyond the provided passage before making inferences. As you practice with drawing inferences, you will find that they require concentration and attention.

➢ **Review Video:** Inference
Visit ***mometrix.com/academy*** *and enter* ***Code:*** **379203**

One of the most important skills in reading comprehension is the identification of **topics** and **main ideas.** There is a subtle difference between these two features. The topic is the subject of a text (i.e., what the text is all about). The main idea, on the other hand, is the most important point being made by the author. The topic is usually expressed in a few words at the most while the main idea often needs a full sentence to be completely defined. As an example, a short passage might have the topic of penguins and the main idea could be written as *Penguins are different from other birds in many ways.* In most nonfiction writing, the topic and the main idea will be stated directly and often appear in a sentence at the very beginning or end of the text. When being tested on an understanding of the author's topic, you may be able to skim the passage for the general idea, by reading only the first sentence of each paragraph. A body paragraph's first sentence is often--but not always--the main topic sentence which gives you a summary of the content in the paragraph.

However, there are cases in which the reader must figure out an unstated topic or main idea. In these instances, you must read every sentence of the text and try to come up with an overarching idea that is supported by each of those sentences.

Note: A thesis statement should not be confused with the main idea of the passage. While the main idea gives a brief, general summary of a text, the thesis statement provides a specific perspective on an issue that the author supports with evidence.

> ➢ **Review Video:** Topics and Main Ideas
> *Visit* ***mometrix.com/academy*** *and enter* ***Code:*** **691033**

Supporting details provide evidence and backing for the main point. In order to show that a main idea is correct, or valid, authors add details that prove their point. All texts contain details, but they are only classified as supporting details when they serve to reinforce some larger point. Supporting details are most commonly found in informative and persuasive texts. In some cases, they will be clearly indicated with terms like *for example* or *for instance*, or they will be enumerated with terms like *first*, *second*, and *last*. However, you need to be prepared for texts that do not contain those indicators. As a reader, you should consider whether the author's supporting details really back up his or her main point. Supporting details can be factual and correct, yet they may not be relevant to the author's point. Conversely, supporting details can seem pertinent, but they can be ineffective because they are based on opinion or assertions that cannot be proven.

> ➢ **Review Video:** Supporting Details
> *Visit* ***mometrix.com/academy*** *and enter* ***Code:*** **396297**

An example of a main idea is: *Giraffes live in the Serengeti of Africa*. A supporting detail about giraffes could be: *A giraffe in this region benefits from a long neck by reaching twigs and leaves on tall trees.* The main idea gives the general idea that the text is about giraffes. The supporting detail gives a specific fact about how the giraffes eat.

Readers must often **draw conclusions** about the information they have read. When asked for a *conclusion* that may be drawn, look for critical "hedge" phrases, such as *likely, may, can, will often*, among many others. When you are being tested on this knowledge, remember the question that writers insert into these hedge phrases to cover every possibility. Often an answer will be wrong simply because there is no room for exception. Extreme positive or negative answers (such as always or never) are usually not correct. The reader should not use any outside knowledge that is not gathered from the passage to answer the related questions. Correct answers can be derived straight from the passage.

Reasoning

Inductive and Deductive Reasoning

Inductive reasoning is a method of logic that uses particulars to draw a general conclusion. The inductive reasoning process starts with data. For example, if someone observes for several months that zebras have stripes, then they may conclude that all zebras in existence have stripes. This individual's conclusion (e.g., that all zebras in existence have stripes) is not considered definite since every zebra in existence has not been observed. Unless every piece of data is examined, conclusions are based on probabilities. As another example, inductive reasoning is used to make inferences about the universe. The entire universe has not been examined, but inferences can be made based on observations about what has been examined from the universe. These inferences may be proven false when more data is available, but they are valid at the time they are made from observable data.

Deductive reasoning involves the use of general facts or premises to come to a specific conclusion. For example: *Susan is a sophomore in high school*, and *all sophomores take geometry*. Thus, one can infer that *Susan takes geometry*. The word *all* does not allow for exceptions. If all sophomores take geometry, then the assertion that Susan has a geometry class is a logical conclusion. As an intelligent reader, you need to recognize inductive and deductive reasoning so you can follow the line of an argument and determine if the inference or conclusion is valid.

> ➢ **Review Video:** Inductive and Deductive Reasoning
> *Visit **mometrix.com/academy** and enter **Code:*** **507014**

Logical Fallacies

A logical fallacy is a failure of reasoning. As a reader, you want to recognize logical fallacies because they diminish the value of the author's message. The four most common logical fallacies in writing are the false analogy, circular reasoning, false dichotomy, and overgeneralization.

In a **false analogy**, the author suggests that two things are similar when they are different. This fallacy is committed when the author is attempting to convince readers that something unknown is like something relatively familiar. The author takes advantage of the reader's ignorance to make this false comparison. One example might be the following statement: *Failing to tip a waitress is like stealing money out of somebody's wallet*. To compare stingy diners with thieves is a false analogy. While failing to tip is considered very rude, people are not arrested for their failure to tip as they would be for stealing money from someone's wallet.

> ➢ **Review Video:** False Analogy
> *Visit **mometrix.com/academy** and enter **Code:*** **865045**

Circular reasoning is a difficult logical fallacy to identify because the fallacy is typically hidden behind dense language and complicated sentences. Reasoning is described as circular when the argument offers no support for assertions other than restating them in different words. Put another way, a circular argument refers to itself as evidence of truth. A simple example of a circular argument is when a person uses a word to define itself, such as: *Niceness is the state of being nice*. If you do not know what *nice* means, then this definition will not be very useful. In a text, circular reasoning is more complex. For instance, an author may write: *Poverty is a problem for society because poverty creates trouble for people throughout the community*. Do you notice the redundancy within the statement that poverty is a problem because it creates trouble? When authors engage in circular reasoning, they either have not given sufficient thought to the argument, or they have not come up with any legitimate justifications for the argument.

> ➢ **Review Video:** Circular Reasoning
> *Visit **mometrix.com/academy** and enter **Code:*** **398925**

A common logical fallacy is the **false dichotomy**. With this logical fallacy, the author creates an artificial sense that there are only two possible options in a situation. This fallacy is common when the author has an agenda and wants to give the impression that his or her view is the only sensible one. A false dichotomy has the effect of limiting the reader's options and imagination. An example of a false dichotomy: *You need to go to the party with me, otherwise you'll just be bored at home*. The speaker suggests that the only other possibility besides being at the party is being bored at home. Of course, this is not a true statement. Since, one is able to be entertained at home or to go somewhere other than the party. When authors limit alternatives, you are always wise to ask whether they are being valid.

➢ **Review Video:** False Dichotomy
Visit ***mometrix.com/academy*** *and enter* ***Code:*** **484397**

Overgeneralization is a logical fallacy where the author makes a broad claim that cannot be proved or disproved. In most cases, overgeneralization occurs when authors want to create an illusion of authority, or when they are using sensational language to sway the opinion of the reader. For example: *Everybody knows that she is a terrible teacher.* In this sentence, the author makes an assumption that cannot be true. This kind of statement is made when the author wants to create the illusion of consensus when none exists. Perhaps most people have a negative view of the teacher but to say that *everybody* feels that way is an exaggeration. When you spot overgeneralization, you should become skeptical about the author's argument because the author may hide a weak or unsupported assertion behind authoritative language.

➢ **Review Video:** Overgeneralization
Visit ***mometrix.com/academy*** *and enter* ***Code:*** **367357**

When considering problems and solutions, the full range of possible options should be mentioned before recommending one solution above others. It is unfair to say that there are only two options, when there can be more options. When you are faced with a choice between a preferred option and a clearly inferior one, the author is committing the "either...or" fallacy. All reasonable alternatives should be included in the possible solutions.

Assumptions are claims that are taken to be true without proof. If a claim is controversial, proof should be provided to verify the assumption. When a claim is made that few would agree with, the writer is guilty of a *non sequitur* (i.e., "does not follow" in Latin) fallacy. So, any assumption that is subject to debate and cannot be accepted without supporting evidence is suspect.

Critical Comprehension

Purposes for Writing

In order to be an effective reader, one must pay attention to the author's **position** and purpose. Even those texts that seem objective and impartial, like textbooks, have a position and bias. Readers need to take these positions into account when considering the author's message. When an author uses emotional language or clearly favors one side of an argument, his or her position is clear. However, the author's position may be evident not only in what he or she writes, but also in what he or she doesn't write. In a normal setting, a reader would want to review some other texts on the same topic in order to develop a view of the author's position. If this was not possible, then you would want to acquire some background about the author. However, since you are in the middle of an exam and the only source of information is the text, you should look for language and argumentation that seems to indicate a particular stance on the subject.

> **Review Video:** Author's Position
> *Visit* ***mometrix.com/academy*** *and enter* ***Code:*** **478923**

Usually, identifying the **purpose** of an author is easier than identifying his or her position. In most cases, the author has no interest in hiding his or her purpose. A text that is meant to entertain, for instance, should be written to please the reader. Most narratives, or stories, are written to entertain, though they may also inform or persuade. Informative texts are easy to identify, while the most difficult purpose of a text to identify is persuasion because the author has an interest in making this purpose hard to detect. When a reader discovers that the author is trying to persuade, he or she should be skeptical of the argument. For this reason persuasive texts often try to establish an entertaining tone and hope to amuse the reader into agreement. On the other hand, an informative tone may be implemented to create an appearance of authority and objectivity.

An author's purpose is evident often in the organization of the text (e.g., section headings in bold font points to an informative text). However, you may not have such organization available to you in your exam. Instead, if the author makes his or her main idea clear from the beginning, then the likely purpose of the text is to inform. If the author begins by making a claim and provides various arguments to support that claim, then the purpose is probably to persuade. If the author tells a story or seems to want the attention of the reader more than to push a particular point or deliver information, then his or her purpose is most likely to entertain. As a reader, you must judge authors on how well they accomplish their purpose. In other words, you need to consider the type of passage (e.g., technical, persuasive, etc.) that the author has written and if the author has followed the requirements of the passage type.

> **Review Video:** Purpose of an Author
> *Visit* ***mometrix.com/academy*** *and enter* ***Code:*** **497555**

The author's purpose for writing will affect his or her writing style and the response of the reader. In a **persuasive essay**, the author is attempting to change the reader's mind or convince him or her of something that he or she did not believe previously. There are several identifying characteristics of persuasive writing. One is opinion presented as fact. When authors attempt to persuade readers, they often present their opinions as if they were fact. Readers must be on guard for statements that sound factual but which cannot be subjected to research, observation, or experiment. Another characteristic of persuasive writing is emotional language. An author will often try to play on the emotions of readers by appealing to their sympathy or sense of morality. When an author uses colorful or evocative language with the intent of arousing the reader's passions, then the author may be attempting to persuade. Finally, in many cases, a persuasive text will give an unfair explanation of opposing positions, if these positions are mentioned at all.

An informative text is written to educate and enlighten readers. Informative texts are almost always nonfiction and are rarely structured as a story. The intention of an informative text is to deliver information in the most comprehensible way. So, look for the structure of the text to be very clear. In an informative text, the thesis statement is one--or two--sentence(s) that normally appears at the end of the first paragraph. The author may use some colorful language, but he or she is likely to put more emphasis on clarity and precision. Informative essays do not typically appeal to the emotions. They often contain facts and figures and rarely include the opinion of the author; however, readers should remain aware of the possibility for a bias as those facts are presented. Sometimes a persuasive essay can resemble an informative essay, especially if the author maintains an even tone and presents his or her views as if they were established fact.

The success or failure of an author's intent to **entertain** is determined by those who read the author's work. Entertaining texts may be either fiction or nonfiction, and they may describe real or imagined people, places, and events. Entertaining texts are often narratives or poems. A text that is written to entertain is likely to contain colorful language that engages the imagination and the emotions. Such writing often features a great deal of figurative language, which typically enlivens the subject matter with images and analogies.

Though an entertaining text is not usually written to persuade or inform, authors may accomplish both of these tasks in their work. An entertaining text may appeal to the reader's emotions and cause him or her to think differently about a particular subject. In any case, entertaining texts tend to showcase the personality of the author more than other types of writing.

When an author intends to **express feelings,** he or she may use expressive and bold language. An author may write with emotion for any number of reasons. Sometimes, authors will express feelings because they are describing a personal situation of great pain or happiness. In other situations, authors will attempt to persuade the reader and will use emotion to stir up the passions. This kind of expression is easy to identify when the writer uses phrases like *I felt* and *I sense*. However, readers may find that the author will simply describe feelings without introducing them. As a reader, you must know the importance of recognizing when an author is expressing emotion and not to become overwhelmed by sympathy or passion. Readers should maintain some detachment so that they can still evaluate the strength of the author's argument or the quality of the writing.

In a sense, almost all writing is descriptive, insofar as an author seeks to describe events, ideas, or people to the reader. Some texts, however, are primarily concerned with **description**. A descriptive text focuses on a particular subject and attempts to depict the subject in a way that will be clear to readers. Descriptive texts contain many adjectives and adverbs (i.e., words that give shades of meaning and create a more detailed mental picture for the reader). A descriptive text fails when it is unclear to the reader. A descriptive text will certainly be informative, and the passage may be persuasive and entertaining as well.

As opposed to a main idea, themes are seldom expressed directly in a text and can be difficult to identify. A **theme** is an issue, an idea, or a question raised by the text. For instance, a theme of *Cinderella* (the Charles Perrault version) is perseverance as the title character serves her stepsisters and step-mother, and the prince seeks to find the girl with the missing slipper. A passage may have many themes, and you--as a dedicated reader--must take care to identify only themes that you are asked to find. One common characteristic of themes is that they raise more questions than they answer. In a good piece of fiction, authors are trying to elevate the reader's perspective and encourage him or her to consider the themes in a deeper way. In the process of reading, one can identify themes by constantly asking about the general issues that the text is addressing. A good way to evaluate an author's approach to a theme is to begin reading with a question in mind (e.g., How does this text approach the theme of love?) and to look for evidence in the text that addresses that question.

> **Review Video:** Theme
> *Visit* ***mometrix.com/academy*** *and enter* ***Code:*** **732074**

Comparison and Contrast

Authors will use different stylistic and writing devices to make their meaning clear for readers. One of those devices is comparison and contrast. When an author describes the ways in which two things are alike, he or she is **comparing** them. When the author describes the ways in which two things are different, he or she is **contrasting** them. The "compare and contrast" essay is one of the most common forms in nonfiction. These passages are often signaled with certain words: a comparison may have indicating terms such as *both*, *same*, *like*, *too*, and *as well*; while a contrast may have terms like *but*, *however*, *on the other hand*, *instead*, and *yet*. Of course, comparisons and contrasts may be implicit without using any such signaling language. A single sentence may both compare and contrast. Consider the sentence *Brian and Sheila love ice cream, but Brian prefers vanilla and Sheila prefers strawberry*. In one sentence, the author has described both a similarity (love of ice cream) and a difference (favorite flavor).

Opinions, Facts, and Predictions

Critical thinking skills are mastered through understanding various types of writing and the different purposes of authors in writing their passages. Every author writes for a purpose. When you understand their purpose and how they accomplish their goal, you will be able to analyze their writing and determine whether or not you agree with their conclusions.

Readers must always be conscious of the distinction between fact and opinion. A **fact** can be subjected to analysis and can be either proved or disproved. An **opinion**, on the other hand, is the author's personal thoughts or feelings which may not be alterable by research or evidence. If the author writes that the distance from New York to Boston is about two hundred miles, then he or she is stating a fact. If an author writes that New York is too crowded, then he or she is giving an opinion because there is no objective standard for overpopulation. An opinion may be indicated by words like *believe*, *think*, or *feel*. Readers must be aware that an opinion may be supported by facts. For instance, the author might give the population density of New York as a reason for an overcrowded population. An opinion supported by fact tends to be more convincing. On the other hand, when authors support their opinions with other opinions, readers should not be persuaded by the argument to any degree.

When you have an argumentative passage, you need to be sure that facts are presented to the reader from reliable sources. An opinion is what the author thinks about a given topic. An opinion is not common knowledge or proven by expert sources, instead the information is the personal beliefs and thoughts of the author. To distinguish between fact and opinion, a reader needs to consider the type of source that is presenting information, the information that backs-up a claim, and the author's motivation to have a certain point-of-view on a given topic. For example, if a panel of scientists has conducted multiple studies on the effectiveness of taking a certain vitamin, then the results are more likely to be factual than a company that is selling a vitamin and claims that taking the vitamin can produce positive effects. The company is motivated to sell their product, and the scientists are using the scientific method to prove a theory. Remember: if you find sentences that contain phrases such as "I think...", then the statement is an opinion.

> **Review Video:** Fact or Opinion
> *Visit* ***mometrix.com/academy*** *and enter* ***Code:*** **870899**

In their attempts to persuade, writers often make mistakes in their thinking patterns and writing choices. These patterns and choices are important to understand so you can make an informed decision. Every author has a point-of-view, but authors demonstrate a bias when they ignore reasonable counterarguments or distort opposing viewpoints. A bias is evident whenever the author is unfair or inaccurate in his or her presentation. Bias may be intentional or unintentional, and readers should be skeptical of the author's argument. Remember that a biased author may still be correct; however, the author will be correct in spite of his or her bias, not because of the bias. A **stereotype** is like a bias, yet a stereotype is applied specifically to a group or place. Stereotyping is considered to be particularly abhorrent because the practice promotes negative generalizations about people. Readers should be very cautious of authors who stereotype in their writing. These faulty assumptions typically reveal the author's ignorance and lack of curiosity.

> **Review Video:** Bias and Stereotype
> *Visit* ***mometrix.com/academy*** *and enter* ***Code:*** **456336**

When reading a good passage, readers are moved to engage actively in the text. One part of being an active reader involves making predictions. A **prediction** is a guess about what will happen next. Readers constantly make predictions based on what they have read and what they already know. Consider the following sentence: *Staring at the computer screen in shock, Kim blindly reached over for the brimming glass of water on the shelf to her side.* The sentence suggests that Kim is agitated, and that she is not looking at the glass that she is going to pick up. So, a reader might predict that Kim is going to knock over the glass. Of course, not every prediction will be accurate: perhaps Kim will pick the glass up cleanly. Nevertheless, the author has certainly created the expectation that the water might be spilled. Predictions are always subject to revision as the reader acquires more information.

> **Review Video:** Predictions
> *Visit* ***mometrix.com/academy*** *and enter* ***Code:*** **437248**

Test-taking tip: To respond to questions requiring future predictions, your answers should be based on evidence of past or present behavior.

Vocabulary

The **denotative** meaning of a word is the literal meaning. The **connotative** meaning goes beyond the denotative meaning to include the emotional reaction that a word may invoke. The connotative meaning often takes the denotative meaning a step further due to associations which the reader makes with the denotative meaning. Readers can differentiate between the denotative and connotative meanings by first recognizing how authors use each meaning. Most non-fiction, for example, is fact-based and authors do not use flowery, figurative language. The reader can assume that the writer is using the denotative meaning of words. In fiction, the author may use the connotative meaning. Readers can determine whether the author is using the denotative or connotative meaning of a word by implementing context clues.

> ➢ **Review Video:** Denotative and Connotative Meanings
> *Visit **mometrix.com/academy** and enter **Code:*** **736707**

Readers can use contrasts to define an unfamiliar word in context. In many sentences, the author will not describe the unfamiliar word directly; instead, he or she will describe the opposite of the unfamiliar word. Thus, you are provided with some information that will bring you closer to defining the word. Consider the following example: *Despite his intelligence, Hector's low brow and bad posture made him look obtuse.* The author writes that Hector's appearance does not convey intelligence. Therefore, *obtuse* must mean unintelligent. Here is another example: *Despite the horrible weather, we were beatific about our trip to Alaska*. The word *despite* indicates that the speaker's feelings were at odds with the weather. Since the weather is described as *horrible*, then *beatific* must mean something positive.

In some cases, there will be very few contextual clues to help a reader define the meaning of an unfamiliar word. When this happens, one strategy that readers may employ is **substitution**. A good reader will brainstorm some possible synonyms for the given word, and he or she will substitute these words into the sentence. If the sentence and the surrounding passage continue to make sense, then the substitution has revealed at least some information about the unfamiliar word. Consider the sentence: *Frank's admonition rang in her ears as she climbed the mountain.* A reader unfamiliar with *admonition* might come up with some substitutions like *vow, promise, advice, complaint*, or *compliment*. All of these words make general sense of the sentence though their meanings are diverse. The process has suggested; however, that an admonition is some sort of message. The substitution strategy is rarely able to pinpoint a precise definition, but this process can be effective as a last resort.

Occasionally, you will be able to define an unfamiliar word by looking at the descriptive words in the context. Consider the following sentence: *Fred dragged the recalcitrant boy kicking and screaming up the stairs.* The words *dragged, kicking*, and *screaming* all suggest that the boy does not want to go up the stairs. The reader may assume that *recalcitrant* means something like unwilling or protesting. In this example, an unfamiliar adjective was identified.

Additionally, using description to define an unfamiliar noun is a common practice compared to unfamiliar adjectives, as in this sentence: *Don's wrinkled frown and constantly shaking fist identified him as a curmudgeon of the first order.* Don is described as having a *wrinkled frown and constantly shaking fist* suggesting that a *curmudgeon* must be a grumpy man. Contrasts do not always provide detailed information about the unfamiliar word, but they at least give the reader some clues.

When a word has more than one meaning, readers can have difficulty with determining how the word is being used in a given sentence. For instance, the verb *cleave*, can mean either *join* or *separate*. When readers come upon this word, they will have to select the definition that makes the most sense. Consider the following sentence: *Hermione's knife cleaved the bread cleanly*. Since, a knife cannot join bread together, the word must indicate separation. A slightly more difficult example would be the sentence: *The birds cleaved together as they flew from the oak tree.* Immediately, the presence of the word *together* should suggest that in this sentence *cleave* is being used to mean *join*. Discovering the intent of a word with multiple meanings requires the same tricks as defining an unknown word: look for contextual clues and evaluate the substituted words.

Grammar Review

The Eight Parts of Speech

Nouns

When you talk about a person, place, thing, or idea, you are talking about nouns. The two main types of nouns are common and proper nouns. Also, nouns can be abstract (i.e., general) or concrete (i.e., specific).

Common nouns are the class or group of people, places, and things (Note: Do not capitalize common nouns). Examples of common nouns:
People: boy, girl, worker, manager
Places: school, bank, library, home
Things: dog, cat, truck, car

Proper nouns are the names of a specific person, place, or thing (Note: Capitalize all proper nouns). Examples of proper nouns:
People: Abraham Lincoln, George Washington, Martin Luther King, Jr.
Places: Los Angeles, California / New York / Asia
Things: Statue of Liberty, Earth*, Lincoln Memorial

*Note: When you talk about the planet that we live on, you capitalize *Earth*. When you mean the dirt, rocks, or land, you lowercase *earth*.

General nouns are the names of conditions or ideas. **Specific nouns** name people, places, and things that are understood by using your senses.

General nouns:
Condition: beauty, strength
Idea: truth, peace

Specific nouns:
People: baby, friend, father
Places: town, park, city hall
Things: rainbow, cough, apple, silk, gasoline

Collective nouns are the names for a person, place, or thing that may act as a whole. The following are examples of collective nouns: *class, company, dozen, group, herd, team,* and *public*.

Pronouns

Pronouns are words that are used to stand in for a noun. A pronoun may be grouped as personal, intensive, relative, interrogative, demonstrative, indefinite, and reciprocal.

Personal: Nominative is the case for nouns and pronouns that are the subject of a sentence. Objective is the case for nouns and pronouns that are an object in a sentence. Possessive is the case for nouns and pronouns that show possession or ownership.

Singular

	Nominative	**Objective**	**Possessive**
First Person	I	me	my, mine
Second Person	you	you	your, yours
Third Person	he, she, it	him, her, it	his, her, hers, its

Plural

	Nominative	**Objective**	**Possessive**
First Person	we	us	our, ours
Second Person	you	you	your, yours
Third Person	they	them	their, theirs

Intensive: I myself, you yourself, he himself, she herself, the (thing) itself, we ourselves, you yourselves, they themselves

Relative: which, who, whom, whose

Interrogative: what, which, who, whom, whose

Demonstrative: this, that, these, those

Indefinite: all, any, each, everyone, either/neither, one, some, several

Reciprocal: each other, one another

➢ **Review Video: Nouns and Pronouns**
*Visit **mometrix.com/academy** and enter **Code:*** **312073**

Verbs

If you want to write a sentence, then you need a verb in your sentence. Without a verb, you have no sentence. The verb of a sentence explains action or being. In other words, the verb shows the subject's movement or the movement that has been done to the subject.

Transitive and Intransitive Verbs

A transitive verb is a verb whose action (e.g., drive, run, jump) points to a receiver (e.g., car, dog, kangaroo). Intransitive verbs do not point to a receiver of an action. In other words, the action of the verb does not point to a subject or object.

Transitive: He plays the piano. | The piano was played by him.

Intransitive: He plays. | John writes well.

A dictionary will let you know whether a verb is transitive or intransitive. Some verbs can be transitive and intransitive.

Action Verbs and Linking Verbs

An action verb is a verb that shows what the subject is doing in a sentence. In other words, an action verb shows action. A sentence can be complete with one word: an action verb. Linking verbs are intransitive verbs that show a condition (i.e., the subject is described but does no action).

Linking verbs link the subject of a sentence to a noun or pronoun, or they link a subject with an adjective. You always need a verb if you want a complete sentence. However, linking verbs are not able to complete a sentence.

Common linking verbs include *appear, be, become, feel, grow, look, seem, smell, sound,* and *taste.* However, any verb that shows a condition and has a noun, pronoun, or adjective that describes the subject of a sentence is a linking verb.

Action: He sings. | Run! | Go! | I talk with him every day. | She reads.

Linking:
Incorrect: I am.
Correct: I am John. | I smell roses. | I feel tired.

Note: Some verbs are followed by words that look like prepositions, but they are a part of the verb and a part of the verb's meaning. These are known as phrasal verbs and examples include *call off, look up*, and *drop off.*

Voice

Transitive verbs come in active or passive voice. If the subject does an action or receives the action of the verb, then you will know whether a verb is active or passive. When the subject of the sentence is doing the action, the verb is active voice. When the subject receives the action, the verb is passive voice.

Active: Jon drew the picture. (The subject *Jon* is doing the action of *drawing a picture.*)

Passive: The picture is drawn by Jon. (The subject *picture* is receiving the action from Jon.)

Verb Tenses

A verb tense shows the different form of a verb to point to the time of an action. The present and past tense are shown by changing the verb's form. An action in the present *I talk* can change form for the past: *I talked.* However, for the other tenses, an auxiliary (i.e., helping) verb is needed to show the change in form. These helping verbs include *am, are, is* | *have, has, had* | *was, were, will* (or *shall*).

Present: I talk	Present perfect: I have talked
Past: I talked	Past perfect: I had talked
Future: I will talk	Future perfect: I will have talked

Present: The action happens at the current time.
Example: He *walks* to the store every morning.
To show that something is happening right now, use the progressive present tense: I *am walking.*

Past: The action happened in the past.
Example: He *walked* to the store an hour ago.

Future: The action is going to happen later.
Example: I *will walk* to the store tomorrow.

Present perfect: The action started in the past and continues into the present.
Example: I *have walked* to the store three times today.

Past perfect: The second action happened in the past. The first action came before the second.
Example: Before I walked to the store (Action 2), I *had walked* to the library (Action 1).

Future perfect: An action that uses the past and the future. In other words, the action is complete before a future moment.
Example: When she comes for the supplies (future moment), I *will have walked* to the store (action completed in the past).

Conjugating Verbs
When you need to change the form of a verb, you are conjugating a verb. The key parts of a verb are first person singular, present tense (dream); first person singular, past tense (dreamed); and the past participle (dreamed). Note: the past participle needs a helping verb to make a verb tense. For example, I *have dreamed* of this day. | I *am dreaming* of this day.

Present Tense: Active Voice

	Singular	**Plural**
First Person	I dream	We dream
Second Person	You dream	You dream
Third Person	He, she, it dreams	They dream

Mood
There are three moods in English: the indicative, the imperative, and the subjunctive.

The **indicative mood** is used for facts, opinions, and questions.
Fact: You can do this.
Opinion: I think that you can do this.
Question: Do you know that you can do this?

The **imperative** is used for orders or requests.
Order: You are going to do this!
Request: Will you do this for me?

The **subjunctive mood** is for wishes and statements that go against fact.
Wish: I wish that I were going to do this.
Statement against fact: If I were you, I would do this. (This goes against fact because I am not you. You have the chance to do this, and I do not have the chance.)

The mood that causes trouble for most people is the subjunctive mood. If you have trouble with any of the moods, then be sure to practice.

Adjectives

An adjective is a word that is used to modify a noun or pronoun. An adjective answers a question: *Which one?, What kind of?,* or *How many?*. Usually, adjectives come before the words that they modify.

Which one?: The *third* suit is my favorite.
What kind?: The *navy blue* suit is my favorite.
How many?: Can I look over the *four* neckties for the suit?

Articles

Articles are adjectives that are used to mark nouns. There are only three: the definite (i.e., limited or fixed amount) article *the*, and the indefinite (i.e., no limit or fixed amount) articles *a* and *an*. Note: *An* comes before words that start with a vowel sound (i.e., vowels include *a, e, i, o, u,* and *y*). For example, Are you going to get an **u**mbrella?

Definite: I lost *the* bottle that belongs to me.
Indefinite: Does anyone have *a* bottle to share?

Comparison with Adjectives

Some adjectives are relative and other adjectives are absolute. Adjectives that are relative can show the comparison between things. Adjectives that are absolute can show comparison. However, they show comparison in a different way. Let's say that you are reading two books. You think that one book is perfect, and the other book is not exactly perfect. It is <u>not</u> possible for the book to be more perfect than the other. Either you think that the book is perfect, or you think that the book is not perfect.

The adjectives that are relative will show the different degrees of something or someone to something else or someone else. The three degrees of adjectives include positive, comparative, and superlative.

The positive degree is the normal form of an adjective.
Example: This work is *difficult.* | She is *smart.*

The comparative degree compares one person or thing to another person or thing.
Example: This work is *more difficult* than your work. | She is *smarter* than me.

The superlative degree compares more than two people or things.
Example: This is the *most difficult* work of my life. | She is the *smartest* lady in school.

➢ **Review Video: What is an Adjective?**
Visit ***mometrix.com/academy*** *and enter* ***Code:*** **470154**

Adverbs

An adverb is a word that is used to modify a verb, adjective, or another adverb. Usually, adverbs answer one of these questions: *When?, Where?, How?,* and *Why?*. The negatives *not* and *never* are known as adverbs. Adverbs that modify adjectives or other adverbs strengthen or weaken the words that they modify.

Examples:
He walks quickly through the crowd.
The water flows smoothly on the rocks.

Note: While many adverbs end in *-ly*, you need to remember that not all adverbs end in *-ly*. Also, some words that end in *-ly* are adjectives, not adverbs. Some examples include: *early, friendly, holy, lonely, silly*, and *ugly*. To know if a word that ends in *-ly* is an adjective or adverb, you need to check your dictionary.

Examples:
He is *never* angry.
You talk *too* loud.

Comparison with Adverbs
The rules for comparing adverbs are the same as the rules for adjectives.

The positive degree is the standard form of an adverb.
Example: He arrives soon. | She speaks softly to her friends.

The comparative degree compares one person or thing to another person or thing.
Example: He arrives sooner than Sarah. | She speaks more softly than him.

The superlative degree compares more than two people or things.
Example: He arrives soonest of the group. | She speaks most softly of any of her friends.

➢ **Review Video: Adverbs**
*Visit **mometrix.com/academy** and enter **Code:*** **713951**

Prepositions
A preposition is a word placed before a noun or pronoun that shows the relationship between an object and another word in the sentence.

Common prepositions:

about	before	during	on	under
after	beneath	for	over	until
against	between	from	past	up
among	beyond	in	through	with
around	by	of	to	within
at	down	off	toward	without

Examples:
The napkin is *in* the drawer.
The Earth rotates *around* the Sun.
The needle is *beneath* the haystack.
Can you find me *among* the words?

➢ **Review Video: What is a Preposition?**
*Visit **mometrix.com/academy** and enter **Code:*** **946763**

Conjunctions

Conjunctions join words, phrases, or clauses, and they show the connection between the joined pieces. There are coordinating conjunctions that connect equal parts of sentences. Correlative conjunctions show the connection between pairs. Subordinating conjunctions join subordinate (i.e., dependent) clauses with independent clauses.

Coordinating Conjunctions

The coordinating conjunctions include: *and, but, yet, or, nor, for,* and *so*

Examples:

The rock was small, but it was heavy.

She drove in the night, and he drove in the day.

Correlative Conjunctions

The correlative conjunctions are: *either...or* | *neither...nor* | *not only... but also*

Examples:

Either you are coming, *or* you are staying. | He ran *not only* three miles, *but also* swam 200 yards.

> **Review Video: Coordinating and Correlative Conjunctions**
> *Visit* ***mometrix.com/academy*** *and enter* ***Code:*** **390329**

Subordinating Conjunctions

Common subordinating conjunctions include:

after	since	whenever
although	so that	where
because	unless	wherever
before	until	whether
in order that	when	while

Examples:

I am hungry *because* I did not eat breakfast.

He went home *when* everyone left.

> **Review Video: Subordinating Conjunctions**
> *Visit* ***mometrix.com/academy*** *and enter* ***Code:*** **958913**

Interjections

An interjection is a word for exclamation (i.e., great amount of feeling) that is used alone or as a piece to a sentence. Often, they are used at the beginning of a sentence for an introduction. Sometimes, they can be used in the middle of a sentence to show a change in thought or attitude.

Common Interjections: Hey! | Oh,... | Ouch! | Please! | Wow!

Punctuation

End Punctuation

Periods
Use a period to end all sentences except direct questions, exclamations, and questions.

Declarative Sentence
A declarative sentence gives information or makes a statement.
Examples: I can fly a kite. | The plane left two hours ago.

Imperative Sentence
An imperative sentence gives an order or command.
Examples: You are coming with me. | Bring me that note.

Periods for Abbreviations
Examples: 3 P.M. | 2 A.M. | Mr. Jones | Mrs. Stevens | Dr. Smith | Bill Jr. | Pennsylvania Ave.
Note: an abbreviation is a shortened form of a word or phrase.

Question Marks
Question marks should be used following a direct question. A polite request can be followed by a period instead of a question mark.

Direct Question: What is for lunch today? | How are you? | Why is that the answer?

Polite Requests:
Can you please send me the item tomorrow. | Will you please walk with me on the track.

Exclamation Marks
Exclamation marks are used after a word group or sentence that shows much feeling or has special importance. Exclamation marks should not be overused. They are saved for proper exclamatory interjections.

Examples: We're going to the finals! | You have a beautiful car! | That's crazy!

Commas

The comma is a punctuation mark that can help you understand connections in a sentence. Not every sentence needs a comma. However, if a sentence needs a comma, you need to put it in the right place. A comma in the wrong place (or an absent comma) will make a sentence's meaning unclear. These are some of the rules for commas:

1. Use a comma between a coordinating conjunction joining independent clauses
   Example: *Bob caught three fish, and I caught two fish.*

2. Use a comma after an introductory phrase or an adverbial clause
   Examples:
   After the final out, we went to a restaurant to celebrate.
   Studying the stars, I was surprised at the beauty of the sky.

3. Use a comma between items in a series.
Example: I will bring *the turkey, the pie, and the coffee.*

4. Use a comma between coordinate adjectives not joined with *and*
Incorrect: The kind, brown dog followed me home.
Correct: The *kind, loyal* dog followed me home.

Not all adjectives are coordinate (i.e., equal or parallel). There are two simple ways to know if your adjectives are coordinate. One, you can join the adjectives with *and*: *The kind and loyal dog*. Two, you can change the order of the adjectives: *The loyal, kind dog*.

5. Use commas for interjections and after *yes* and *no* responses
Examples:
Interjection: Oh, I had no idea. | Wow, you know how to play this game.
Yes and No: *Yes,* I heard you. | *No,* I cannot come tomorrow.

6. Use commas to separate nonessential modifiers and nonessential appositives
Examples:
Nonessential Modifier: John Frank, who is coaching the team, was promoted today.
Nonessential Appositive: Thomas Edison, an American inventor, was born in Ohio.

7. Use commas to set off nouns of direct address, interrogative tags, and contrast
Examples:
Direct Address: You, *John,* are my only hope in this moment.
Interrogative Tag: This is the last time, *correct*?
Contrast: You are my friend, *not my enemy.*

8. Use commas with dates, addresses, geographical names, and titles
Examples:
Date: *July 4, 1776,* is an important date to remember.
Address: He is meeting me at *456 Delaware Avenue,* tomorrow morning.
Geographical Name: *Paris, France,* is my favorite city.
Title: John Smith, *Ph. D.,* will be visiting your class today.

9. Use commas to separate expressions like *he said* and *she said* if they come between a sentence of a quote
Examples:
"I want you to know," he began, "that I always wanted the best for you."
"You can start," Jane said, "with an apology."

➢ **Review Video: Commas**
Visit ***mometrix.com/academy*** *and enter* **Code: 644254**

Semicolons

The semicolon is used to connect major sentence pieces of equal value. Some rules for semicolons include:

1. Use a semicolon between closely connected independent clauses that are not connected with a coordinating conjunction.
   Examples:
   She is outside; we are inside.
   You are right; we should go with your plan.

2. Use a semicolon between independent clauses linked with a transitional word.
   Examples:
   I think that we can agree on this; *however,* I am not sure about my friends.
   You are looking in the wrong places; *therefore,* you will not find what you need.

3. Use a semicolon between items in a series that has internal punctuation.
   Example: I have visited *New York, New York; Augusta, Maine; and Baltimore, Maryland.*

> ➢ **Review Video: Semicolon Usage**
> *Visit* ***mometrix.com/academy*** *and enter* ***Code:*** **370605**

Colons

The colon is used to call attention to the words that follow it. A colon must come after an independent clause. The rules for colons are as follows:

1. Use a colon after an independent clause to make a list
   Example: I want to learn many languages: Spanish, French, German, and Italian.

2. Use a colon for explanations or to give a quote
   Examples:
   Quote: The man started with an idea: "We are able to do more than we imagine."
   Explanation: There is one thing that stands out on your resume: responsibility.

3. Use a colon after the greeting in a formal letter, to show hours and minutes, and to separate a title and subtitle
   Examples:
   Greeting in a formal letter: Dear Sir: | To Whom It May Concern:
   Time: It is 3:14 P.M.
   Title: The essay is titled "America: A Short Introduction to a Modern Country"

Parentheses

Parentheses are used for additional information. Also, they can be used to put labels for letters or numbers in a series. Parentheses should be not be used very often. If they are overused, parentheses can be a distraction instead of a help.

Examples:
Extra Information: The rattlesnake (see Image 2) is a dangerous snake of North and South America.

Series: Include in the email (1) your name, (2) your address, and (3) your question for the author.

Quotation Marks

Use quotation marks to close off direct quotations of a person's spoken or written words. Do not use quotation marks around indirect quotations. An indirect quotation gives someone's message without using the person's exact words. Use single quotation marks to close off a quotation inside a quotation.

Direct Quote: Nancy said, "I am waiting for Henry to arrive."

Indirect Quote: Henry said that he is going to be late to the meeting.

Quote inside a Quote: The teacher asked, "Has everyone read 'The Gift of the Magi'?"

Quotation marks should be used around the titles of short works: newspaper and magazine articles, poems, short stories, songs, television episodes, radio programs, and subdivisions of books or web sites.
Examples:
"Rip van Winkle" (short story by Washington Irving)
"O Captain! My Captain!" (poem by Walt Whitman)

Quotation marks may be used to set off words that are being used in a different way from a dictionary definition. Also, they can be used to highlight irony.
Examples:
The boss warned Frank that he was walking on "thin ice."
(Frank is not walking on real ice. Instead, Frank is being warned to avoid mistakes.)

The teacher thanked the young man for his "honesty."
(Honesty and truth are not always the same thing. In this example, the quotation marks around *honesty* show that the teacher does not believe the young man's explanation.)

➢ **Review Video: Quotation Marks**
*Visit **mometrix.com/academy** and enter **Code:*** **118471**

Note: Periods and commas are put inside quotation marks. Colons and semicolons are put outside the quotation marks. Question marks and exclamation points are placed inside quotation marks when they are part of a quote. When the question or exclamation mark goes with the whole sentence, the mark is left outside of the quotation marks.
Examples:
Period and comma: We read "Peter Pan," "Alice in Wonderland," and "Cinderella."

Semicolon: They watched "The Nutcracker"; then, they went home.

Exclamation mark that is a part of a quote: The crowd cheered, "Victory!"

Question mark that goes with the whole sentence: Is your favorite book "The Hobbit"?

Apostrophes

An apostrophe is used to show possession or the deletion of letters in contractions. An apostrophe is not needed with the possessive pronouns *his, hers, its, ours, theirs, whose*, and *yours*.

Singular Nouns: David's car | a book's theme | my brother's board game

Plural Nouns with *-s*: the scissors' handle | boys' basketball

Plural Nouns without *-s*: Men's department | the people's adventure

➢ **Review Video: Apostrophes**
*Visit **mometrix.com/academy** and enter **Code:*** **213068**

Hyphen

The hyphen is used to separate compound words. The following are the rules for hyphens:

1. Compound numbers come with a hyphen
   Example: This team needs *twenty-five* points to win the game.

2. Fractions need a hyphen if they are used as an adjective
   Correct: The recipe says that we need a *three-fourths* cup of butter.
   Incorrect: *One-fourth* of the road is under construction.

3. Compound words used as adjectives that come before a noun need a hyphen
   Correct: The *well-fed* dog took a nap.
   Incorrect: The dog was *well-fed* for his nap.

4. To avoid confusion with some words, use a hyphen
   Examples: semi-irresponsible | Re-collect |Re-claim

Note: This is not a complete set of the rules for hyphens. A dictionary is the best tool for knowing if a compound word needs a hyphen.

Capitalization

The rules for capitalization are:

1. Capitalize the first word of a sentence and the first word in a direct quotation
   Examples:
   First Word: *Football* is my favorite sport.
   Direct Quote: She asked, "*What* is your name?"

2. Capitalize proper nouns and adjectives that come from proper nouns
   Examples:
   Proper Noun: My parents are from *Europe*.
   Adjective from Proper Noun: My father is *British,* and my mother is *Italian*.

3. Capitalize the names of days, months, and holidays
   Examples:
   Day: Everyone needs to be here on *Wednesday*.
   Month: I am so excited for *December*.
   Holiday: *Independence Day* comes every July.

4. Capitalize the names on a compass for specific areas, not when they give direction
   Examples:
   Specific Area: James is from the *West*.
   Direction: After three miles, turn *south* toward the highway.

5. Capitalize the first word for each word in a title (Note: Articles, Prepositions, and Conjunctions are not capitalized.)
   Examples:
   Titles: *Romeo and Juliet* is a beautiful drama on love.
   Incorrect: *The Taming Of The Shrew* is my favorite. (Remember that prepositions and articles are not capitalized.)

   Note: Books, movies, plays (more than one act), newspapers, magazines, and long musical pieces are put in italics. The two examples of Shakespeare's plays are underlined to show their use as an example.

Improving Sentences and Paragraphs

Subjects and Predicates

Subjects

Every sentence has two things: a subject and a verb. The subject of a sentence names who or what the sentence is all about. The subject may be directly stated in a sentence, or the subject may be the implied *you*.

In imperative sentences, the verb's subject is understood (e.g., |You| Run to the store). So, the subject may not be in the sentence. Normally, the subject comes before the verb. However, the subject comes after the verb in sentences that begin with *There are* or *There was*.

Direct:
John knows the way to the park.
(Who knows the way to the park? Answer: John)

The cookies need ten more minutes.
(What needs ten minutes? Answer: The cookies)

By five o' clock, Bill will need to leave.
(Who needs to leave? Answer: Bill)

Remember: The subject can come after the verb.
There are five letters on the table for him.
(What is on the table? Answer: Five letters)

There were coffee and doughnuts in the house.
(What was in the house? Answer: Coffee and doughnuts)

Implied:
Go to the post office for me.
(Who is going to the post office? Answer: You are.)

Come and sit with me, please?
(Who needs to come and sit? Answer: You do.)

The complete subject has the simple subject and all of the modifiers. To find the complete subject, ask *Who* or *What* and insert the verb to complete the question. The answer is the complete subject. To find the simple subject, remove all of the modifiers in the complete subject. When you can find the subject of a sentence, you can correct many problems. These problems include sentence fragments and subject-verb agreement.

Examples:
The small red car is the one that he wants for Christmas.
(The complete subject is *the small red car.*)

The young artist is coming over for dinner.
(The complete subject is *the young artist.*)

> **Review Video: Subjects**
> *Visit* ***mometrix.com/academy*** *and enter* ***Code:*** **444771**

Predicates
In a sentence, you always have a predicate and a subject. A predicate is what remains when you have found the subject. The subject tells what the sentence is about, and the predicate explains or describes the subject.

Think about the sentence: *He sings*. In this sentence, we have a subject (He) and a predicate (sings). This is all that is needed for a sentence to be complete. Would we like more information? Of course, we would like to know more. However, if this all the information that you are given, you have a complete sentence.

Now, let's look at another sentence:
John and Jane sing on Tuesday nights at the dance hall.

What is the subject of this sentence?
Answer: John and Jane.

What is the predicate of this sentence?
Answer: Everything else in the sentence besides John and Jane.

Subject-Verb Agreement

Verbs agree with their subjects in number. In other words, singular subjects need singular verbs. Plural subjects need plural verbs. Singular is for one person, place, or thing. Plural is for more than one person, place, or thing. Subjects and verbs must also agree in person: first, second, or third. The present tense ending *-s* is used on a verb if its subject is third person singular; otherwise, the verb takes no ending.

> **Review Video: Subjects and Verbs**
> *Visit **mometrix.com/academy** and enter **Code:*** **987207**

Number Agreement Examples:
Single Subject and Verb: *Dan calls home.*
(Dan is one person. So, the singular verb *calls* is needed.)

Plural Subject and Verb: *Dan and Bob call home.*
(More than one person needs the plural verb *call.*)

Person Agreement Examples:
First Person: I *am* walking.
Second Person: You *are* walking.
Third Person: He *is* walking.

Problems with Subject-Verb Agreement

- Words between Subject and Verb
  The joy of my life returns home tonight.
  (**Singular Subject**: joy. **Singular Verb**: returns)
  The phrase *of my life* does not influence the verb *returns*.

The question that still remains unanswered is "Who are you?"
(**Singular Subject**: question. **Singular Verb**: is)
Don't let the phrase "*that still remains*..." trouble you. The subject *questions* goes with *is.*

- Compound Subjects
  You and Jon are invited to come to my house.
  (**Plural Subject**: You and Jon. **Plural Verb**: are)

  The pencil and paper belong to me.
  (**Plural Subject**: pencil and paper. **Plural Verb**: belong)

- Subjects Joined by *Or* and *Nor*
  Today or tomorrow is the day.
  (**Subject**: Today / tomorrow. **Verb**: is)

  Stan or Phil wants to read the book.
  (**Subject**: Stan / Phil. **Verb**: wants)

  Neither the books nor the *pen is* on the desk.
  (**Subject**: Books / Pen. **Verb**: was)

  Either the blanket or *pillows arrive* this afternoon.
  (**Subject**: Blanket / Pillows. **Verb**: arrive)

  Note: Singular subjects that are joined with the conjunction *or* need a singular verb. However, when one subject is singular and another is plural, you make the verb agree with the closer subject. The example about books and the pen has a singular verb because the pen (singular subject) is closer to the verb.

- Indefinite Pronouns: Either, Neither, and Each
  Is either of you ready for the game?
  (**Singular Subject**: Either. **Singular Verb**: is)

  Each man, woman, and child is unique.
  (**Singular Subject**: Each. **Singular Verb**: is)

- The adjective Every and compounds: Everybody, Everyone, Anybody, Anyone
  Every day passes faster than the last.
  (**Singular Subject**: Every day. **Singular Verb**: passes)

  Anybody is welcome to bring a tent.
  (**Singular Subject**: Anybody. **Singular Verb**: is)

- Collective Nouns
  The family eats at the restaurant every Friday night.
  (The members of the family are one at the restaurant.)

  The team are leaving for their homes after the game.
  (The members of the team are leaving as individuals to go to their own homes.)

- Who, Which, and That as Subject
  This is the man who is helping me today.
  He is a good man who serves others before himself.
  This painting that is hung over the couch is very beautiful.

- Plural Form and Singular Meaning
  Some nouns that are singular in meaning but plural in form: news, mathematics, physics, and economics
  The news is coming on now.
  Mathematics is my favorite class.

  Some nouns that are plural in meaning: athletics, gymnastics, scissors, and pants
  Do these pants come with a shirt?
  The scissors are for my project.

  Note: There are more nouns in plural form and are singular in meaning than plural in meaning. Look to your dictionary for help when you don't know about the meaning of a verb.

  Addition, Multiplication, Subtraction, and Division are normally singular.
  One plus one is two.
  Three times three is nine.

Complements

A complement is a noun, pronoun, or adjective that is used to give more information about the verb in the sentence.

Direct Objects

A direct object is a noun that takes or receives the action of a verb. Remember: a complete sentence does not need a direct object. A sentence needs only a subject and a verb. When you are looking for a direct object, find the verb and ask *who* or *what*.

Example: I took the blanket. (Who or what did I take? *The blanket*)
Jane read books. (Who or what does Jane read? *Books*)

Indirect Objects

An indirect object is a word or group of words that show how an action had an influence on someone or something. If there is an indirect object in a sentence, then you always have a direct object in the sentence. When you are looking for the indirect object, find the verb and ask *to/for whom or what.*

Examples: We taught the old dog a new trick.
(To/For Whom or What was taught? *The old dog*)

I gave them a math lesson.
(To/For Whom or What was given? *Them*)

Predicate Nouns are nouns that modify the subject and finish linking verbs.

Example: My father is a lawyer.
Father is the subject. Lawyer is the predicate noun.

Predicate Adjectives are adjectives that modify the subject and finish linking verbs.
Example: Your mother is patient.
Mother is the subject. Patient is the predicate adjective.

Pronoun Usage

Pronoun - antecedent agreement - The antecedent is the noun that has been replaced by a pronoun. A pronoun and the antecedent agree when they are singular or plural.

Singular agreement: *John* came into town, and *he* played for us.
(The word *He* replaces *John*.)

Plural agreement: *John and Rick* came into town, and *they* played for us.
(The word *They* replaces *John* and *Rick*.)

To know the correct pronoun for a compound subject, try each pronoun separately with the verb. Your knowledge of pronouns will tell you which one is correct.
Example: Bob and (I, me) will be going.
(Answer: Bob and I will be going.)

Test: (1) *I will be going* or (2) *Me will be going*. The second choice cannot be correct because *me* is not used as a subject of a sentence. Instead, *me* is used as an object.

When a pronoun is used with a noun immediately following (as in "we boys"), try the sentence without the added noun.
Example: (We/Us) boys played football last year.
(Answer: We boys played football last year.)

Test: (1) *We* played football last year or (2) *Us* played football last year. Again, the second choice cannot be correct because *us* is not used as a subject of a sentence. Instead, *us* is used as an object.

➢ **Review Video: Pronoun Usage**
*Visit **mometrix.com/academy** and enter **Code:*** **666500**

Pronoun reference - A pronoun should point clearly to the antecedent. Here is how a pronoun reference can be unhelpful if it is not directly stated or puzzling.

Unhelpful: Ron and Jim went to the store, and he bought soda.
(Who bought soda? Ron or Jim?)

Helpful: Jim went to the store, and he bought soda.
(The sentence is clear. Jim bought the soda.)

Personal pronouns - Some pronouns change their form by their placement in a sentence. A pronoun that is a subject in a sentence comes in the subjective case. Pronouns that serve as objects appear in the objective case. Finally, the pronouns that are used as possessives appear in the possessive case.

Subjective case: *He* is coming to the show.
(The pronoun *He* is the subject of the sentence.)

Objective case: Josh drove *him* to the airport.
(The pronoun *him* is the object of the sentence.)

Possessive case: The flowers are *mine*.
(The pronoun *mine* shows ownership of the flowers.)

Who or whom - *Who*, a subjective-case pronoun, can be used as a subject. *Whom*, an objective case pronoun, can be used as an object. The words *who* and *whom* are common in subordinate clauses or in questions.

Subject: He knows who wants to come.
(*Who* is the subject of the verb *wants*.)

Object: He knows whom we want at the party.
(*Whom* is the object of *we want*.)

Clauses

There are two groups of clauses: independent and dependent. Unlike phrases, a clause has a subject and a verb. So, what is the difference between a clause that is independent and one that is dependent? An independent clause gives a complete thought. A dependent clause does not share a complete thought. Instead, a dependent clause has a subject and a verb, but it needs an independent clause. Subordinate (i.e., dependent) clauses look like sentences. They may have a subject, a verb, and objects or complements. They are used within sentences as adverbs, adjectives, or nouns.

Examples:
Independent Clause: I am running outside.
(The sentence has a subject *I* and a verb *am running*.)

Dependent Clause: I am running <u>because I want to stay in shape</u>.

The clause *I am running* is an independent clause. The underlined clause is dependent. Remember: a dependent clause does not give a complete thought. Think about the dependent clause: *because I want to stay in shape.*

Without any other information, you think: So, you want to stay in shape. What are you are doing to stay in shape? Answer: *I am running.*

<u>Types of Dependent Clauses</u>
An **adjective clause** is a dependent clause that modifies nouns and pronouns. Adjective clauses begin with a relative pronoun (*who, whose, whom, which,* and *that*) or a relative adverb (*where, when,* and *why*). Also, adjective clauses come after the noun that the clause needs to explain or rename. This is done to have a clear connection to the independent clause.
Examples:
I learned the reason *why I won the award.*
This is the place *where I started my first job.*

An adjective clause can be an essential or nonessential clause. An essential clause is very important to the sentence. Essential clauses explain or define a person or thing. Nonessential clauses give more information about a person or thing. However, they are not necessary to the sentence.
Examples:
Essential: A person *who works hard at first* can rest later in life.
Nonessential: Neil Armstrong, *who walked on the moon*, is my hero.

An **adverb clause** is a dependent clause that modifies verbs, adjectives, and other adverbs. To show a clear connection to the independent clause, put the adverb clause immediately before or after the independent clause. An adverb clause can start with *after, although, as, as if, before, because, if, since, so, so that, unless, when, where*, or *while*.
Examples:
When you walked outside, I called the manager.
I want to go with you *unless you want to stay.*

A **noun clause** is a dependent clause that can be used as a subject, object, or complement. Noun clauses can begin with *how, that, what, whether, which, who*, or *why*. These words can also come with an adjective clause. Remember that the entire clause makes a noun or an adjective clause, not the word that starts a clause. So, be sure to look for more than the word that begins the clause. To show a clear connection to the independent clause, be sure that a noun clause comes after the verb. The exception is when the noun clause is the subject of the sentence.
Examples:
The fact *that you were alone* alarms me.
What you learn from each other depends on your honesty with others.

Phrases

A phrase is not a complete sentence. So, a phrase cannot be a statement and cannot give a complete thought. Instead, a phrase is a group of words that can be used as a noun, adjective, or adverb in a sentence. Phrases strengthen sentences by adding explanation or renaming something.

Prepositional Phrases - A phrase that can be found in many sentences is the prepositional phrase. A prepositional phrase begins with a preposition and ends with a noun or pronoun that is used as an object. Normally, the prepositional phrase works as an adjective or an adverb.

Examples:
The picnic is *on the blanket.*
I am sick *with a fever* today.
Among the many flowers, a four-leaf clover was found by John.

Verbals and Verbal Phrases
A verbal looks like a verb, but it is not used as a verb. Instead, a verbal is used as a noun, adjective, or adverb. Be careful with verbals. They do not replace a verb in a sentence.

Correct: Walk a mile daily.
(*Walk* is the verb of this sentence. As in, "*You* walk a mile daily.")

Incorrect: To walk a mile.
(*To walk* is a type of verbal. But, verbals cannot be a verb for a sentence.)

A verbal phrase is a verb form that does not function as the verb of a clause. There are three major types of verbal phrases: participial, gerund, and infinitive phrases.

Participles - A participle is a verbal that is used as an adjective. The present participle always ends with *-ing*. Past participles end with *-d, -ed, -n,* or *-t.*

Examples: Verb: *dance* | Present Participle: *dancing* | Past Participle: *danced*

Participial phrases are made of a participle and any complements or modifiers. Often, they come right after the noun or pronoun that they modify.

Examples:
Shipwrecked on an island, the boys started to fish for food.
Having been seated for five hours, we got out of the car to stretch our legs.
Praised for their work, the group accepted the first place trophy.

Gerunds - A gerund is a verbal that is used as a noun. Gerunds can be found by looking for their *-ing* endings. However, you need to be careful that you have found a gerund, not a present participle. Since gerunds are nouns, they can be used as a subject of a sentence and the object of a verb or preposition.

Gerund Phrases are built around present participles (i.e., *-ing* endings to verbs) and they are always used as nouns. The gerund phrase has a gerund and any complements or modifiers.

Examples:
We want to be known for *teaching the poor.* (Object of Preposition)
Coaching this team is the best job of my life. (Subject)
We like *practicing our songs* in the basement. (Object of the verb: *like*)

Infinitives - An infinitive is a verbal that can be used as a noun, an adjective, or an adverb. An infinitive is made of the basic form of a verb with the word *to* coming before the verb.

Infinitive Phrases are made of an infinitive and all complements and modifiers. They are used as nouns, adjectives, or adverbs.

Examples:
To join the team is my goal in life. (Noun)
The animals have enough food *to eat for the night.* (Adjective)
People lift weights *to exercise their muscles.* (Adverb)

Appositive Phrases

An appositive is a word or phrase that is used to explain or rename nouns or pronouns. In a sentence they can be noun phrases, prepositional phrases, gerund phrases, or infinitive phrases.

Examples:
Terriers, *hunters at heart*, have been dressed up to look like lap dogs.
(The phrase *hunters at heart* renames the noun *terriers.*)

His plan, *to save and invest his money*, was proven as a safe approach.
(The italicized infinitive phrase renames the plan.)

Appositive phrases can be essential or nonessential. An appositive phrase is essential if the person, place, or thing being described or renamed is too general.
Essential: Two Founding Fathers George Washington and Thomas Jefferson served as presidents.

Nonessential: George Washington and Thomas Jefferson, two Founding Fathers, served as presidents.

Absolute Phrases
An absolute phrase is a phrase with a participle that comes after a noun. The absolute phrase is never the subject of a sentence. Also, the phrase does not explain or add to the meaning of a word in a sentence. Absolute phrases are used independently from the rest of the sentence. However, they are still a phrase, and phrases cannot give a complete thought.

Examples:
The alarm ringing, he pushed the snooze button.
The music paused, she continued to dance through the crowd.

Note: Appositive and absolute phrases can be confusing in sentences. So, don't be discouraged if you have a difficult time with them.

Modes of Sentence Patterns

Sentence patterns fall into five common modes with some exceptions. They are:

- Subject + linking verb + subject complement
- Subject + transitive verb + direct object
- Subject + transitive verb + indirect object + direct object
- Subject + transitive verb + direct object + object complement
- Subject + intransitive verb

Common exceptions to these patterns are questions and commands, sentences with delayed subjects, and passive transformations.

Types of Sentences

For a sentence to be complete, it must have a subject and a verb or predicate. A complete sentence will express a complete thought, otherwise it is known as a fragment. An example of a fragment is: *As the clock struck midnight.* A complete sentence would be: *As the clock struck midnight, she ran home.* The types of sentences are declarative, imperative, interrogative, and exclamatory.

A declarative sentence states a fact and ends with a period. The following is an example:

The football game starts at seven o'clock.

An imperative sentence tells someone to do something and ends with a period. The following is an example:

Go to the store and buy milk.

An interrogative sentence asks a question and ends with a question mark. The following is an example:

Are you going to the game on Friday?

An exclamatory sentence shows strong emotion and ends with an exclamation point. The following is an example:

I can't believe we won the game!

Sentence Structures

The four major types of sentence structure are:

1. Simple Sentences – Simple sentences have one independent clause with no subordinate clauses. A simple sentence can have compound elements (e.g., a compound subject or verb).
   Examples:
   Judy watered the lawn. (Singular Subject & Singular Predicate)
   Judy and Alan watered the lawn. (Compound Subject: Judy and Alan)

2. Compound Sentences – Compound sentences have two or more independent clauses with no dependent clauses. Usually, the independent clauses are joined with a comma and a coordinating conjunction, or they can be joined with a semicolon.
   Example:
   The time has come, and we are ready.
   I woke up at dawn; then I went outside to watch the sun rise.

3. Complex Sentences – A complex sentence has one independent clause and one or more dependent clauses.
   Examples:
   Although he had the flu, Harry went to work.
   Marcia got married after she finished college.

4. Compound-Complex Sentences – A compound-complex sentence has at least two independent clauses and at least one dependent clause.
   Examples:
   John is my friend who went to India, and he brought souvenirs for us.
   You may not know, but we heard the music that you played last night.

➢ **Review Video:** Sentence Structure
Visit ***mometrix.com/academy*** *and enter* ***Code:*** **700478**

Sentence Fragments

A part of a sentence should not be treated like a complete sentence. A sentence must be made of at least one independent clause. An independent clause has a subject and a verb. Remember that the independent clause can stand alone as a sentence. Some fragments are independent clauses that begin with a subordinating word (e.g., as, because, so, etc.). Other fragments may not have a subject, a verb, or both.

A sentence fragment can be repaired in several ways. One way is to put the fragment with a neighbor sentence. Another way is to be sure that punctuation is not needed. You can also turn the fragment into a sentence by adding any missing pieces. Sentence fragments are allowed for writers who want to show off their art. However, for your exam, sentence fragments are not allowed.

Fragment: Because he wanted to sail for Rome.
Correct: He dreamed of Europe because he wanted to sail for Rome.

Run-on Sentences

Run-on sentences are independent clauses that have not been joined by a conjunction. When two or more independent clauses appear in one sentence, they must be joined in one of these ways:

1. Correction with a comma and a coordinating conjunction.
   Incorrect: I went on the trip and I had a good time.
   Correct: I went on the trip, and I had a good time.

2. Correction with a semicolon, a colon, or a dash. Used when independent clauses are closely related and their connection is clear without a coordinating conjunction.
   Incorrect: I went to the store and I bought some eggs.
   Correct: I went to the store; I bought some eggs.

3. Correction by separating sentences. This correction may be used when both independent clauses are long. Also, this can be used when one sentence is a question and one is not.
   Incorrect: The drive to New York takes ten hours it makes me very tired.
   Correct: The drive to New York takes ten hours. So, I become very tired.

4. Correction by changing parts of the sentence. One way is to turn one of the independent clauses into a phrase or subordinate clause.
   Incorrect: The drive to New York takes ten hours it makes me very tired.
   Correct: During the ten hour drive to New York, I become very tired.

Note: Normally, one of these choices will be a clear correction to a run-on sentence. The fourth way can be the best correction but needs the most work.

➢ **Review Video: Fragments and Run-on Sentences**
Visit ***mometrix.com/academy*** *and enter* ***Code:*** **541989**

Dangling and Misplaced Modifiers

Dangling Modifiers
A dangling modifier is a verbal phrase that does not have a clear connection to a word. A dangling modifier can also be a dependent clause (the subject and/or verb are not included) that does not have a clear connection to a word.

Examples:
Dangling: *Reading each magazine article*, the stories caught my attention.
Corrected: Reading each magazine article, *I* was entertained by the stories.

In this example, the word *stories* cannot be modified by *Reading each magazine article*. People can read, but stories cannot read. So, the pronoun *I* is needed for the modifying phrase *Reading each magazine article*.

Dangling: Since childhood, my grandparents have visited me for Christmas.
Corrected: Since childhood, I have been visited by my grandparents for Christmas.

In this example, the dependent adverb clause *Since childhood* cannot modify grandparents. So, the pronoun *I* is needed for the modifying adverb clause.

Misplaced Modifiers
In some sentences, a modifier can be put in more than one place. However, you need to be sure that there is no confusion about which word is being explained or given more detail.

Incorrect: He read the book to a crowd that was filled with beautiful pictures.
Correct: He read the book that was filled with beautiful pictures to a crowd.

The crowd is not filled with pictures. The book is filled with pictures.

Incorrect: John only ate fruits and vegetables for two weeks.
Correct: John ate *only* fruits and vegetables for two weeks.

John may have done nothing else for two weeks but eat fruits and vegetables and sleep. However, it is reasonable to think that John had fruits and vegetables for his meals. Then, he continued to work on other things.

Split Infinitives
A split infinitive is when something comes between the word *to* and the verb that pairs with *to*.
Incorrect: To *clearly* explain | To *softly* sing
Correct: *To explain* clearly | *To sing* softly

Double Negatives

Standard English allows two negatives when a positive meaning is intended. For example, "The team was not displeased with their performance." Double negatives that are used to emphasize negation are not part of Standard English.

Negative modifiers (e.g., never, no, and not) should not be paired with other negative modifiers or negative words (e.g., none, nobody, nothing, or neither). The modifiers *hardly, barely*, and *scarcely* are also considered negatives in Standard English. So, they should not be used with other negatives.

Parallelism and Subordination

Parallelism
Parallel structures are used in sentences to highlight similar ideas and to connect sentences that give similar information. Parallelism pairs parts of speech, phrases, or clauses together with a matching piece. To write, *I enjoy reading and to study* would be incorrect. An infinitive does not match with a gerund. Instead, you should write *I enjoy reading and studying*.

Be sure that you continue to use certain words (e.g., articles, linking verbs, prepositions, infinitive sign (to), and the introductory word for a dependent clause) in sentences.

Incorrect: Will you bring the paper and pen with you?
Correct: Will you bring *the* paper and *a* pen with you?

Incorrect: The animals can come to eat and play.
Correct: The animals can come *to* eat and *to* play.

Incorrect: You are the person who remembered my name and cared for me.
Correct: You are the person *who* remembered my name and *who* cared for me.

<u>Subordination</u>
When two items are not equal to each other, you can join them by making the more important piece an independent clause. The less important piece can become subordinate. To make the less important piece subordinate, you make it a phrase or a dependent clause. The piece of more importance should be the one that readers want or will need to remember.
Example:
(1) The team had a perfect regular season. (2) The team lost the championship.
Despite having a perfect regular season, *the team lost the championship*.

Spelling

Spelling Rules

Words Ending with a Consonant

Usually the final consonant is doubled on a word before adding a suffix. This is the rule for single syllable words, words ending with one consonant, and multi-syllable words with the last syllable accented. The following are examples:

- *beg* becomes *begging* (single syllable)
- *shop* becomes *shopped* (single syllable)
- *add* becomes *adding* (already ends in double consonant, do not add another *d*)
- *deter* becomes *deterring* (multi-syllable, accent on last syllable)
- *regret* becomes *regrettable* (multi-syllable, accent on last syllable)
- *compost* becomes *composting* (do not add another *t* because the accent is on the first syllable)

Words Ending with *y* or *c*

The general rule for words ending in *y* is to keep the *y* when adding a suffix if the *y* is preceded by a vowel. If the word ends in a consonant and *y* the *y* is changed to an *i* before the suffix is added (unless the suffix itself begins with *i*). The following are examples:

- *pay* becomes *paying* (keep the *y*)
- *bully* becomes *bullied* (change to *i*)
- *bully* becomes *bullying* (keep the *y* because the suffix is *–ing*)

If a word ends with *c* and the suffix begins with an *e, i,* or *y*, the letter *k* is usually added to the end of the word. The following are examples:

- *panic* becomes *panicky*
- *mimic* becomes *mimicking*

Words Containing *ie* or *ei*, and/or Ending with *e*

Most words are spelled with an *i* before *e*, except when they follow the letter *c*, **or** sound like *a*. For example, the following words are spelled correctly according to these rules:

- piece, friend, believe (*i* before *e*)
- receive, ceiling, conceited (except after *c*)
- weight, neighborhood, veil (sounds like *a*)

To add a suffix to words ending with the letter *e*, first determine if the *e* is silent. If it is, the *e* will be kept if the added suffix begins with a consonant. If the suffix begins with a vowel, the *e* is dropped. The following are examples:

- *age* becomes *ageless* (keep the *e*)
- *age* becomes *aging* (drop the *e*)

An exception to this rule occurs when the word ends in *ce* or *ge* and the suffix *able* or *ous* is added; these words will retain the letter *e*. The following are examples:

- *courage* becomes *courageous*
- *notice* becomes *noticeable*

Words Ending with *ise* or *ize*

A small number of words end with *ise*. Most of the words in the English language with the same sound end in *ize*. The following are examples:

- advertise, advise, arise, chastise, circumcise, and comprise
- compromise, demise, despise, devise, disguise, enterprise, excise, and exercise
- franchise, improvise, incise, merchandise, premise, reprise, and revise
- supervise, surmise, surprise, and televise

Words that end with *ize* include the following:

- accessorize, agonize, authorize, and brutalize
- capitalize, caramelize, categorize, civilize, and demonize
- downsize, empathize, euthanize, idolize, and immunize
- legalize, metabolize, mobilize, organize, and ostracize
- plagiarize, privatize, utilize, and visualize

(Note that some words may technically be spelled with *ise*, especially in British English, but it is more common to use *ize*. Examples include *symbolize/symbolise,* and *baptize/baptise.*)

Words Ending with *ceed, sede,* or *cede*

There are only three words in the English language that end with *ceed*: *exceed, proceed,* and *succeed.* There is only one word in the English language that ends with *sede*: *supersede*. Most other words that sound like *sede* or *ceed* end with *cede*. The following are examples:

- concede, recede, and precede

Words Ending in *able* or *ible*

For words ending in *able* or *ible*, there are no hard and fast rules. The following are examples:

- adjustable, unbeatable, collectable, deliverable, and likeable
- edible, compatible, feasible, sensible, and credible

There are more words ending in *able* than *ible*; this is useful to know if guessing is necessary.

Words Ending in *ance* or *ence*

The suffixes *ence, ency,* and *ent* are used in the following cases:

- the suffix is preceded by the letter *c* but sounds like *s* – *innocence*
- the suffix is preceded by the letter *g* but sounds like *j* – *intelligence, negligence*

The suffixes *ance, ancy,* and *ant* are used in the following cases:

- the suffix is preceded by the letter *c* but sounds like *k* – *significant, vacant*
- the suffix is preceded by the letter *g* with a hard sound – *elegant, extravagance*

If the suffix is preceded by other letters, there are no clear rules. For example: *finance, abundance,* and *assistance* use the letter *a,* while *decadence, competence,* and *excellence* use the letter *e.*

Words Ending in *tion, sion,* or *cian*
Words ending in *tion, sion,* or *cian* all sound like *shun* or *zhun*. There are no rules for which ending is used for words. The following are examples:

- action, agitation, caution, fiction, nation, and motion
- admission, expression, mansion, permission, and television
- electrician, magician, musician, optician, and physician (note that these words tend to describe occupations)

Words with the *ai* or *ia* Combination
When deciding if *ai* or *ia* is correct, the combination of *ai* usually sounds like one vowel sound, as in *Britain*, while the vowels in *ia* are pronounced separately, as in *guardian*. The following are examples:

- captain, certain, faint, hair, malaise, and praise (*ai* makes one sound)
- bacteria, beneficiary, diamond, humiliation, and nuptial (*ia* makes two sounds)

Plural Forms of Nouns

Nouns Ending in *ch, sh, s, x,* or *z*
When a noun ends in the letters *ch, sh, s, x,* or *z*, an *es* instead of a singular *s* is added to the end of the word to make it plural. The following are examples:

- *church* becomes *churches*
- *bush* becomes *bushes*
- *bass* becomes *basses*
- *mix* becomes *mixes*
- *buzz* becomes *buzzes*

This is the rule with proper names as well; the Ross family would become the Rosses.

Nouns Ending in *y* or *ay/ey/iy/oy/uy*
If a noun ends with a consonant and y, the plural is formed by replacing the *y* with *ies*. For example, *fly* becomes *flies* and *puppy* becomes *puppies*. If a noun ends with a vowel and *y*, the plural is formed by adding an *s*. For example, *alley* becomes *alleys* and *boy* becomes *boys*.

Nouns Ending in *f* or *fe*
Most nouns ending in *f* or *fe* are pluralized by replacing the *f* with *v* and adding *es*. The following are examples:

- *knife* becomes *knives; self* becomes *selves; wolf* becomes *wolves.*

An exception to this rule is the word *roof; roof* becomes *roofs.*

Nouns Ending in *o*
Most nouns ending with a consonant and *o* are pluralized by adding *es*. The following are examples:

- *hero* becomes *heroes; tornado* becomes *tornadoes; potato* becomes *potatoes*

Most nouns ending with a vowel and *o* are pluralized by adding *s*. The following are examples:

- *portfolio* becomes *portfolios; radio* becomes *radios; cameo* becomes *cameos.*

An exception to these rules is seen with musical terms ending in *o*. These words are pluralized by adding *s* even if they end in a consonant and *o*. The following are examples: *soprano* becomes *sopranos; banjo* becomes *banjos; piano* becomes *pianos.*

Exceptions to the Rules of Plurals

Some words do not fall into any specific category for making the singular form plural. They are irregular. Certain words become plural by changing the vowels within the word. The following are examples:

- *woman* becomes *women; goose* becomes *geese; foot* becomes *feet*

Some words change in unusual ways in the plural form. The following are examples:

- *mouse* becomes *mice; ox* becomes *oxen*; *person* becomes *people*

Some words are the same in both the singular and plural forms. The following are examples:

- *Salmon*, *deer*, and *moose* are the same whether singular or plural.

Plural Forms of Letters, Numbers, Symbols, and Compound Nouns with Hyphens

Letters and numbers become plural by adding an apostrophe and *s*. The following are examples:

- The *L's* are the people whose names begin with the letter *L*.
- They broke the teams down into groups of *3's*.
- The sorority girls were all *KD's*.

A compound noun is a noun that is made up of two or more words; they can be written with hyphens. For example, *mother-in-law* or *court-martial* are compound nouns. To make them plural, an *s* or *es* is added to the noun portion of the word. The following are examples: *mother-in-law* becomes *mothers-in-law; court-martial* becomes *courts-martial.*

➢ **Review Video: Spelling Tips**
Visit ***mometrix.com/academy*** *and enter* ***Code:*** **138869**

Commonly Misspelled Words

accidentally
accommodate
accompanied
accompany
achieved
acknowledgment
across
address
aggravate
aisle
ancient
anxiety
apparently
appearance
arctic
argument
arrangement
attendance
auxiliary
awkward
bachelor
barbarian
beggar
beneficiary
biscuit
brilliant
business
cafeteria
calendar
campaign
candidate
ceiling
cemetery
changeable
changing
characteristic
chauffeur
colonel
column
commit
committee
comparative
compel
competent
competition
conceive
congratulations
conqueror
conscious
coolly
correspondent
courtesy
curiosity
cylinder
deceive
deference
deferred
definite
describe
desirable
desperate
develop
diphtheria
disappear
disappoint
disastrous
discipline
discussion
disease
dissatisfied
dissipate
drudgery
ecstasy
efficient
eighth
eligible
embarrass
emphasize
especially
exaggerate
exceed
exhaust
exhilaration
existence
explanation
extraordinary
familiar
fascinate
February
fiery
finally
forehead
foreign
foreigner
foremost
forfeit
ghost
glamorous
government
grammar
grateful
grief
grievous
handkerchief
harass
height
hoping
hurriedly
hygiene
hypocrisy
imminent
incidentally
incredible
independent
indigestible
inevitable
innocence
intelligible
intentionally
intercede
interest
irresistible
judgment
legitimate
liable
library
likelihood
literature
maintenance
maneuver
manual
mathematics
mattress
miniature
mischievous

Commonly Misspelled Words

misspell
momentous
mortgage
neither
nickel
niece
ninety
noticeable
notoriety
obedience
obstacle
occasion
occurrence
omitted
operate
optimistic
organization
outrageous
pageant
pamphlet
parallel
parliament
permissible
perseverance
persuade
physically
physician
possess
possibly
practically
prairie
preceding
prejudice
prevalent
professor
pronunciation
pronouncement
propeller
protein
psychiatrist
psychology
quantity
questionnaire
rally
recede
receive
recognize
recommend
referral
referred
relieve
religious
resistance
restaurant
rhetoric
rhythm
ridiculous
sacrilegious
salary
scarcely
schedule
secretary
sentinel
separate
severely
sheriff
shriek
similar
soliloquy
sophomore
species
strenuous
studying
suffrage
supersede
suppress
surprise
symmetry
temperament
temperature
tendency
tournament
tragedy
transferred
truly
twelfth
tyranny
unanimous
unpleasant
usage
vacuum
valuable
vein
vengeance
vigilance
villain
Wednesday
weird
wholly

Paragraph Development

Level of Formality

The relationship between writer and reader is important in choosing a level of formality as most writing requires some degree of formality. Formal writing is for addressing a superior in a school or work environment. Business letters, textbooks, and newspapers use a moderate to high level of formality. Informal writing is appropriate for private letters, personal e-mails, and business correspondence between close associates.

For your exam, you will want to be aware of informal and formal writing. One way that this can be accomplished is to watch for shifts in point of view in the essay. For example, unless writers are using a personal example, they will rarely refer to themselves (e.g., "*I* think that *my* point is very clear.") to avoid being informal when they need to be formal. Also, be mindful of an author who addresses his or her audience directly in their writing (e.g., "Readers, *like you*, will understand this argument.") as this can be a sign of informal writing. Good writers understand the need to be consistent with their level of formality. Shifts in levels of formality or point of view can confuse readers and discount the message of an author's writing.

<u>Clichés</u>
Clichés are phrases that have been overused to the point that the phrase has no importance or has lost the original meaning. The phrases have no originality and add very little to a passage. Therefore, most writers will avoid the use of clichés. Another option is to make changes to a cliché so that it is not predictable and empty of meaning.

Examples
When life gives you lemons, make lemonade.
Every cloud has a silver lining.

<u>Jargon</u>
Jargon is a specialized vocabulary that is used among members of a trade or profession. Since jargon is understood by a small audience, writers tend to leave them to passages where certain readers will understand the vocabulary. Jargon includes exaggerated language that tries to impress rather than inform. Sentences filled with jargon are not precise and difficult to understand.

Examples
"He is going to *toenail* these frames for us." (Toenail is construction jargon for nailing at an angle.)
"They brought in a *kip* of material today." (Kip refers to 1000 pounds in architecture and engineering.)

<u>Slang</u>
Slang is an informal and sometimes private language that is understood by some individuals. Slang has some usefulness, but the language can have a small audience. So, most formal writing will not include this kind of language.

Examples
"Yes, the event was a blast!" (In this sentence, *blast* means that the event was a great experience.)
"That attempt was an epic fail." (By *epic fail*, the speaker means that his or her attempt was not a success.)

Colloquialism
A colloquialism is a word or phrase that is found in informal writing. Unlike slang, colloquial language will be familiar to a greater range of people. Colloquial language can include some slang, but these are limited to contractions for the most part.

Examples
"Can *y'all* come back another time?" (Y'all is contraction of "you all" which has become a colloquialism.)
"Will you stop him from building this *castle in the air*?" (A "castle in the air" is an improbable or unlikely event.)

Point of View

Point of view is the perspective from which writing occurs. There are several possibilities:

- *First person* is written so that the *I* of the story is a participant or observer.
- *Second person* is a device to draw the reader in more closely. It is really a variation or refinement of the first-person narrative.
- *Third person*, the most traditional form of point of view, is the omniscient narrator, in which the narrative voice, presumed to be the writer's, is presumed to know everything about the characters, plot, and action. Most novels use this point of view.
- A multiple point of view is narration delivered from the perspective of several characters.

➢ **Review Video:** Points of View
Visit ***mometrix.com/academy*** *and enter* ***Code:*** **383336**

Practice Makes Prepared Writers

Writing is a skill that continues to need development throughout a person's life. For some people, writing seems to be a natural gift. They rarely struggle with writer's block. When you read their papers, they have persuasive ideas. For others, writing is an intimidating task that they endure. As you prepare for the TEAS, believe that you can improve your skills and be better prepared for reviewing several types of writing.

A traditional way to prepare for the English and Language Usage Section is to read. When you read newspapers, magazines, and books, you learn about new ideas. You can read newspapers and magazines to become informed about issues that affect many people. As you think about those issues and ideas, you can take a position and form opinions. Try to develop these ideas and your opinions by sharing them with friends. After you develop your opinions, try writing them down as if you were going to spread your ideas beyond your friends.

Remember that you are practicing for more than an exam. Two of the most valuable things in life are the abilities to read critically and to write clearly. When you work on evaluating the arguments of a passage and explain your thoughts well, you are developing skills that you will use for a lifetime.

Brainstorming
Brainstorming is a technique that is used to find a creative approach to a subject. This can be accomplished by simple free-association with a topic. For example, with paper and pen, you write

every thought that you have about the topic in a word or phrase. This is done without critical thinking. Everything that comes to your mind about the topic, you should put on your scratch paper. Then, you need to read the list over a few times. Next, you look for patterns, repetitions, and clusters of ideas. This allows a variety of fresh ideas to come as you think about the topic.

Free Writing

Free writing is a form of brainstorming, but the method occurs in a structured way. The method involves a limited amount of time (e.g., 2 to 3 minutes) and writing everything that comes to mind about the topic in complete sentences. When time expires, you need to review everything that has been written down. Many of your sentences may make little or no sense, but the insights and observations that can come from free writing make this method a valuable approach. Usually, free writing results in a fuller expression of ideas than brainstorming because thoughts and associations are written in complete sentences. However, both techniques can be used to complement the other.

Revisions

A writer's choice of words is a signature of their style. Careful thought about the use of words can improve a piece of writing. A passage can be an exciting piece to read when attention is given to the use of specific nouns rather than general ones.
Example:
General: His kindness will never be forgotten.

Specific: His thoughtful gifts and bear hugs will never be forgotten.

Attention should also be given to the kind of verbs that are used in sentences. Active verbs (e.g., run, swim) should be about an action. Whenever possible, an active verb should replace a linking verb to provide clear examples for arguments and to strengthen a passage overall.
Example:
Passive: The winners were called to the stage by the judges.

Active: The judges called the winners to the stage.

Revising sentences is done to make writing more effective. Editing sentences is done to correct any errors. Sentences are the building blocks of writing, and they can be changed by paying attention to sentence length, sentence structure, and sentence openings. You should add variety to sentence length, structure, and openings so that the essay does not seem boring or repetitive. A careful analysis of a piece of writing will expose these stylistic problems, and they can be corrected before you finish your essay. Changing up your sentence structure and sentence length can make your essay more inviting and appealing to readers.

Recursive Writing Process

However you approach writing, you may find comfort in knowing that the revision process can occur in any order. The recursive writing process is not as difficult as the phrase appears to you. Simply put, the recursive writing process means that the steps in the writing process occur in no particular order. For example, planning, drafting, and revising (all a part of the writing process) take place at about the same time and you may not notice that all three happen so close together. Truly, the writing process is a series of moving back and forth between planning, drafting, and revising. Then, more planning, more drafting, and more revising until the writing is complete.

> ➢ **Review Video: Recursive Writing Process**
> *Visit **mometrix.com/academy** and enter **Code:*** **951611**

Transitions

Transitions are bridges between what has been read and what is about to be read. Transitions smooth the reader's path between sentences and inform the reader of major connections to new ideas forthcoming in the text. Transitional phrases should be used with care, selecting the appropriate phrase for a transition. Tone is another important consideration in using transitional phrases, varying the tone for different audiences. For example, in a scholarly essay, *in summary* would be preferable to the more informal *in short.*

When working with transitional words and phrases, writers usually find a natural flow that indicates when a transition is needed. In reading a draft of the text, it should become apparent where the flow is uneven or rough. At this point, the writer can add transitional elements during the revision process. Revising can also afford an opportunity to delete transitional devices that seem heavy handed or unnecessary.

Transitional words and phrases are used to transition between paragraphs and also to transition within a single paragraph. Transitions assist the flow of ideas and help to unify an essay. A writer can use certain words to indicate that an example or summary is being presented. The following phrases, among others, can be used as this type of transition: *as a result, as I have said, for example, for instance, in any case, in any event, in brief, in conclusion, in fact, in other words, in short, on the whole,* and *to sum it up.*

> ➢ **Review Video: Transitions**
> *Visit **mometrix.com/academy** and enter **Code:*** **707563**

Transitional Words

Link Similar Ideas

When a writer links ideas that are similar in nature, there are a variety of words and phrases he or she can choose, including but not limited to: *also, and, another, besides, equally important, further, furthermore, in addition, likewise, too, similarly, nor, of course,* and *for instance.*

Link Dissimilar or Contradictory Ideas

Writers can link contradictory ideas in an essay by using, among others, the following words and phrases: *although, and yet, even if, conversely, but, however, otherwise, still, yet, instead, in spite of, nevertheless, on the contrary,* and *on the other hand.*

Indicate Cause, Purpose, or Result
Writers may need to indicate that one thing is the cause, purpose, or result of another thing. To show this relationship, writers can use, among others, the following linking words and phrases: *as, as a result, because, consequently, hence, for, for this reason, since, so, then, thus,* and *therefore.*

Indicate Time or Position
Certain words can be used to indicate the time and position of one thing in relation to another. Writers can use, for example, the following terms to create a timeline of events in an essay: *above, across, afterward, before, beyond, eventually, meanwhile, next, presently, around, at once, at the present time, finally, first, here, second, thereafter,* and *upon*. These words can show the order or placement of items or ideas in an essay.

Paragraphs

After the introduction of a passage, a series of body paragraphs will carry a message through to the conclusion. A paragraph should be unified around a main point. Normally, a good topic sentence summarizes the paragraph's main point. A topic sentence is a general sentence that gives an introduction to the paragraph. The sentences that follow are a support to the topic sentence. However, the topic sentence can come as the final sentence to the paragraph if the earlier sentences give a clear explanation of the topic sentence. Overall, the paragraphs need to stay true to the main point. This means that any unnecessary sentences that do not advance the main point should be removed.

The main point of a paragraph requires adequate development (i.e., a substantial paragraph that covers the main point). A paragraph of two or three sentences does not cover a main point. This is true when the main point of the paragraph gives strong support to the argument of the thesis. An occasional short paragraph is fine as a transitional device. However, a well-developed argument will have paragraphs with more than a few sentences.

Methods of Developing Paragraphs
A common method of development with paragraphs can be done with **examples**. These examples are the supporting details to the main idea of a paragraph or a passage. When authors write about something that their audience may not understand, they can provide an example to show their point. When authors write about something that is not easily accepted, they can give examples to prove their point.

Illustrations are extended examples that require several sentences. Well selected illustrations can be a great way for authors to develop a point that may not be familiar to their audience.

Analogies make comparisons between items that appear to have nothing in common. Analogies are employed by writers to provoke fresh thoughts about a subject. These comparisons may be used to explain the unfamiliar, to clarify an abstract point, or to argue a point. Although analogies are effective literary devices, they should be used carefully in arguments. Two things may be alike in some respects but completely different in others.

Cause and effect is an excellent device used when the cause and effect are accepted as true. One way that authors can use cause and effect is to state the effect in the topic sentence of a paragraph and add the causes in the body of the paragraph. With this method, an author's paragraphs can have structure which always strengthens writing.

Types of Paragraphs

A **paragraph of narration** tells a story or a part of a story. Normally, the sentences are arranged in chronological order (i.e., the order that the events happened). However, flashbacks (i.e., beginning the story at an earlier time) can be included.

A **descriptive paragraph** makes a verbal portrait of a person, place, or thing. When specific details are used that appeal to one or more of the senses (i.e., sight, sound, smell, taste, and touch), authors give readers a sense of being present in the moment.

A **process paragraph** is related to time order (i.e., First, you open the bottle. Second, you pour the liquid, etc.). Usually, this describes a process or teaches readers how to perform a process.

Comparing two things draws attention to their similarities and indicates a number of differences. When authors contrast, they focus only on differences. Both comparisons and contrasts may be used point-by-point or in following paragraphs.

Reasons for starting a new paragraph include:

1. To mark off the introduction and concluding paragraphs
2. To signal a shift to a new idea or topic
3. To indicate an important shift in time or place
4. To explain a point in additional detail
5. To highlight a comparison, contrast, or cause and effect relationship

Paragraph Length

Most readers find that their comfort level for a paragraph is between 100 and 200 words. Shorter paragraphs cause too much starting and stopping, and give a choppy effect. Paragraphs that are too long often test the attention span of readers. Two notable exceptions to this rule exist. In scientific or scholarly papers, longer paragraphs suggest seriousness and depth. In journalistic writing, constraints are placed on paragraph size by the narrow columns in a newspaper format.

The first and last paragraphs of a text will usually be the introduction and conclusion. These special-purpose paragraphs are likely to be shorter than paragraphs in the body of the work. Paragraphs in the body of the essay follow the subject's outline; one paragraph per point in short essays and a group of paragraphs per point in longer works. Some ideas require more development than others, so it is good for a writer to remain flexible. A paragraph of excessive length may be divided, and shorter ones may be combined.

Coherent Paragraphs

A smooth flow of sentences and paragraphs without gaps, shifts, or bumps will lead to paragraph coherence. Ties between old and new information can be smoothed by several methods:

- Linking ideas clearly, from the topic sentence to the body of the paragraph, is essential for a smooth transition. The topic sentence states the main point, and this should be followed by specific details, examples, and illustrations that support the topic sentence. The support may be direct or indirect. In indirect support, the illustrations and examples may support a sentence that in turn supports the topic directly.
- The repetition of key words adds coherence to a paragraph. To avoid dull language, variations of the key words may be used.
- Parallel structures are often used within sentences to emphasize the similarity of ideas and connect sentences giving similar information.
- Maintaining a consistent verb tense throughout the paragraph helps. Shifting tenses affects the smooth flow of words and can disrupt the coherence of the paragraph.

Mathematics and Quantitative Skills Test

Numbers and Operations

Numbers and Their Classifications

There are several different kinds of numbers. When you learn to count as a child, you typical start with *Natural Numbers*. These are sometimes called "counting numbers" and begin with 1, 2, 3 ... etc. *Whole Numbers* include all natural numbers as well as 0. *Integers* include all whole numbers as well as their associated negative values (...-2, -1, 0, 1, 2...). Fractions with an integer in the numerator and a non-zero integer in the denominator are called *Rational Numbers*. Numbers such as π, that are non-terminating and non-repeating and cannot be expressed as a fraction, are considered *Irrational Numbers*. Any number that contains the imaginary number *i*, where $i^2 = -1$ and $i = \sqrt{-1}$, is referred to as a *Complex Number*. All natural numbers, whole numbers, integers, rational numbers, and irrational numbers are *Real Numbers*; complex numbers are not real numbers.

Aside from the number 1, all natural numbers can either be classified as prime or composite. *Prime Numbers* are natural numbers greater than 1 whose only factors are 1 and itself. On the other hand, *Composite Numbers* are natural numbers greater than 1 that are not prime numbers. 1 is a special case in that it is neither a prime number nor composite number. According to the *Fundamental Theorem of Arithmetic*, every composite number can be uniquely written as the product of prime numbers.

Numbers are the basic building blocks of mathematics. Specific features of numbers are identified by the following terms:

Integers – The set of positive and negative numbers, including zero. Integers do not include fractions $\left(\frac{1}{3}\right)$, decimals (0.56), or mixed numbers $\left(7\frac{3}{4}\right)$.

Even number – Any integer that can be divided by 2 without leaving a remainder. For example: 2, 4, 6, 8, and so on.

Odd number – Any integer that cannot be divided evenly by 2. For example: 3, 5, 7, 9, and so on.

Decimal number – a number that uses a decimal point to show the part of the number that is less than one. Example: 1.234.

Decimal point – a symbol used to separate the ones place from the tenths place in decimals or dollars from cents in currency.

Decimal place – the position of a number to the right of the decimal point. In the decimal 0.123, the 1 is in the first place to the right of the decimal point, indicating tenths; the 2 is in the second place, indicating hundredths; and the 3 is in the third place, indicating thousandths.

➢ **Review Video: Numbers and Their Classifications**
*Visit **mometrix.com/academy** and enter **Code:*** **461071**

Operations

There are four basic mathematical operations:
Addition increases the value of one quantity by the value of another quantity. Example: $2 + 4 = 6$; $8 + 9 = 17$. The result is called the sum. With addition, the order does not matter. $4 + 2 = 2 + 4$.

Subtraction is the opposite operation to addition; it decreases the value of one quantity by the value of another quantity. Example: $6 - 4 = 2$; $17 - 8 = 9$. The result is called the difference. Note that with subtraction, the order does matter. $6 - 4 \neq 4 - 6$.

Multiplication can be thought of as repeated addition. One number tells how many times to add the other number to itself. Example: 3×2 (three times two) $= 2 + 2 + 2 = 6$. With multiplication, the order does not matter. 2×3 (or $3 + 3$) $= 3 \times 2$ (or $2 + 2 + 2$).

Division is the opposite operation to multiplication; one number tells us how many parts to divide the other number into. Example: $20 \div 4 = 5$; if 20 is split into 4 equal parts, each part is 5. With division, the order of the numbers does matter. $20 \div 4 \neq 4 \div 20$.

Parentheses and Exponents

An exponent is a superscript number placed next to another number at the top right. It indicates how many times the base number is to be multiplied by itself. Exponents provide a shorthand way to write what would be a longer mathematical expression. Example: $a^2 = a \times a$; $2^4 = 2 \times 2 \times 2 \times 2$. A number with an exponent of 2 is said to be "squared," while a number with an exponent of 3 is said to be "cubed." The value of a number raised to an exponent is called its power. So, 8^4 is read as "8 to the 4th power," or "8 raised to the power of 4." A negative exponent is the same as the reciprocal of a positive exponent. Example: $a^{-2} = 1/a^2$.

Parentheses are used to designate which operations should be done first when there are multiple operations. Example: $4 - (2 + 1) = 1$; the parentheses tell us that we must add 2 and 1, and then subtract the sum from 4, rather than subtracting 2 from 4 and then adding 1 (this would give us an answer of 3).

Order of Operations

Order of Operations is a set of rules that dictates the order in which we must perform each operation in an expression so that we will evaluate at accurately. If we have an expression that includes multiple different operations, Order of Operations tells us which operations to do first. The most common mnemonic for Order of Operations is PEMDAS, or "Please Excuse My Dear Aunt Sally." PEMDAS stands for Parentheses, Exponents, Multiplication, Division, Addition, Subtraction. It is important to understand that multiplication and division have equal precedence, as do addition and subtraction, so those pairs of operations are simply worked from left to right in order.

Example: Evaluate the expression $5 + 20 \div 4 \times (2 + 3)^2 - 6$ using the correct order of operations.
P: Perform the operations inside the parentheses, $(2 + 3) = 5$.
E: Simplify the exponents, $(5)^2 = 25$.
The equation now looks like this: $5 + 20 \div 4 \times 25 - 6$.
MD: Perform multiplication and division from left to right, $20 \div 4 = 5$; then $5 \times 25 = 125$.
The equation now looks like this: $5 + 125 - 6$.
AS: Perform addition and subtraction from left to right, $5 + 125 = 130$; then $130 - 6 = 124$.

> **Review Video: Order of Operations**
> *Visit **mometrix.com/academy** and enter **Code:** **259675***

Roots and Square Roots

A root, such as a square root, is another way of writing a fractional exponent. Instead of using a superscript, roots use the radical symbol ($\sqrt{}$) to indicate the operation. A radical will have a number underneath the bar, and may sometimes have a number in the upper left: $\sqrt[n]{a}$, read as "the nth root of a." The relationship between radical notation and exponent notation can be described by this equation: $\sqrt[n]{a} = a^{1/n}$. The two special cases of n = 2 and n = 3 are called square roots and cube roots. If there is no number to the upper left, it is understood to be a square root (n = 2). Nearly all of the roots you encounter will be square roots. A square root is the same as a number raised to the one-half power. When we say that a is the square root of b ($a = \sqrt{b}$), we mean that a multiplied by itself equals b: ($a \times a = b$).

A perfect square is a number that has an integer for its square root. There are 10 perfect squares from 1 to 100: 1, 4, 9, 16, 25, 36, 49, 64, 81, 100 (the squares of integers 1 through 10).

Factors and Multiples

Factors are numbers that are multiplied together to obtain a product. For example, in the equation $2 \times 3 = 6$, the numbers 2 and 3 are factors. A prime number has only two factors (1 and itself), but other numbers can have many factors.

> **Review Video: Factors**
> *Visit **mometrix.com/academy** and enter **Code:** **920086***

A common factor is a number that divides exactly into two or more other numbers. For example, the factors of 12 are 1, 2, 3, 4, 6, and 12, while the factors of 15 are 1, 3, 5, and 15. The common factors of 12 and 15 are 1 and 3. A prime factor is also a prime number. Therefore, the prime factors of 12 are 2 and 3. For 15, the prime factors are 3 and 5.

The greatest common factor (GCF) is the largest number that is a factor of two or more numbers. For example, the factors of 15 are 1, 3, 5, and 15; the factors of 35 are 1, 5, 7, and 35. Therefore, the greatest common factor of 15 and 35 is 5.

The least common multiple (LCM) is the smallest number that is a multiple of two or more numbers. For example, the multiples of 3 include 3, 6, 9, 12, 15, etc.; the multiples of 5 include 5, 10, 15, 20, etc. Therefore, the least common multiple of 3 and 5 is 15.

> ➤ **Review Video: Multiples**
> *Visit **mometrix.com/academy** and enter **Code:** **626738***

Fractions

A fraction is a number that is expressed as one integer written above another integer, with a dividing line between them ($\frac{x}{y}$). It represents the quotient of the two numbers "x divided by y." It can also be thought of as x out of y equal parts.

The top number of a fraction is called the numerator, and it represents the number of parts under consideration. The 1 in $\frac{1}{4}$ means that 1 part out of the whole is being considered in the calculation. The bottom number of a fraction is called the denominator, and it represents the total number of equal parts. The 4 in $\frac{1}{4}$ means that the whole consists of 4 equal parts. A fraction cannot have a denominator of zero; this is referred to as "undefined."

Fractions can be manipulated by multiplying or dividing (but not adding or subtracting) both the numerator and denominator by the same number, without changing the value of the fraction. If you divide both numbers by a common factor, you are reducing or simplifying the fraction. Two fractions that have the same value, but are expressed differently are known as equivalent fractions. For example, $\frac{2}{10}, \frac{3}{15}, \frac{4}{20}$, and $\frac{5}{25}$ are all equivalent fractions. They can also all be reduced or simplified to $\frac{1}{5}$.

When two fractions are manipulated so that they have the same denominator, this is known as finding a common denominator. The number chosen to be that common denominator should be the least common multiple of the two original denominators. Example: $\frac{3}{4}$ and $\frac{5}{6}$; the least common multiple of 4 and 6 is 12. Manipulating to achieve the common denominator: $\frac{3}{4} = \frac{9}{12}; \frac{5}{6} = \frac{10}{12}$.

A fraction whose denominator is greater than its numerator is known as a proper fraction, while a fraction whose numerator is greater than its denominator is known as an improper fraction. Proper fractions have values less than one and improper fractions have values greater than one.

A mixed number is a number that contains both an integer and a fraction. Any improper fraction can be rewritten as a mixed number. Example: $\frac{8}{3} = \frac{6}{3} + \frac{2}{3} = 2 + \frac{2}{3} = 2\frac{2}{3}$. Similarly, any mixed number can be rewritten as an improper fraction. Example: $1\frac{3}{5} = 1 + \frac{3}{5} = \frac{5}{5} + \frac{3}{5} = \frac{8}{5}$.

A fraction that contains a fraction in the numerator, denominator, or both is called a *Complex Fraction*. These can be solved in a number of ways; with the simplest being by following the order of operations as stated earlier. For example, $\left(\frac{4}{7}\right)\Big/\left(\frac{5}{8}\right) = 0.571/_{0.625} = 0.914$. Another way to solve this problem is to multiply the fraction in the numerator by the recipricol of the fraction in the denominator. For example, $\left(\frac{4}{7}\right)\Big/\left(\frac{5}{8}\right) = \frac{4}{7} \times \frac{8}{5} = \frac{32}{35} = 0.914$.

> **Review Video: Fractions**
> *Visit **mometrix.com/academy** and enter **Code:*** **262335**

Operations with Fractions

Adding and Subtracting Fractions

If two fractions have a common denominator, they can be added or subtracted simply by adding or subtracting the two numerators and retaining the same denominator. Example: $\frac{1}{2} + \frac{1}{4} = \frac{2}{4} + \frac{1}{4} = \frac{3}{4}$. If the two fractions do not already have the same denominator, one or both of them must be manipulated to achieve a common denominator before they can be added or subtracted.

Multiplying Fractions

Two fractions can be multiplied by multiplying the two numerators to find the new numerator and the two denominators to find the new denominator. Example: $\frac{1}{3} \times \frac{2}{3} = \frac{1\times2}{3\times3} = \frac{2}{9}$.

Dividing Fractions

Two fractions can be divided by flipping the numerator and denominator of the second fraction and then proceeding as though it were a multiplication. Example: $\frac{2}{3} \div \frac{3}{4} = \frac{2}{3} \times \frac{4}{3} = \frac{8}{9}$.

Operations with Decimals

Adding and Subtracting Decimals

When adding and subtracting decimals, the decimal points must always be aligned. Adding decimals is just like adding regular whole numbers. Example: 4.5 + 2 = 6.5.

If the problem-solver does not properly align the decimal points, an incorrect answer of 4.7 may result. An easy way to add decimals is to align all of the decimal points in a vertical column visually. This will allow one to see exactly where the decimal should be placed in the final answer. Begin adding from right to left. Add each column in turn, making sure to carry the number to the left if a column adds up to more than 9. The same rules apply to the subtraction of decimals.

> **Review Video: Adding and Subtracting Decimals**
> *Visit **mometrix.com/academy** and enter **Code:*** **381101**

Multiplying Decimals

A simple multiplication problem has two components: a multiplicand and a multiplier. When multiplying decimals, work as though the numbers were whole rather than decimals. Once the final product is calculated, count the number of places to the right of the decimal in both the multiplicand and the multiplier. Then, count that number of places from the right of the product and place the decimal in that position. For example, 12.3 × 2.56 has three places to the right of the respective decimals. Multiply 123 × 256 to get 31488. Now, beginning on the right, count three places to the left and insert the decimal. The final product will be 31.488.

> ➢ **Review Video: Multiplying Decimals**
> *Visit **mometrix.com/academy** and enter **Code:*** **731574**

Dividing Decimals

Every division problem has a divisor and a dividend. The dividend is the number that is being divided. In the problem 14 ÷ 7, 14 is the dividend and 7 is the divisor. In a division problem with decimals, the divisor must be converted into a whole number. Begin by moving the decimal in the divisor to the right until a whole number is created. Next, move the decimal in the dividend the same number of spaces to the right. For example, 4.9 into 24.5 would become 49 into 245. The decimal was moved one space to the right to create a whole number in the divisor, and then the same was done for the dividend. Once the whole numbers are created, the problem is carried out normally: 245 ÷ 49 = 5.

> ➢ **Review Video: Dividing Decimals**
> *Visit **mometrix.com/academy** and enter **Code:*** **560690**

Percentages

Percentages can be thought of as fractions that are based on a whole of 100; that is, one whole is equal to 100%. The word percent means "per hundred." Fractions can be expressed as percents by finding equivalent fractions with a denomination of 100. Example: $\frac{7}{10} = \frac{70}{100} = 70\%$; $\frac{1}{4} = \frac{25}{100} = 25\%$.

To express a percentage as a fraction, divide the percentage number by 100 and reduce the fraction to its simplest possible terms. Example: $60\% = \frac{60}{100} = \frac{3}{5}$; $96\% = \frac{96}{100} = \frac{24}{25}$.

Converting decimals to percentages and percentages to decimals is as simple as moving the decimal point. To convert from a decimal to a percent, move the decimal point two places to the right. To convert from a percent to a decimal, move it two places to the left. Example: 0.23 = 23%; 5.34 = 534%; 0.007 = 0.7%; 700% = 7.00; 86% = 0.86; 0.15% = 0.0015.
It may be helpful to remember that the percentage number will always be larger than the equivalent decimal number.

A percentage problem can be presented three main ways: (1) Find what percentage of some number another number is. Example: What percentage of 40 is 8? (2) Find what number is some percentage of a given number. Example: What number is 20% of 40? (3) Find what number another number is a given percentage of. Example: What number is 8 20% of? The three components in all of these cases are the same: a whole (W), a part (P), and a percentage (%). These are related by the equation: P = W × %. This is the form of the equation you would use to solve problems of type (2). To solve types (1) and (3), you would use these two forms: % = P/W and W = P/%.

The thing that frequently makes percentage problems difficult is that they are most often also word problems, so a large part of solving them is figuring out which quantities are what. Example: In a school cafeteria, 7 students choose pizza, 9 choose hamburgers, and 4 choose tacos. Find the percentage that chooses tacos. To find the whole, you must first add all of the parts: 7 + 9 + 4 = 20. The percentage can then be found by dividing the part by the whole (% = P/W): $\frac{4}{20} = \frac{20}{100} = 20\%$.

> ➢ **Review Video: Percentages**
> *Visit* ***mometrix.com/academy*** *and enter* ***Code:*** **141911**

Converting Percents, Fractions, and Decimals

Example 1

15% can be written as a fraction and as a decimal. 15% written as a fraction is $\frac{15}{100}$ which equals $\frac{3}{20}$. 15% written as a decimal is 0.15.

To convert a percent to a fraction, follow these steps:

1) Write the percent over 100 because percent means "per one hundred." So, 15% can be written as $\frac{15}{100}$.
2) Fractions should be written in simplest form, which means that the numbers in the numerator and denominator should be reduced if possible. Both 15 and 100 can be divided by 5.
3) Therefore, $\frac{15 \div 5}{100 \div 5} = \frac{3}{20}$.

To convert a percent to a decimal, follow these steps:

1) Write the percent over 100 because percent means "per one hundred." So, 15% can be written as $\frac{15}{100}$.
2) 15 divided by 100 equals 0.15, so 15% = 0.15. In other words, when converting from a percent to a decimal, drop the percent sign and move the decimal two places to the left.

Example 2

Write 24.36% as a fraction and then as a decimal. Explain how you made these conversions.

24.36% written as a fraction is $\frac{24.36}{100}$, or $\frac{2436}{10{,}000}$, which reduces to $\frac{609}{2500}$. 24.36% written as a decimal is 0.2436. Recall that dividing by 100 moves the decimal two places to the left.

> ➢ **Review Video: Converting Percentages to Decimals and Fractions**
> *Visit* ***mometrix.com/academy*** *and enter* ***Code:*** **287297**

Example 3

Convert $\frac{4}{5}$ to a decimal and to a percent.

To convert a fraction to a decimal, simply divide the numerator by the denominator in the fraction. The numerator is the top number in the fraction and the denominator is the bottom number in a fraction. So $\frac{4}{5} = 4 \div 5 = 0.80 = 0.8$.
Percent means "per hundred." $\frac{4 \times 20}{5 \times 20} = \frac{80}{100} = 80\%$.

Example 4

Convert $3\frac{2}{5}$ to a decimal and to a percent.

The mixed number $3\frac{2}{5}$ has a whole number and a fractional part. The fractional part $\frac{2}{5}$ can be written as a decimal by dividing 5 into 2, which gives 0.4. Adding the whole to the part gives 3.4. Alternatively, note that $3\frac{2}{5} = 3\frac{4}{10} = 3.4$
To change a decimal to a percent, multiply it by 100.
$3.4(100) = 340\%$. Notice that this percentage is greater than 100%. This makes sense because the original mixed number $3\frac{2}{5}$ is greater than 1.

- **Review Video:** Converting Fractions to Percentages and Decimals
  *Visit **mometrix.com/academy** and enter **Code:*** **306233**

- **Review Video:** Converting Decimals to Fractions and Percentages
  *Visit **mometrix.com/academy** and enter **Code:*** **986765**

Ratios

A ratio is a comparison of two quantities in a particular order. Example: If there are 14 computers in a lab, and the class has 20 students, there is a student to computer ratio of 20 to 14, commonly written as 20:14.

Two more comparisons used frequently in algebra are ratios and proportions. A *Ratio* is a comparison of two quantitites, expressed in a number of different ways. Ratios can be listed as "a to b", "a:b", or "a/b". Examples of ratios are miles per hour (miles/hour), meters per second (meters/second), miles per gallon (miles/gallon), etc..

- **Review Video:** Ratios
  *Visit **mometrix.com/academy** and enter **Code:*** **996914**

Proportions and Cross Products

A proportion is a relationship between two quantities that dictates how one changes when the other changes. A direct proportion describes a relationship in which a quantity increases by a set amount for every increase in the other quantity, or decreases by that same amount for every decrease in the other quantity. Example: For every 1 sheet cake, 18 people can be served cake. The number of sheet cakes, and the number of people that can be served from them is directly proportional.

A statement of two equal ratios is a *Proportion*, such as $\frac{m}{b} = \frac{w}{z}$. If Fred travels 2 miles in 1 hour and Jane travels 4 miles in 2 hours, their speeds are said to be proportional because $\frac{2}{1} = \frac{4}{2}$. In a proportion, the product of the numerator of the first ratio and the denominator of the second ratio is equal to the product of the denominator of the first ratio and the numerator of the second ratio. Using the previous example we see that $m \times z = b \times w$, thus $2 \times 2 = 1 \times 4$.

➢ **Review Video: Proportions**
Visit ***mometrix.com/academy*** *and enter* ***Code:*** **505355**

Inverse proportion is a relationship in which an increase in one quantity is accompanied by a decrease in the other, or vice versa. Example: the time required for a car trip decreases as the speed increases, and increases as the speed decreases, so the time required is inversely proportional to the speed of the car.

Scientific Notation

Scientific notation is a way of writing long numbers in a shorter form. The form $a \times 10^n$ is used in scientific notation. This form means that *a* is greater than or equal to 1 but less than 10. Also, *n* is the number of places the decimal must move to get from the original number to *a*.

Example: The number 230,400,000 is long to write. To see this value in scientific notation, place a decimal point between the first and second numbers. This includes all digits through the last non-zero digit (a = 2.304).

To find the correct power of 10, count the number of places the decimal point had to move (n = 8). The number is positive if the decimal moved to the left. Thus, the number is negative if it moved to the right. So, 230,400,000 can be written as 2.304×10^8.

Now, let's look at the number 0.00002304. We have the same value for *a*. However, this time the decimal moved 5 places to the right (n = -5). So, 0.00002304 can be written as 2.304×10^{-5}. This notation makes it easy to compare very large or very small numbers. By comparing exponents, you can see that 3.28×10^4 is smaller than 1.51×10^5 because 4 is less than 5.

Addition and Subtraction
To add and subtract numbers in scientific notation, you need the numbers to have the same power of 10. Next, you can add the constants. Then, you can use the power of 10 with the result.

If the constant is greater than 10 or less than 1, you need to move the decimal place. For constants less than 1, the decimal is moved to the right. For constants greater than 10, the decimal is moved to the left. Also, the power of 10 needs to change as you move the decimal place.

Example 1
In the problem $(4.8 \times 10^4) + (2.2 \times 10^4)$, the numbers have the same power of 10. So, add 4.8 and 2.2. So, you have 7 as the result. Now, the number can be written as (7×10^4).

Example 2

In the problem $(3.1 \times 10^8) - (2.4 \times 10^8)$, the numbers have the same power of 10. So, subtract 3.4 and 1.1. So, you have 0.7 as the result. Remember that you cannot have a constant that is less than 1. So, you need to move the decimal place one time to the right: (7×10^8). Also, the power of 10 has to change. Now, the number can be written as (7×10^{-1}).

The power of 10 is -1 because we moved the decimal place one time to the right. Now you have $(7 \times 10^{-1}) \times 10^8$. The reason is that we still have the power of 10 as 8. Now, you can add the -1 to the +8 for an answer of (7×10^7).

Example 3

In the problem$(5.3 \times 10^6) + (2.7 \times 10^7)$, the numbers do not have the same power of 10. So, you need one of the terms to have the same power. So, take (5.3×10^6) and change it to (0.53×10^7). Now, you can add 0.53 and 2.7. So, the number can be written as (3.23×10^7).

Multiplication

In the problem $(2.4 \times 10^3) \times (5.7 \times 10^5)$, you need to multiply 2.4 and 5.7. Then, you need to add the powers of 10 which are 3 and 5 for this example. So, you have (13.68×10^8). Remember that this cannot be an answer for scientific notation. The 13.68 for a constant is higher than 10. So, move the decimal to the left one time and change the exponent. Now, you have (1.368×10^9) as the answer.

Division

In the problem $(5.6 \times 10^6) \div (2.3 \times 10^2)$, you need to divide 5.6 and 2.3. Then, you need to subtract the powers of 10 which are 6 and 2 for this example. So, you have (2.43×10^4).

Functions

Example 1

The table below is the value of each part of an ordered pair. An ordered pair is written as: (x, y)

x	*y*
2	6
4	12
6	18
8	24

You can find y if you know x. The number in the y column is three times the number in the x column. Multiply the x number by 3 to get the y number.

x	*y*
2	$2 \times 3 = 6$
4	$4 \times 3 = 12$
6	$6 \times 3 = 18$
8	$8 \times 3 = 24$

Example 2
The table shows some data points for a linear function. What is the missing value in the table?

x	*y*
0	?
3	50
5	80

The data in the table represent a linear function. For a linear function, the rate of change is equal to the slope. To find the slope, calculate the change in *y* divided by the change in *x* for the two given points from the table: $m = \frac{80-50}{5-3} = \frac{30}{2} = 15$

The rate of change of the linear function is 15. This means for each increase of 1 in the value of *x*, the value of *y* increases by 15. Similarly, each decrease of 1 in the value of *x* decreases the value of *y* by 15. The *x*-value 0 is 3 less than 3, so subtract $3 \cdot 15 = 45$ from 50 to get $y = 5$. This is the missing value in the table.

Sequencing

Example 1
Use the sequence to find each of the following.
6, 13, 20, 27, 34, 41, ...
a) Find the position of 34.
b) Find the value of the term in position 7.

a) The position of a term is its place in the sequence. The sequence begins with 6, in position 1, 13 is position 2, etc. The term 34 has a position of 5.
b) The terms in positions 1 through 6 are given. To find the term in position 7, identify the difference between each term.
13 – 6 = 7
20 – 13 = 7
27 – 20 = 7
34 – 27 = 7
41 – 34 = 7
The terms are increasing by 7. To find the 7th term, add 7 to the sixth term, 41:
41 + 7 = 48
The term in position 7 is 48.

Example 2
The *n*th term of a sequence is: $4n - 6$. Find the terms in position: 1, 4, and 10.

To find the terms in each given position, evaluate the expression for the *n*th term at the given position values.
1st term: 4(1) – 6 = 4 – 6 = –2
4th term: 4(4) – 6 = 16 – 6 = 10
10th term: 4(10) – 6 = 40 – 6 = 34

Example 3
Write an algebraic expression to determine the *n*th term of the arithmetic sequence:
31, 25, 19, 13, ...

To find the *n*th term, find the common difference between each pair of given terms.
2nd term – 1st term: $25 - 31 = -6$
3rd term – 2nd term: $19 - 25 = -6$
4th term – 3rd term: $13 - 19 = -6$
The first term is 31, so when $n = 1$, the term is 31.
1st term: $31 + -6(n - 1)$

Simplify this expression and check it for terms 2, 3, and 4 by evaluating the expression at $n = 2, 3$, and 4.
$31 + -6(n - 1) = 31 - 6n + 6 = -6n + 37$
2nd term: $-6(2) + 37 = -12 + 37 = 25$
3rd term: $-6(3) + 37 = -18 + 37 = 19$
4th term: $-6(4) + 37 = -24 + 37 = 13$
The *n*th term of the arithmetic sequence is $-6n + 37$.

Algebra

Absolute Value

A precursor to working with negative numbers is understanding what absolute values are. A number's *Absolute Value* is simply the distance away from zero a number is on the number line. The absolute value of a number is always positive and is written $|x|$.

Example
Show that $|3| = |-3|$.

The absolute value of 3, written as $|3|$, is 3 because the distance between 0 and 3 on a number line is three units. Likewise, the absolute value of –3, written as $|-3|$, is 3 because the distance between 0 and –3 on a number line is three units. So, $|3| = |-3|$.

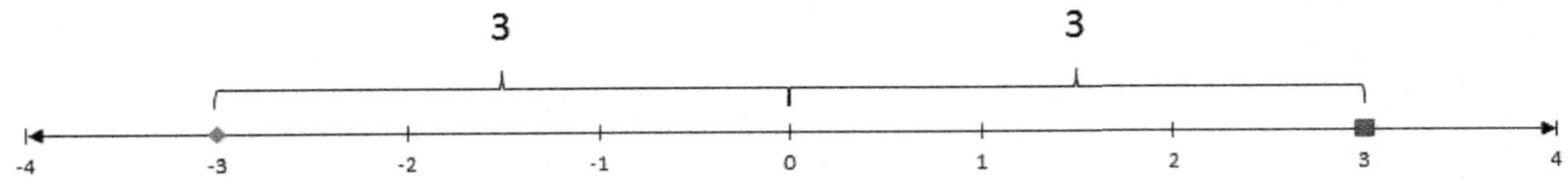

Working with Positive & Negative Numbers

A precursor to working with negative numbers is understanding what absolute values are. A number's *Absolute Value* is simply the distance away from zero a number is on the number line. The absolute value of a number is always positive and is written $|x|$.

When adding signed numbers, if the signs are the same simply add the absolute values of the addends and apply the original sign to the sum. For example, $(+4) + (+8) = +12$ and $(-4) + (-8) = -12$. When the original signs are different, take the absolute values of the addends and subtract the smaller value from the larger value, then apply the original sign of the larger value to the difference. For instance, $(+4) + (-8) = -4$ and $(-4) + (+8) = +4$.

For subtracting signed numbers, change the sign of the number after the minus symbol and then follow the same rules used for addition. For example, $(+4) - (+8) = (+4) + (-8) = -4$.

If the signs are the same the product is positive when multiplying signed numbers. For example, $(+4) \times (+8) = +32$ and $(-4) \times (-8) = +32$. If the signs are opposite, the product is negative. For example, $(+4) \times (-8) = -32$ and $(-4) \times (+8) = -32$. When more than two factors are multiplied together, the sign of the product is determined by how many negative factors are present. If there are an odd number of negative factors then the product is negative, whereas an even number of negative factors indicates a positive product. For instance, $(+4) \times (-8) \times (-2) = +64$ and $(-4) \times (-8) \times (-2) = -64$.

The rules for dividing signed numbers are similar to multiplying signed numbers. If the dividend and divisor have the same sign, the quotient is positive. If the dividend and divisor have opposite signs, the quotient is negative. For example, $(-4) \div (+8) = -0.5$.

Solving for a Variable

Similar to order of operation rules, algebraic rules must be obeyed to ensure a correct answer. Begin by locating all parentheses and brackets, and then solving the equations within them. Then, perform the operations necessary to remove all parentheses and brackets. Next, convert all fractions into whole numbers and combine common terms on each side of the equation.

Beginning on the left side of the expression, solve operations involving multiplication and division. Then, work left to right solving operations involving addition and subtraction. Finally, cross-multiply if necessary to reach the final solution.

Example 1:
$4a-10=10$

Constants are the numbers in equations that do not change. The variable in this equation is a. Variables are most commonly presented as either x or y, but they can be any letter. Every variable is equal to a number; one must solve the equation to determine what that number is. In an algebraic expression, the answer will usually be the number represented by the variable. In order to solve this equation, keep in mind that what is done to one side must be done to the other side as well. The first step will be to remove 10 from the left side by adding 10 to both sides. This will be expressed as $4a-10+10=10+10$, which simplifies to $4a=20$. Next, remove the 4 by dividing both sides by 4. This step will be expressed as $4a\div4=20\div4$. The expression now becomes $a=5$.

Since variables are the letters that represent an unknown number, you must solve for that unknown number in single variable problems. The main thing to remember is that you can do anything to one side of an equation as long as you do it to the other.

Example 2:
Solve for x in the equation $2x + 3 = 5$.

Answer: First you want to get the "2x" isolated by itself on one side. To do that, first get rid of the 3. Subtract 3 from both sides of the equation $2x + 3 - 3 = 5 - 3$ or $2x = 2$. Now since the x is being multiplied by the 2 in "2x", you must divide by 2 to get rid of it. So, divide both sides by 2, which gives $2x / 2 = 2 / 2$ or $x = 1$.

Manipulating Equations

Sometimes you will have variables missing in equations. So, you need to find the missing variable. To do this, you need to remember one important thing: whatever you do to one side of an equation, you need to do to the other side. If you subtract 100 from one side of an equation, you need to subtract 100 from the other side of the equation. This will allow you to change the form of the equation to find missing values.

Example
Ray earns $10 an hour. This can be given with the expression $10x$, where x is equal to the number of hours that Ray works. This is the independent variable. The independent variable is the amount that can change. The money that Ray earns is in y hours. So, you would write the equation: $10x = y$. The variable y is the dependent variable. This depends on x and cannot be changed. Now, let's say that Ray makes $360. How many hours did he work to make $360?

$$10x = 360$$

Now, you want to know how many hours that Ray worked. So, you want to get x by itself. To do that, you can divide both sides of the equation by 10.

$$\frac{10x}{10} = \frac{360}{10}$$

So, you have: $x = 36$. Now, you know that Ray worked 36 hours to make $360.

Laws of Exponents

The laws of exponents are as follows:

1) Any number to the power of 1 is equal to itself: $a^1 = a$.
2) The number 1 raised to any power is equal to 1: $1^n = 1$.
3) Any number raised to the power of 0 is equal to 1: $a^0 = 1$.
4) Add exponents to multiply powers of the same base number: $a^n \times a^m = a^{n+m}$.
5) Subtract exponents to divide powers of the same number; that is $a^n \div a^m = a^{n-m}$.
6) Multiply exponents to raise a power to a power: $(a^n)^m = a^{n \times m}$.
7) If multiplied or divided numbers inside parentheses are collectively raised to a power, this is the same as each individual term being raised to that power: $(a \times b)^n = a^n \times b^n$; $(a \div b)^n = a^n \div b^n$.

Note: Exponents do not have to be integers. Fractional or decimal exponents follow all the rules above as well. Example: $5^{\frac{1}{4}} \times 5^{\frac{3}{4}} = 5^{\frac{1}{4}+\frac{3}{4}} = 5^1 = 5$.

➢ **Review Video:** Law of Exponents
*Visit **mometrix.com/academy** and enter **Code:*** **532558**

Polynomial Algebra

Equations are made up of monomials and polynomials. A *Monomial* is a single variable or product of constants and variables, such as *x*, *2x*, or $\frac{2}{x}$. There will never be addition or subtraction symbols in a monomial. Like monomials have like variables, but they may have different coefficients. *Polynomials* are algebraic expressions which use addition and subtraction to combine two or more monomials. Two terms make a binomial; three terms make a trinomial; etc.. The *Degree of a Monomial* is the sum of the exponents of the variables. The *Degree of a Polynomial* is the highest degree of any individual term.

Add Polynomials

To add polynomials, you need to add like terms. These terms have the same variable part. An example is $4x^2$ and $3x^2$ have x^2 terms. To find the sum of like terms, find the sum of the coefficients. Then, keep the same variable part. You can use the distributive property to distribute the plus sign to each term of the polynomial. For example:

$(4x^2 - 5x + 7) + (3x^2 + 2x + 1) =$
$(4x^2 - 5x + 7) + 3x^2 + 2x + 1 =$
$(4x^2 + 3x^2) + (-5x + 2x) + (7 + 1) =$
$7x^2 - 3x + 8$

Subtract Polynomials

To subtract polynomials, you need to subtract like terms. To find the difference of like terms, find the difference of the coefficients. Then, keep the same variable part. You can use the distributive property to distribute the minus sign to each term of the polynomial. For example:

$(-2x^2 - x + 5) - (3x^2 - 4x + 1) =$
$(-2x^2 - x + 5) - 3x^2 + 4x - 1 =$
$(-2x^2 - 3x^2) + (-x + 4x) + (5 - 1) =$
$-5x^2 + 3x + 4$

Multiply Polynomials

To multiply two binomials, follow the *FOIL* method. FOIL stands for:

- First: Multiply the first term of each binomial
- Outer: Multiply the outer terms of each binomial
- Inner: Multiply the inner terms of each binomial
- Last: Multiply the last term of each binomial

Using FOIL $(Ax + By)(Cx + Dy) = ACx^2 + ADxy + BCxy + BDy^2$.

Example: $(3x + 6)(4x - 2)$

First: $3x \times 4x = 12x^2$
Outer: $3x \times -2 = -6x$ | Current Expression: $12x^2 - 6x$
Inner: $6 \times 4x = 24x$ | Current Expression: $12x^2 - 6x + 24x$
Last: $6 \times -2 = -12$ | Final Expression: $12x^2 - 6x + 24x - 12$

Now, combine like terms. For this example, that is $-6x + 24x$. Then, the expression looks like: $12x^2 + 18x - 12$. Each number is a multiple of 6. So, the expression becomes $6(2x^2 + 3x - 2)$, and the polynomial has been expanded.

Divide Polynomials

To divide polynomials, start with placing the terms of each polynomial in order of one variable. You may put them in ascending or descending order. Also, be consistent with both polynomials. To get the first term of the quotient, divide the first term of the dividend by the first term of the divisor. Next, multiply the first term of the quotient by the entire divisor. Then, subtract that product from the dividend and repeat for the following terms.

You want to end with a remainder of zero or a remainder with a degree that is less than the degree of the divisor. If the quotient has a remainder, write the answer as a mixed expression in the form: $\text{quotient} + \frac{\text{remainder}}{\text{divisor}}$.

Example: Divide $4x^5 + 3x^2 - x$ by x

$$\frac{4x^5}{x} + \frac{3x^2}{x} - \frac{x}{x} = 4x^4 + 3x - 1$$

Below are patterns of some special products to remember: *perfect trinomial squares*, the *difference between two squares*, the *sum and difference of two cubes*, and *perfect cubes*.

- Perfect Trinomial Squares: $x^2 + 2xy + y^2 = (x + y)^2$ or $x^2 - 2xy + y^2 = (x - y)^2$
- Difference between Two Squares: $x^2 - y^2 = (x + y)(x - y)$

- Sum of Two Cubes: $x^3 + y^3 = (x + y)(x^2 - xy + y^2)$
  Note: the second factor is NOT the same as a perfect trinomial square. So, do not try to factor it further.
- Difference between Two Cubes: $x^3 - y^3 = (x - y)(x^2 + xy + y^2)$
  Again, the second factor is NOT the same as a perfect trinomial square.
- Perfect Cubes: $x^3 + 3x^2y + 3xy^2 + y^3 = (x + y)^3$ and $x^3 - 3x^2y + 3xy^2 - y^3 = (x - y)^3$

Factor a Polynomial

1. Check for a common monomial factor.
2. Factor out the greatest common monomial factor
3. Look for patterns of special products: differences of two squares, the sum or difference of two cubes for binomial factors, or perfect trinomial squares for trinomial factors.

Example

Solve the equation $2x^2 - 5x - 12 = 0$ by factoring.

The expression $2x^2 - 5x - 12$ splits into two factors of the form $(2x + a)(x + b)$. To find *a* and *b,* you must find two factors of -12 that sum to -5 after one of them is doubled.

-12 can be factored in the following ways: 1 and -12 | 2 and -6 | 3 and -4 |
4 and -3 | 6 and -2 | 12 and -1.

Of these factors, only 3 and -4 will sum to -5 after we double one of them. Since -4 is the factor that must be doubled, it should go in position *b*, where it will be multiplied by $2x$ when the FOIL method is used. The factored expression is $(2x + 3)(x - 4)$. So, you are left with $(2x + 3)(x - 4) = 0$.

By the zero product property, each value of *x* that will make one of the factors equal zero is a solution to this equation. The first factor equals zero when $x = -1.5$, and the second factor equals zero when $x = 4$. So, those are the solutions.

Note: The factor may be a trinomial but not a perfect trinomial square. So, look for a factorable form: $x^2 + (a + b)x + ab = (x + a)(x + b)$
or $(ac)x^2 + (ad + bc)x + bd = (ax + b)(cx + d)$

Some factors may have four terms. So, look for groups to factor. After you have found the factors, write the original polynomial as the product of all the factors. Make sure that all of the polynomial factors are prime. Monomial factors may be prime or composite. Check your work by multiplying the factors to make sure you get the original polynomial.

➢ **Review Video: Polynomials**
*Visit **mometrix.com/academy** and enter **Code:*** **305005**

Inequalities

In algebra and higher areas of math, you will work with problems that do not equal each other. The statement comparing such expressions with symbols such as < (less than) or > (greater than) is called an *Inequality*.

One way to remember these symbols is to see that the sign for "less than" looks like an *L* for *L*ess. Also, the sign for "greater than" looks like half of an *R* in g*R*eater. The terms *less than or equal to, at most*, or *no more than* are for the symbol ≤. Also, the terms *greater than or equal to, at least*, and *no less than* are for the symbol ≥.

Graphing and Solving Inequalities

Solving inequalities can be done with the same rules as for solving equations. However, when multiplying or dividing by a negative number, the direction of the inequality sign must be flipped or reversed.

Example 1

An example of an inequality is $7x > 5$. To solve for x, divide both sides by 7,and the solution is $x > \frac{5}{7}$. Graphs of the solution set of inequalities are given on a number line. Open circles are used to show that an expression approaches a number. However, the open circle points out that it is not equal to that number.

Example 2

Graph $10 > -2x + 4$.

In order to graph the inequality $10 > -2x + 4$, you need to solve for *x*. The opposite of addition is subtraction. So, subtract 4 from both sides. This gives you $6 > -2x$.

Next, the opposite of multiplication is division. So, divide both sides by -2. Don't forget to flip the inequality symbol because you are dividing by a negative number. Now, you have $-3 < x$. You can rewrite this as $x > -3$.

To graph an inequality, you make a number line. Then, put a circle around the value that is being compared to *x*. If you are graphing a *greater than* or *less than* inequality, the circle remains open. This stands for all of the values except -3. If the inequality is *greater than or equal to* or *less than or equal to*, you draw a closed circle around the value. This would stand for all of the values including the number.

Finally, look over the values that the solution stands for. Then, shade the number line in the needed direction. This example calls for graphing all of the values greater than -3. This is all of the numbers to the right of -3. So, you shade this area on the number line.

Other Inequalities

Conditional Inequalities are those with certain values for the variable that will make the condition true. So, other values for the variable where the condition will be false. *Absolute Inequalities* can have any real number as the value for the variable to make the condition true. So, there is no real number value for the variable that will make the condition false.

Double Inequalities are when two inequality statements are part of the same variable expression. An example of this is $-c < ax + b < c$.

Solving Quadratic Equations

The *Quadratic Formula* is used to solve quadratic equations when other methods are more difficult. To use the quadratic formula to solve a quadratic equation, begin by rewriting the equation in standard form $ax^2 + bx + c = 0$, where a, b, and c are coefficients. Once you have identified the values of the coefficients, substitute those values into the quadratic formula $= \frac{-b \pm \sqrt{b^2 - 4ac}}{2a}$. Evaluate the equation and simplify the expression. Again, check each root by substituting into the original equation. In the quadratic formula, the portion of the formula under the radical $(b^2 - 4ac)$ is called the *Discriminant*. If the discriminant is zero, there is only one root: zero. If the discriminant is positive, there are two different real roots. If the discriminant is negative, there are no real roots.

To solve a quadratic equation by *Factoring*, begin by rewriting the equation in standard form, if necessary. Factor the side with the variable then set each of the factors equal to zero and solve the resulting linear equations. Check your answers by substituting the roots you found into the original equation. If, when writing the equation in standard form, you have an equation in the form $x^2 + c = 0$ or $x^2 - c = 0$, set $x^2 = -c$ or $x^2 = c$ and take the square root of c. If $c = 0$, the only real root is zero. If c is positive, there are two real roots—the positive and negative square root values. If c is negative, there are no real roots because you cannot take the square root of a negative number.

To solve a quadratic equation by *Completing the Square*, rewrite the equation so that all terms containing the variable are on the left side of the equal sign, and all the constants are on the right side of the equal sign. Make sure the coefficient of the squared term is 1. If there is a coefficient with the squared term, divide each term on both sides of the equal side by that number. Next, work with the coefficient of the single-variable term. Square half of this coefficient, and add that value to both sides. Now you can factor the left side (the side containing the variable) as the square of a binomial. $x^2 + 2ax + a^2 = C \Rightarrow (x + a)^2 = C$, where x is the variable, and a and C are constants. Take the square root of both sides and solve for the variable. Substitute the value of the variable in the original problem to check your work.

In order to solve a *Radical Equation*, begin by isolating the radical term on one side of the equation, and move all other terms to the other side of the equation. Look at the index of the radicand. Remember, if no number is given, the index is 2, meaning square root. Raise both sides of the equation to the power equal to the index of the radical. Solve the resulting equation as you would a normal polynomial equation. When you have found the roots, you must check them in the original problem to eliminate extraneous roots.

> **Review Video:** Solving Quadratic Equations
> *Visit* ***mometrix.com/academy*** *and enter* ***Code:*** **305005**

Geometry and Measurement

Lines and Planes

A point is a fixed location in space; has no size or dimensions; commonly represented by a dot.

A line is a set of points that extends infinitely in two opposite directions. It has length, but no width or depth. A line can be defined by any two distinct points that it contains. A line segment is a portion of a line that has definite endpoints. A ray is a portion of a line that extends from a single point on that line in one direction along the line. It has a definite beginning, but no ending.

A plane is a two-dimensional flat surface defined by three non-collinear points. A plane extends an infinite distance in all directions in those two dimensions. It contains an infinite number of points, parallel lines and segments, intersecting lines and segments, as well as parallel or intersecting rays. A plane will never contain a three-dimensional figure or skew lines. Two given planes will either be parallel or they will intersect to form a line. A plane may intersect a circular conic surface, such as a cone, to form conic sections, such as the parabola, hyperbola, circle or ellipse.

Perpendicular lines are lines that intersect at right angles. They are represented by the symbol $\perp$. The shortest distance from a line to a point not on the line is a perpendicular segment from the point to the line.

Parallel lines are lines in the same plane that have no points in common and never meet. It is possible for lines to be in different planes, have no points in common, and never meet, but they are not parallel because they are in different planes.

A bisector is a line or line segment that divides another line segment into two equal lengths. A perpendicular bisector of a line segment is composed of points that are equidistant from the endpoints of the segment it is dividing.

Intersecting lines are lines that have exactly one point in common. Concurrent lines are multiple lines that intersect at a single point.

A transversal is a line that intersects at least two other lines, which may or may not be parallel to one another. A transversal that intersects parallel lines is a common occurrence in geometry.

Coordinate Plane

When algebraic functions and equations are shown graphically, they are usually shown on a *Cartesian Coordinate Plane*. The Cartesian coordinate plane consists of two number lines placed perpendicular to each other, and intersecting at the zero point, also known as the origin. The horizontal number line is known as the x-axis, with positive values to the right of the origin, and negative values to the left of the origin. The vertical number line is known as the y-axis, with positive values above the origin, and negative values below the origin.

Any point on the plane can be identified by an ordered pair in the form (*x*,*y*), called coordinates. The *x*-value of the coordinate is called the abscissa, and the *y*-value of the coordinate is called the ordinate. The two number lines divide the plane into four quadrants: I, II, III, and IV.

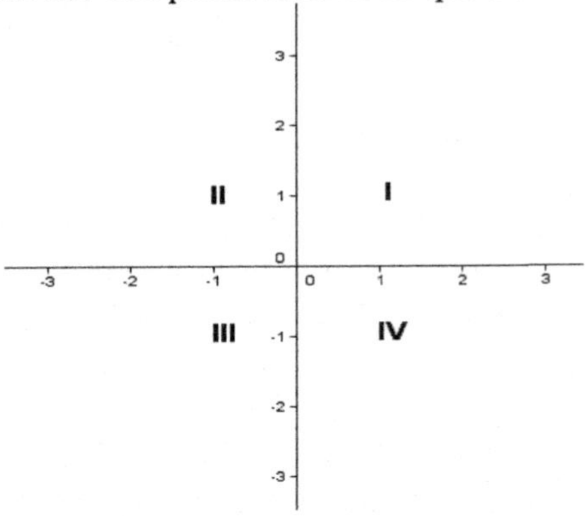

Before learning the different forms equations can be written in, it is important to understand some terminology. A ratio of the change in the vertical distance to the change in horizontal distance is called the *Slope*. On a graph with two points, (x_1, y_1) and (x_2, y_2), the slope is represented by the formula $= \frac{y_2 - y_1}{x_2 - x_1}$; $x_1 \neq x_2$. If the value of the slope is positive, the line slopes upward from left to right. If the value of the slope is negative, the line slopes downward from left to right. If the *y*-coordinates are the same for both points, the slope is 0 and the line is a *Horizontal Line*. If the *x*-coordinates are the same for both points, there is no slope and the line is a *Vertical Line*. Two or more lines that have equal slopes are *Parallel Lines*. *Perpendicular Lines* have slopes that are negative reciprocals of each other, such as $\frac{a}{b}$ and $\frac{-b}{a}$.

As mentioned previously, equations can be written many ways. Below is a list of the many forms equations can take.

- *Standard Form*: $Ax + By = C$; the slope is $\frac{-A}{B}$ and the *y*-intercept is $\frac{C}{B}$
- *Slope Intercept Form*: $y = mx + b$, where m is the slope and b is the *y*-intercept
- *Point-Slope Form*: $y - y_1 = m(x - x_1)$, where m is the slope and (x_1, y_1) is a point on the line
- *Two-Point Form*: $\frac{y - y_1}{x - x_1} = \frac{y_2 - y_1}{x_2 - x_1}$, where (x_1, y_1) and (x_2, y_2) are two points on the given line
- *Intercept Form*: $\frac{x}{x_1} + \frac{y}{y_1} = 1$, where $(x_1, 0)$ is the point at which a line intersects the *x*-axis, and $(0, y_1)$ is the point at which the same line intersects the *y*-axis

Equations can also be written as $ax + b = 0$, where $a \neq 0$. These are referred to as *One Variable Linear Equations*. A solution to an equation is called a *Root*. In the case where we have the equation $5x + 10 = 0$, if we solve for x we get a solution of $x = -2$. In other words, the root of the equation is -2. This is found by first subtracting 10 from both sides, which gives $5x = -10$. Next, simply divide both sides by the coefficient of the variable, in this case 5, to get $x = -2$. This can be checked by plugging -2 back into the original equation $(5)(-2) + 10 = -10 + 10 = 0$.

The *Solution Set* is the set of all solutions of an equation. In our example, the solution set would simply be -2. If there were more solutions (there usually are in multivariable equations) then they would also be included in the solution set. When an equation has no true solutions, this is referred to as an *Empty Set*. Equations with identical solution sets are *Equivalent Equations*. An *Identity* is a term whose value or determinant is equal to 1.

Calculations Using Points

Sometimes you need to perform calculations using only points on a graph as input data. Using points, you can determine what the midpoint and distance are. If you know the equation for a line you can calculate the distance between the line and the point.

To find the *Midpoint* of two points (x_1, y_1) and (x_2, y_2), average the x-coordinates to get the x-coordinate of the midpoint, and average the y-coordinates to get the y-coordinate of the midpoint. The formula is midpoint $= \left(\frac{x_1+x_2}{2}, \frac{y_1+y_2}{2}\right)$.

The *Distance* between two points is the same as the length of the hypotenuse of a right triangle with the two given points as endpoints, and the two sides of the right triangle parallel to the x-axis and y-axis, respectively. The length of the segment parallel to the x-axis is the difference between the x-coordinates of the two points. The length of the segment parallel to the y-axis is the difference between the y-coordinates of the two points. Use the Pythagorean Theorem $a^2 + b^2 = c^2$ or $c = \sqrt{a^2 + b^2}$ to find the distance. The formula is: distance $= \sqrt{(x_2 - x_1)^2 + (y_2 - y_1)^2}$.

When a line is in the format $Ax + By + C = 0$, where A, B, and C are coefficients, you can use a point (x_1, y_1) not on the line and apply the formula $d = \frac{|Ax_1+By_1+C|}{\sqrt{A^2+B^2}}$ to find the distance between the line and the point (x_1, y_1).

➢ **Review Video:** Distance & Midpoint for Points on the Coordinate Plane
Visit ***mometrix.com/academy*** *and enter* ***Code:*** **973653**

Transformation

- Rotation: An object is rotated, or turned, between 0 and 360 degrees, around a fixed point. The size and shape of the object are unchanged.
- Reflection: An object is reflected, or flipped, across a line, so that the original object and reflected object are the same distance from the line of reflection. The size and shape of the object are unchanged.
- Translation: An object is translated, or shifted, horizontally and/or vertically to a new location. The orientation, size, and shape of the object are unchanged.

Rotation

A line segment begins at (1, 4) and ends at (5, 4). Draw the line segment and rotate the line segment 90º about the point (3, 4).

The point about which the line segment is being rotated is on the line segment. This point should be on both the original and rotated line. The point (3, 4) is the center of the original line segment, and should still be the center of the rotated line segment. The dashed line is the rotated line segment.

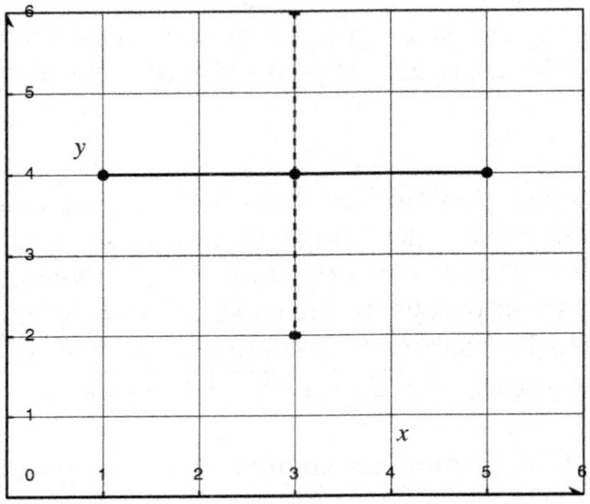

Reflection

Example 1: To create a congruent rectangle by reflecting, first draw a line of reflection. The line can be next to or on the figure. Then draw the image reflected across this line.

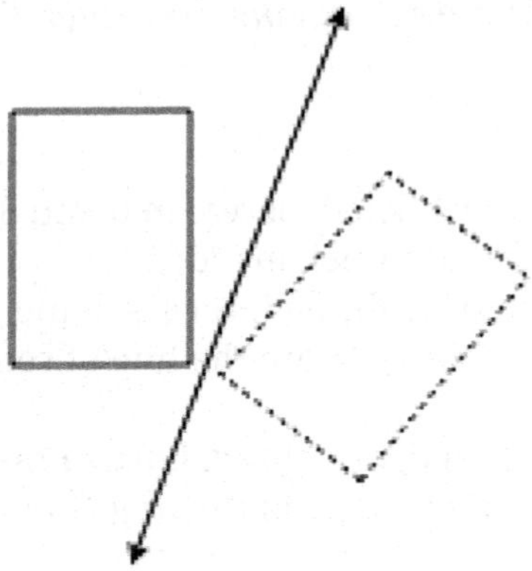

Example 2: A line segment begins at (1, 5) and ends at (5, 4). Draw the line segment, then reflect the line segment across the line $y = 3$.

To reflect a segment, consider folding a piece of paper at the line of reflection. The new image should line up exactly with the old image when the paper is folded. The dashed line is the reflected line se

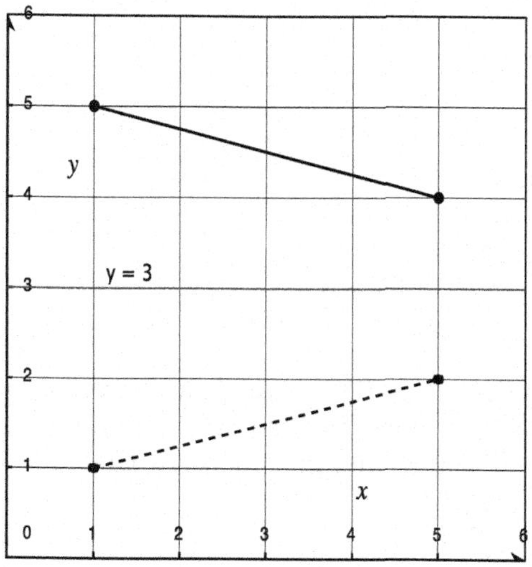

<u>Translation</u>

Example 1: A line segment on an x-y grid starts at (3, 2) and ends at (4, 1). Draw the line segment, and translate the segment up 2 units and left 2 units.

The solid line segment is the original line segment, and the dashed line is the translated line segment. The y-coordinate of each point has increased by 2, because the points moved two units away from 0. The x-coordinate of each point has decreased by 2, because the points moved two units closer to 0.

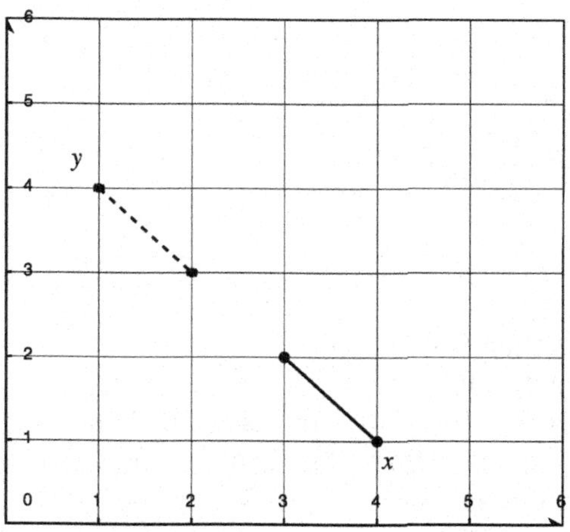

Example 2: Identify a transformation that could have been performed on the solid triangle to result in the dashed triangle.

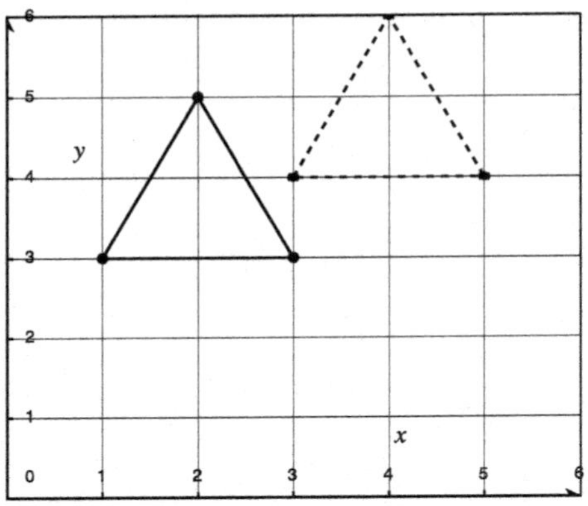

The transformed triangle has the same orientation as the original triangle. It has been shifted up one unit and two units to the right. Because the orientation of the figure has not changed, and its new position can be described using shifts up and to the right, the figure was translated.

Angles

An angle is formed when two lines or line segments meet at a common point. It may be a common starting point for a pair of segments or rays, or it may be the intersection of lines. Angles are represented by the symbol ∠.

The vertex is the point at which two segments or rays meet to form an angle. If the angle is formed by intersecting rays, lines, and/or line segments, the vertex is the point at which four angles are formed. The pairs of angles opposite one another are called vertical angles, and their measures are equal. In the figure below, angles ABC and DBE are congruent, as are angles ABD and CBE.

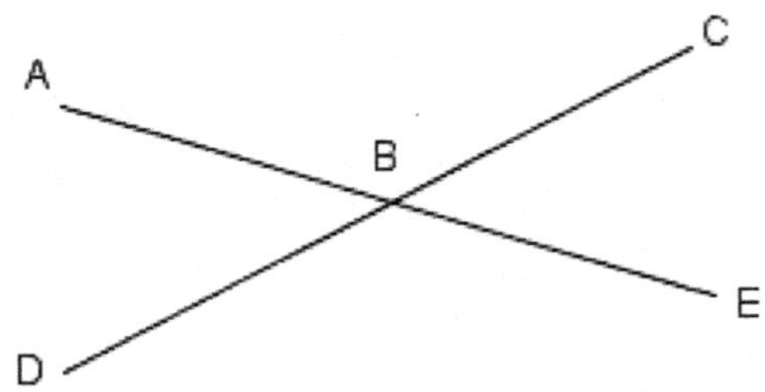

An acute angle is an angle with a degree measure less than 90°.
A right angle is an angle with a degree measure of exactly 90°.
An obtuse angle is an angle with a degree measure greater than 90° but less than 180°.
A straight angle is an angle with a degree measure of exactly 180°. This is also a semicircle.
A reflex angle is an angle with a degree measure greater than 180° but less than 360°.
A full angle is an angle with a degree measure of exactly 360°.

Two angles whose sum is exactly 90° are said to be complementary. The two angles may or may not be adjacent. In a right triangle, the two acute angles are complementary.

Two angles whose sum is exactly 180° are said to be supplementary. The two angles may or may not be adjacent. Two intersecting lines always form two pairs of supplementary angles. Adjacent supplementary angles will always form a straight line.

Two angles that have the same vertex and share a side are said to be adjacent. Vertical angles are not adjacent because they share a vertex but no common side.

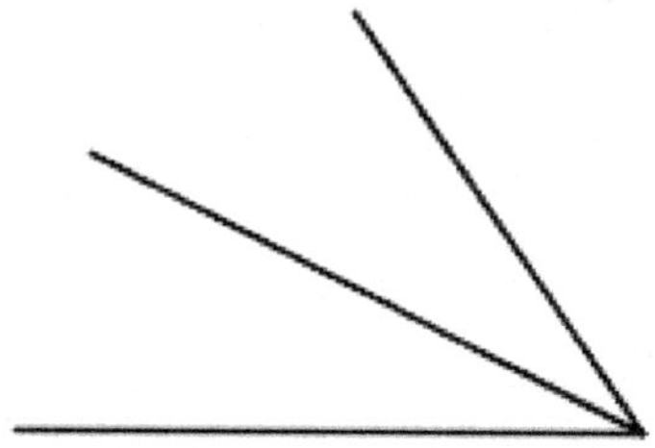

Adjacent

Share vertex and side

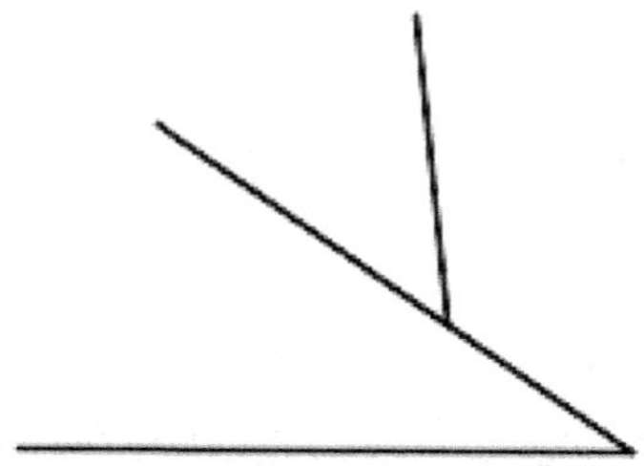

Not adjacent

Share part of side, but not vertex

When two parallel lines are cut by a transversal, the angles that are between the two parallel lines are interior angles. In the diagram below, angles 3, 4, 5, and 6 are interior angles.

When two parallel lines are cut by a transversal, the angles that are outside the parallel lines are exterior angles. In the diagram below, angles 1, 2, 7, and 8 are exterior angles.

When two parallel lines are cut by a transversal, the angles that are in the same position relative to the transversal and a parallel line are corresponding angles. The diagram below has four pairs of corresponding angles: angles 1 and 5; angles 2 and 6; angles 3 and 7; and angles 4 and 8. Corresponding angles formed by parallel lines are congruent.

When two parallel lines are cut by a transversal, the two interior angles that are on opposite sides of the transversal are called alternate interior angles. In the diagram below, there are two pairs of alternate interior angles: angles 3 and 6, and angles 4 and 5. Alternate interior angles formed by parallel lines are congruent.

When two parallel lines are cut by a transversal, the two exterior angles that are on opposite sides of the transversal are called alternate exterior angles. In the diagram below, there are two pairs of alternate exterior angles: angles 1 and 8, and angles 2 and 7. Alternate exterior angles formed by parallel lines are congruent.

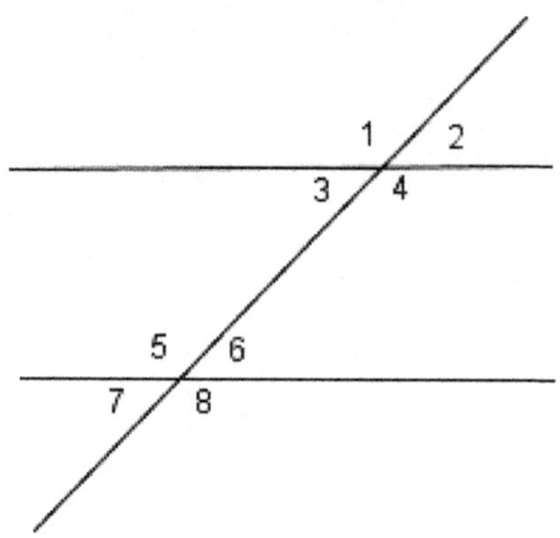

Triangles

An equilateral triangle is a triangle with three congruent sides. An equilateral triangle will also have three congruent angles, each 60°. All equilateral triangles are also acute triangles.

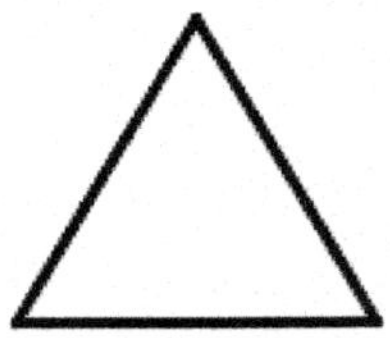

An isosceles triangle is a triangle with two congruent sides. An isosceles triangle will also have two congruent angles opposite the two congruent sides.

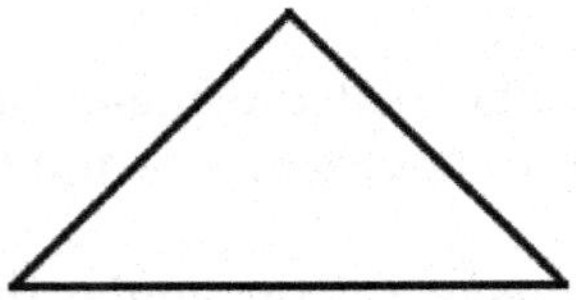

A scalene triangle is a triangle with no congruent sides. A scalene triangle will also have three angles of different measures. The angle with the largest measure is opposite the longest side, and the angle with the smallest measure is opposite the shortest side.

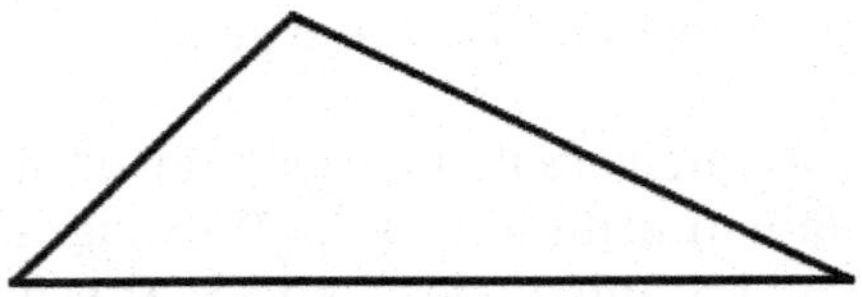

An acute triangle is a triangle whose three angles are all less than 90°. If two of the angles are equal, the acute triangle is also an isosceles triangle. If the three angles are all equal, the acute triangle is also an equilateral triangle.

A right triangle is a triangle with exactly one angle equal to 90°. All right triangles follow the Pythagorean Theorem. A right triangle can never be acute or obtuse.

An obtuse triangle is a triangle with exactly one angle greater than 90°. The other two angles may or may not be equal. If the two remaining angles are equal, the obtuse triangle is also an isosceles triangle.

Triangle Terminology

Altitude of a Triangle: A line segment drawn from one vertex perpendicular to the opposite side. In the diagram below, $\overline{BE}$, $\overline{AD}$, and $\overline{CF}$ are altitudes. The three altitudes in a triangle are always concurrent.

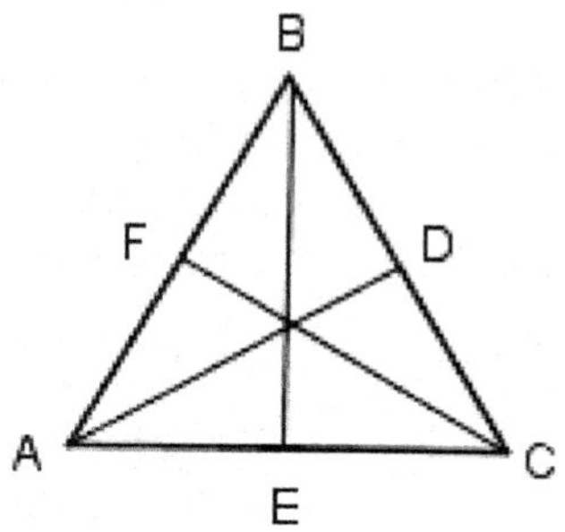

Height of a Triangle: The length of the altitude, although the two terms are often used interchangeably.

Orthocenter of a Triangle: The point of concurrency of the altitudes of a triangle. Note that in an obtuse triangle, the orthocenter will be outside the circle, and in a right triangle, the orthocenter is the vertex of the right angle.

Median of a Triangle: A line segment drawn from one vertex to the midpoint of the opposite side. This is not the same as the altitude, except the altitude to the base of an isosceles triangle and all three altitudes of an equilateral triangle.

Centroid of a Triangle: The point of concurrency of the medians of a triangle. This is the same point as the orthocenter only in an equilateral triangle. Unlike the orthocenter, the centroid is always inside the triangle. The centroid can also be considered the exact center of the triangle. Any shape triangle can be perfectly balanced on a tip placed at the centroid. The centroid is also the point that is two-thirds the distance from the vertex to the opposite side.

- **Review Video: Orthocenter and Centroid of a Triangle**
  *Visit **mometrix.com/academy** and enter **Code:*** **598260**

General Rules for Triangles

The Triangle Inequality Theorem states that the sum of the measures of any two sides of a triangle is always greater than the measure of the third side. If the sum of the measures of two sides were equal to the third side, a triangle would be impossible because the two sides would lie flat across the third side and there would be no vertex. If the sum of the measures of two of the sides was less than the third side, a closed figure would be impossible because the two shortest sides would never meet.

The sum of the measures of the interior angles of a triangle is always 180°. Therefore, a triangle can never have more than one angle greater than or equal to 90°.

In any triangle, the angles opposite congruent sides are congruent, and the sides opposite congruent angles are congruent. The largest angle is always opposite the longest side, and the smallest angle is always opposite the shortest side.

The line segment that joins the midpoints of any two sides of a triangle is always parallel to the third side and exactly half the length of the third side.

Pythagorean Theorem

The side of a triangle opposite the right angle is called the hypotenuse. The other two sides are called the legs. The Pythagorean Theorem states a relationship among the legs and hypotenuse of a right triangle: $a^2 + b^2 = c^2$, where a and b are the lengths of the legs of a right triangle, and c is the length of the hypotenuse. Note that this formula will only work with right triangles.

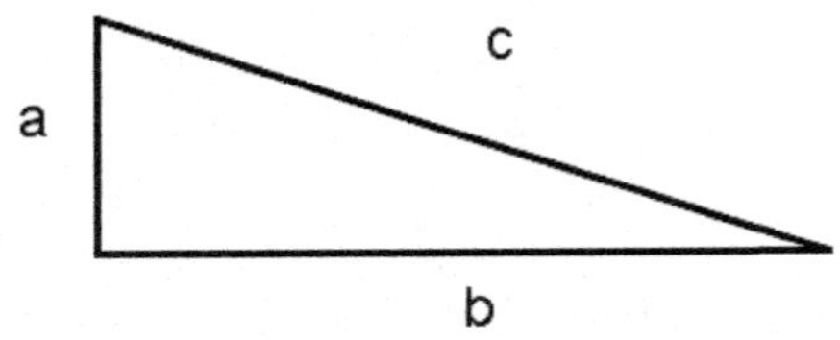

➢ **Review Video: Pythagorean Theorem**
*Visit **mometrix.com/academy** and enter **Code:** **906576***

The theorem is most commonly used to find the length of an unknown side of a right triangle, given the lengths of the other two sides. For example, given that the hypotenuse of a right triangle is 5 and one side is 3, the other side can be found using the formula: $a^2 + b^2 = c^2$, $3^2 + b^2 = 5^2$, $9 + b^2 = 25$, $b^2 = 25 - 9 = 16$, $b = \sqrt{16} = 4$.

Polygons

Each straight line segment of a polygon is called a side.

The point at which two sides of a polygon intersect is called the vertex. In a polygon, the number of sides is always equal to the number of vertices.

A polygon with all sides congruent and all angles equal is called a regular polygon.

A line segment from the center of a polygon perpendicular to a side of the polygon is called the apothem. In a regular polygon, the apothem can be used to find the area of the polygon using the formula $A = \frac{1}{2}ap$, where a is the apothem and p is the perimeter.

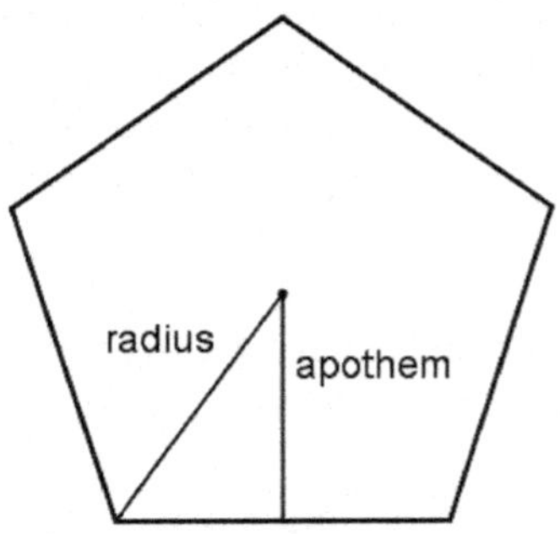

A line segment from the center of a polygon to a vertex of the polygon is called a radius. The radius of a regular polygon is also the radius of a circle that can be circumscribed about the polygon.

Triangle – 3 sides
Quadrilateral – 4 sides
Pentagon – 5 sides
Hexagon – 6 sides
Heptagon – 7 sides
Octagon – 8 sides
Nonagon – 9 sides
Decagon – 10 sides
Dodecagon – 12 sides

More generally, an n-gon is a polygon that has n angles and n sides.

Quadrilateral: A closed two-dimensional geometric figure composed of exactly four straight sides. The sum of the interior angles of any quadrilateral is 360°.

Parallelogram: A quadrilateral that has exactly two pairs of opposite parallel sides. The sides that are parallel are also congruent. The opposite interior angles are always congruent, and the consecutive interior angles are supplementary. The diagonals of a parallelogram bisect each other. Each diagonal divides the parallelogram into two congruent triangles.

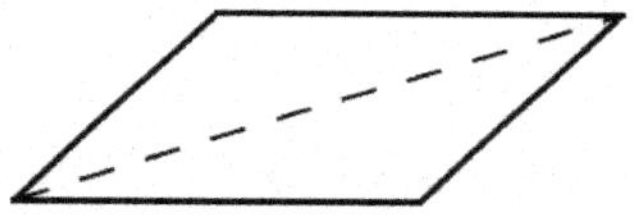

Trapezoid: Traditionally, a quadrilateral that has exactly one pair of parallel sides. Some math texts define trapezoid as a quadrilateral that has at least one pair of parallel sides. Because there are no rules governing the second pair of sides, there are no rules that apply to the properties of the diagonals of a trapezoid.

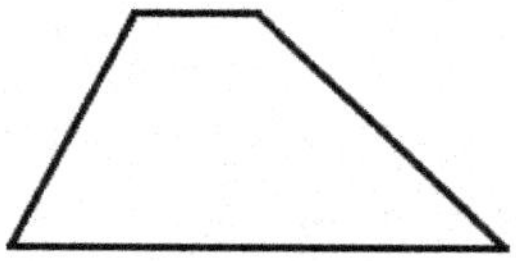

Rectangles, rhombuses, and squares are all special forms of parallelograms.
Rectangle: A parallelogram with four right angles. All rectangles are parallelograms, but not all parallelograms are rectangles. The diagonals of a rectangle are congruent.

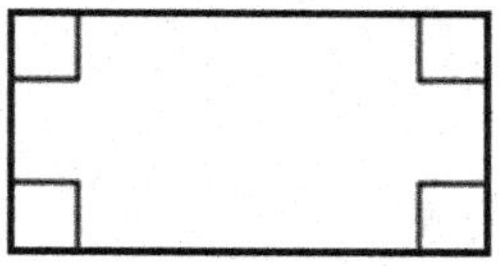

Rhombus: A parallelogram with four congruent sides. All rhombuses are parallelograms, but not all parallelograms are rhombuses. The diagonals of a rhombus are perpendicular to each other.

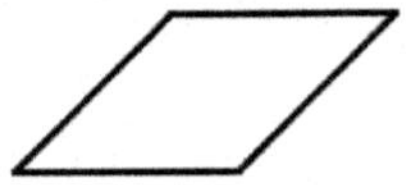

Square: A parallelogram with four right angles and four congruent sides. All squares are also parallelograms, rhombuses, and rectangles. The diagonals of a square are congruent and perpendicular to each other.

A quadrilateral whose diagonals bisect each other is a parallelogram. A quadrilateral whose opposite sides are parallel (2 pairs of parallel sides) is a parallelogram.

A quadrilateral whose diagonals are perpendicular bisectors of each other is a rhombus. A quadrilateral whose opposite sides (both pairs) are parallel and congruent is a rhombus.

A parallelogram that has a right angle is a rectangle. (Consecutive angles of a parallelogram are supplementary. Therefore if there is one right angle in a parallelogram, there are four right angles in that parallelogram.)

A rhombus with one right angle is a square. Because the rhombus is a special form of a parallelogram, the rules about the angles of a parallelogram also apply to the rhombus.

Circles

The center is the single point inside the circle that is equidistant from every point on the circle. (Point O in the diagram below.)

The radius is a line segment that joins the center of the circle and any one point on the circle. All radii of a circle are equal. (Segments OX, OY, and OZ in the diagram below.)

The diameter is a line segment that passes through the center of the circle and has both endpoints on the circle. The length of the diameter is exactly twice the length of the radius. (Segment XZ in the diagram below.)

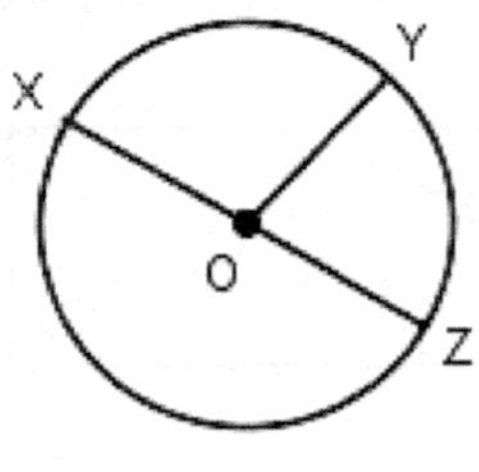

➢ **Review Video:** Points of a Circle
Visit ***mometrix.com/academy*** *and enter* ***Code:*** **420746**

Measurement

Area and Perimeter Formulas

Triangle
The perimeter of any triangle is found by summing the three side lengths; $P = a + b + c$. For an equilateral triangle, this is the same as $P = 3s$, where s is any side length, since all three sides are the same length.

Find the side of a triangle
You may have problems that give you the perimeter of a triangle. So, you are asked to find one of the sides.

Example: The perimeter of a triangle is 35 cm. One side length is 10 cm. Another side length is 20cm. Find the length of the missing side.

First: Set up the equation to set apart a side length.
Now, the equation is $35 = 10 + 20 + c$. So, you are left with $35 = 30 + c$.

Second: Subtract 30 from both sides: $35 - 30 = 30 - 30 + c$
Then, you are left with $5 = c$

The area of any triangle can be found by taking half the product of one side length (base or b) and the perpendicular distance from that side to the opposite vertex (height or h). In equation form, $A = \frac{1}{2}bh$. For many triangles, it may be difficult to calculate h, so using one of the other formulas given here may be easier.

Find the height or the area of the base
You may have problems that give you the area of a triangle. So, you are asked to find the height or the base.

Example: The area of a triangle is 70 cm^2, and the height is 10. Find the base.

First: Set up the equation to set apart the base.
The equation is $70 = \frac{1}{2}10b$.
Now, multiply both sides by 2: $70 \times 2 = \frac{1}{2}10b \times 2$.
So, you are left with: $140 = 10b$.

Second: Divide both sides by 10 to get the base: $\frac{140}{10} = \frac{10b}{10}$
Then, you have $14 = b$.

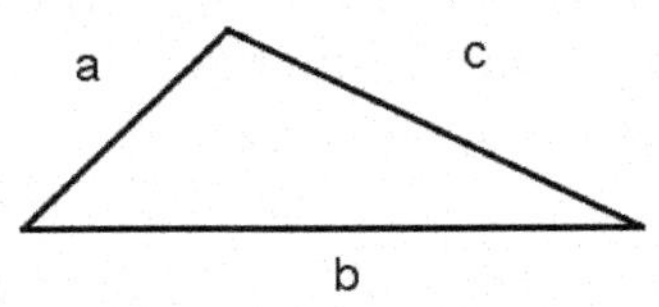

➢ **Review Video:** **Area and Perimeter of a Triangle**
Visit ***mometrix.com/academy*** *and enter* ***Code:*** **817385**

Another formula that works for any triangle is $A = \sqrt{s(s-a)(s-b)(s-c)}$, where A is the area, s is the semiperimeter $s = \frac{a+b+c}{2}$, and a, b, and c are the lengths of the three sides.

The area of an equilateral triangle can found by the formula $A = \frac{\sqrt{3}}{4}s^2$, where A is the area and s is the length of a side. You could use the $30° - 60° - 90°$ ratios to find the height of the triangle and then use the standard triangle area formula, but this is faster.

The area of an isosceles triangle can found by the formula, $A = \frac{1}{2}b\sqrt{a^2 - \frac{b^2}{4}}$, where A is the area, b is the base (the unique side), and a is the length of one of the two congruent sides. If you do not remember this formula, you can use the Pythagorean Theorem to find the height so you can use the standard formula for the area of a triangle.

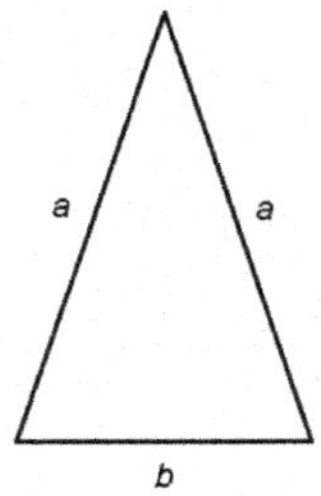

Square
The area of a square is found by using the formula $A = s^2$, where and s is the length of one side.

Find the side of a square
You may have problems that give you the area of a square. So, you are asked to find the side.
Example: The area of a square is 9 cm^2. Find the side.
First: Set up the equation to set apart s.
The equation is $9 = s^2$.

Second: Now, you can take the square root of both sides: $\sqrt{9} = \sqrt{s^2}$.
So, you are left with: $3 = s$

The perimeter of a square is found by using the formula $P = 4s$, where s is the length of one side. Because all four sides are equal in a square, it is faster to multiply the length of one side by 4 than to add the same number four times. You could use the formulas for rectangles and get the same answer.

Find the side of a square
You may have problems that give you the perimeter of a square. So, you are asked to find the side.
Example: The perimeter of a square is 60 cm. Find the side.
First: Set up the equation to set apart s.
The equation is $60 = 4s$.

Second: Now, you can divide both sides by 4: $\frac{60}{4} = \frac{4s}{4}$. You are left with $15 = s$

➢ **Review Video:** Area and Perimeter of a Square
Visit ***mometrix.com/academy*** *and enter* ***Code:*** **620902**

Rectangle

The area of a rectangle is found by the formula $A = lw$, where A is the area of the rectangle, l is the length (usually considered to be the longer side) and w is the width (usually considered to be the shorter side). The numbers for l and w are interchangeable.

Find the width or length of a rectangle

You may have problems that give you the area of a rectangle. So, you are asked to find the width.
Example: The area of a rectangle is 150cm^2, and the length is 10cm. Find the width.

First: Set up the equation to set apart width. The equation is $150 = 10w$.

Second: Divide both sides by 10: $\frac{150}{10} = \frac{10w}{10}$. You are left with $15 = w$

Note: When you need to find the length, you can follow the steps above to find it.

The perimeter of a rectangle is found by the formula $P = 2l + 2w$ or $P = 2(l + w)$, where l is the length, and w is the width. It may be easier to add the length and width first and then double the result, as in the second formula.

Find the width or length of a rectangle

You may have problems that give you the perimeter of a rectangle. So, you are asked to find the width.
Example: The perimeter of a rectangle is 100cm, and the length is 20cm. Find the width.

First: Set up the equation to set apart the width. The equation is $100 = 2(20 + w)$

Second: Distribute the 2 across $(20 + w)$: $100 = 40 + 2w$

Then, subtract 40 from both sides: $100 - 40 = 40 + 2w - 40$

So, you are left with: $60 = 2w$. Then, divide both sides by 2: $\frac{60}{2} = \frac{2w}{2}$.

Now, you have $30 = w$.

Note: When you need to find the length, you can follow the steps above to find it.

➢ **Review Video:** Area and Perimeter of a Rectangle
Visit ***mometrix.com/academy*** *and enter* ***Code:*** **933707**

Parallelogram

The area of a parallelogram is found by the formula $A = bh$, where b is the length of the base, and h is the height. Note that the base and height correspond to the length and width in a rectangle, so this formula would apply to rectangles as well. Do not confuse the height of a parallelogram with the length of the second side. The two are only the same measure in the case of a rectangle.

Find the length of the base or the height of a parallelogram

You may have problems that give you the area of a parallelogram. So, you are asked to find the area of the base or the height.
Example: The area of the parallelogram is 84 cm^2. The base is 7cm. Find the height.

Set up the equation to set apart the height.

So, you have $84 = 7h$. Now, divide both sides by 7: $\frac{84}{7} = \frac{7h}{7}$.

Then, you are left with $12 = h$

The perimeter of a parallelogram is found by the formula $P = 2a + 2b$ or $P = 2(a + b)$, where a and b are the lengths of the two sides.

Find the missing side of a parallelogram
You may have problems that give you the perimeter of a parallelogram. So, you are asked to find one of the sides. Example: The perimeter of a parallelogram is 100cm, and one side is 20cm. Find the other side.

First: Set up the equation to set apart one of the side lengths.
The equation is $100 = 2(20 + b)$

Second: Distribute the 2 across $(20 + b)$: $100 = 40 + 2b$
Then, subtract 40 from both sides: $100 - 40 = 40 + 2b - 40$
So, you are left with: $60 = 2b$. Then, divide both sides by 2: $\frac{60}{2} = \frac{2b}{2}$
Now, you have $30 = b$.

➢ **Review Video: Area and Perimeter of a Parallelogram**
Visit ***mometrix.com/academy*** *and enter* ***Code:*** **718313**

Trapezoid

The area of a trapezoid is found by the formula $A = \frac{1}{2}h(b_1 + b_2)$, where h is the height (segment joining and perpendicular to the parallel bases), and b_1 and b_2 are the two parallel sides (bases). Do not use one of the other two sides as the height unless that side is also perpendicular to the parallel bases.

Find the height of a trapezoid
You may have problems that give you the area of a trapezoid. So, you are asked to find the height. Example: The area of a trapezoid is 30cm^2. B_1 is 3cm, and B_2 is 9cm. Find the height.

First: Set up the equation to set apart the height. The equation is $30 = \frac{1}{2}h(3 + 9)$.

Second: Now, multiply both sides by 2: $30 \times 2 = \frac{1}{2}(12)h \times 2$.
So, you are left with: $60 = (12)h$.

Third: Divide both sides by 12: $\frac{60}{12} = \frac{(12)h}{12}$. Now, you have $5 = h$

Find a base of a trapezoid
You may have problems that give you the area of a trapezoid and the height. So, you are asked to find one of the bases.
Example: The area of a trapezoid is 90cm^2. b_1 is 5cm, and the height is 12cm. Find b_2.

First: Set up the equation to set apart b_2.
The equation is $90 = \frac{1}{2}12(5 + b_2)$.

Second: Now, multiply the height by $\frac{1}{2}$: $90 = 6(5 + b_2)$.
So, you can distribute the 6 across $(5 + b_2)$: $90 = 30 + 6b_2$

Third: Subtract 30 from both sides $90 - 30 = 30 + 6b_2 - 30$.
Now, you have $60 = 6b_2$.
Then, divide both sides by 6: $\frac{60}{6} = \frac{6b_2}{6}$. So, $b_2 = 10$.

The perimeter of a trapezoid is found by the formula $P = a + b_1 + c + b_2$, where a, b_1, c, and b_2 are the four sides of the trapezoid.

Find the missing side of a trapezoid
Example: The perimeter of a trapezoid is 50cm. B_1 is 20cm, B_2 is 10cm, and a is 5cm. Find the length of side c.

First: Set up the equation to set apart the missing side.
The equation is $50 = 5 + 20 + c + 10$. So, you have $50 = 35 + c$

Second: Subtract 35 from both sides: $50 - 35 = 35 + c - 35$.
So, you are left with $15 = c$

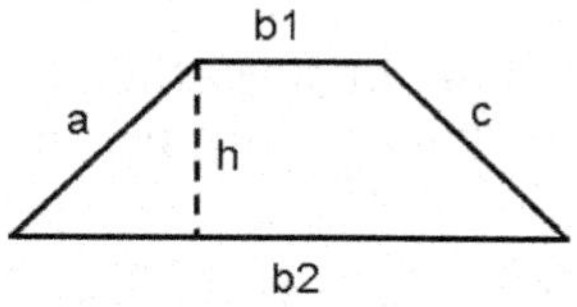

➢ **Review Video:** Area and Perimeter of a Trapezoid
Visit ***mometrix.com/academy*** *and enter* ***Code:*** **587523**

Circles
The area of a circle is found by the formula $A = \pi r^2$, where r is the length of the radius. If the diameter of the circle is given, remember to divide it in half to get the length of the radius before proceeding.

Find the radius of a circle
You may have problems that give you the area of a circle. So, you are asked to find the radius.
Example: The area of a circle is 30cm². Find the radius.

First: Set up the equation to set apart the radius.
The equation is $30 = \pi r^2$. Now, divide both sides by π: $\frac{30}{\pi} = \frac{\pi r^2}{\pi}$

Second: Take the square root of both sides: $\sqrt{9.55} = \sqrt{r^2}$.
So, you are left with: $3.09 = r$.

Note: You may have the area, and you are asked to find the diameter of the circle. So, follow the steps above to find the radius. Then, multiply the radius by 2 for the diameter.

The circumference of a circle is found by the formula $C = 2\pi r$, where r is the radius. Again, remember to convert the diameter if you are given that measure rather than the radius.

Find the radius of a circle
You may have problems that give you the circumference of a circle. So, you are asked to find the radius. Example: The circumference is 20cm. Find the radius.

First: Set up the equation to set apart the radius.
The equation is $20 = 2\pi r$. Now divide both sides by 2: $\frac{20}{2} = \frac{2\pi r}{2}$.

Second: Divide both sides by π: $\frac{10}{\pi} = \frac{\pi r}{\pi}$. So, you are left with $3.18 = r$

Note: You may have the circumference, and you are asked to find the diameter of the circle. So, follow the steps above to find the radius. Then, multiply the radius by 2 for the diameter.

➢ **Review Video: Area and Circumference of a Circle**
*Visit **mometrix.com/academy** and enter **Code:*** **243015**

Volume and Surface Area

The surface area of a solid object is the area of all sides or exterior surfaces. For objects such as prisms and pyramids, a further distinction is made between base surface area (B) and lateral surface area (LA). For a prism, the total surface area (SA) is $SA = LA + 2B$. For a pyramid or cone, the total surface area is $SA = LA + B$.

Sphere

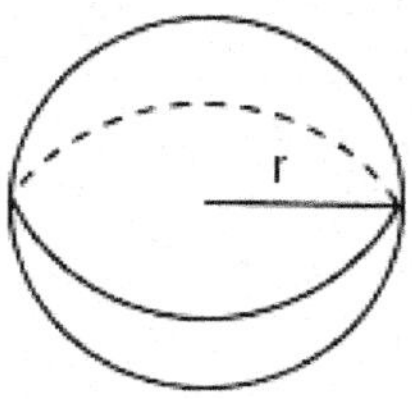

The surface area of a sphere can be found by the formula $A = 4\pi r^2$, where r is the radius.

Find the radius of a sphere
You may have problems that give you the surface area of a sphere. So, you are asked to find the radius.
Example: The surface area of a sphere is 100 cm^2. Find the radius.

First: Set up the equation to set apart the radius.
You begin with: $SA = 4\pi r^2$. Then, you move 4π to the other side of the equal sign and cancel out the 4π on the right side of the formula: $\frac{SA}{4\pi} = r^2$.
Next, you square both sides to set apart the radius:
$\sqrt{\frac{SA}{4\pi}} = \sqrt{r^2}$. So, you are left with $r = \sqrt{\frac{SA}{4\pi}}$

Second: Solve the equation.
$\sqrt{\frac{100}{4\pi}} = \sqrt{\frac{100}{12.57}} = 2.82$. So, the radius equals 2.82 cm.

The volume is given by the formula $V = \frac{4}{3}\pi r^3$, where r is the radius. Both quantities are generally given in terms of π.

Find the radius of a sphere

You may have problems that give you the volume of a sphere. So, you are asked to find the radius.
Example: The volume of a sphere is 100 cm^3. Find the radius.

First: Set up the equation and cancel out the fraction.

$\frac{3}{4} \times \frac{4}{3}\pi r^3 = 100 \times \frac{3}{4}$. So, you are left with: $\pi r^3 = 75$

Second: Cancel out π.

$\frac{\pi r^3}{\pi} = \frac{75}{\pi}$. So, you are left with: $r^3 = \frac{75}{\pi} = 23.87$

Third: Take the cubed root of r^3 and 23.87 to solve for the radius.

$\sqrt[3]{r^3} = \sqrt[3]{23.87}$. So, you have the result of r= 2.88

➢ **Review Video:** <u>Volume and Surface Area of a Sphere</u>
Visit ***mometrix.com/academy*** *and enter* ***Code:*** **786928**

<u>Prisms</u>

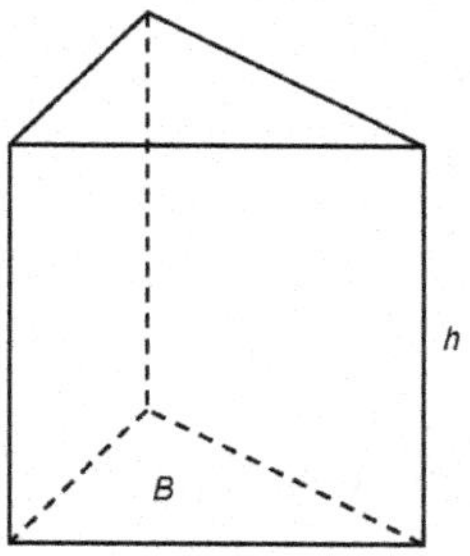

The volume of any prism is found by the formula $V = Bh$, where B is the area of the base, and h is the height (perpendicular distance between the bases).

Find the area of the base or the height of a prism

You may have problems that give you the volume of a prism. So, you are asked to find the area of the base or the height.
Example: The volume of the prism is 200 cm^3. The area of the base is 10cm. Find the height.

First: Set up the equation to set apart the height. So, you have $200 = 10h$.

Second: Now, divide both sides by 10: $\frac{200}{10} = \frac{10h}{10}$. Then, you are left with $20 = h$

Note: When you need to find the area of the base, you can follow the steps above to solve for it.

The surface area of any prism is the sum of the areas of both bases and all sides. It can be calculated as $SA = 2B + Ph$, where P is the perimeter of the base.

Find the area of the base
You may have problems that give you the surface area of a prism. So, you are asked to find the area of the base.
Example: The surface area of the prism is 100 cm². The perimeter of the base is 10cm, and the height is 2cm. Find the area of the base.

First: Set up the equation to set apart the area of the base.
So, you have $100 = 2B + 20$.

Second: Subtract 20 from both sides: $100 - 20 = 2B + 20 - 20$.
Now, you are left with $80 = 2B$. So, divide both sides by 2.
Then, you have $40 = B$.

Find the perimeter of the base or the height of a prism
You may have problems that give you the surface area of a prism and the area of the base. So, you are asked to find the perimeter of the base or the height.
Example: The surface area of the prism is 280 cm². The area of the base is 15cm², and the perimeter of the base is 10cm. Find the height.

First: Set up the equation to set apart the height.
The equation is $280 = 2(15) + (10)h$. So, you have $250 = 30 + (10)h$

Second: Subtract 30 from both sides: $280 - 30 = 30 + (10)h - 30$.
Now, you are left with: $250 = (10)h$. Then, divide both sides by 10.
$\frac{250}{10} = \frac{(10)h}{10} = 25$. So, the height of the prism is 25cm.

Note: When you need to find the perimeter of the base, you can follow the steps above to find it.

Rectangular Prism

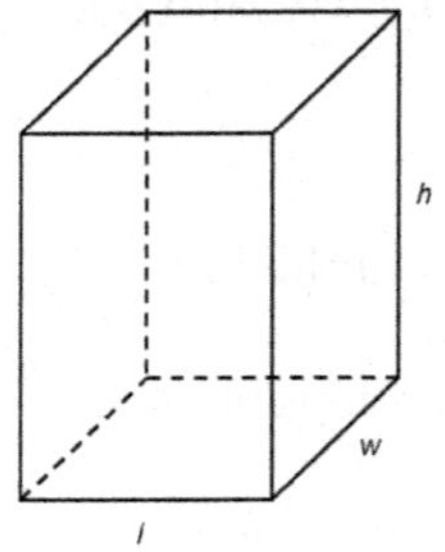

For a rectangular prism, the volume can be found by the formula $V = lwh$, where V is the volume, l is the length, w is the width, and h is the height.

Find the length, width, or height of a rectangular prism
You may have problems that give you the volume of a rectangular prism. So, you are asked to find the length, width, or height.
Example: The volume of the rectangular prism is 200 cm³. The width is 10cm, and the height is 10cm. Find the length.

First: Set up the equation to set apart the length.
So, you have $200 = l(10)(10)$ that becomes $200 = (100)l$.

Second: Divide both sides by 100.
Now, you have $\frac{200}{100} = \frac{(100)l}{100}$. So, you are left with $2 = l$.

Note: When you need to find the width or height, you can follow the steps above to solve for either.

The surface area can be calculated as $SA = 2lw + 2hl + 2wh$ or $SA = 2(lw + hl + wh)$.

Find the length, width, or height of a rectangular prism
You may have problems that give you the surface area of a rectangular prism. So, you are asked to find the length, width, or height.
Example: The surface area of the rectangular prism is 200 cm². The width is 15cm, and the height is 5cm. Find the length.

First: Set up the equation to set apart the length.
So, you have $200 = 2(15)l + 2(5)l + 2(15)(5)$ that becomes:
$200 = (40)l + 150$.

Second: Subtract 150 from both sides.
So, $200 - 150 = (40)l + 150 - 150$ becomes $50 = (40)l$.
Then, divide both sides by 40 to set apart l: $\frac{50}{40} = \frac{(40)l}{40}$.
You are left with $1.25 = l$.

Note: When you need to find the width or height, you can follow the steps above to solve for either.

<u>Cube</u>
The volume of a cube can be found by the formula $V = s^3$, where s is the length of a side.

Find the side of a cube
You may have problems that give you the volume of a cube. So, you are asked to find the side.
Example: The volume of a cube is 20 cm³. Find the side.

First: Set up the equation to set apart the side length. Then, take the cube root of both sides. So, $20 = s^3$ becomes $\sqrt[3]{20} = \sqrt[3]{s^3}$ Then, you are left with $\sqrt[3]{20} = s$

Second: Solve for the side length.
$\sqrt[3]{20} = 2.71$. So, s equals 2.71.

The surface area of a cube is calculated as $SA = 6s^2$, where SA is the total surface area and s is the length of a side. These formulas are the same as the ones used for the volume and surface area of a rectangular prism, but simplified since all three quantities (length, width, and height) are the same.

Find the side of a cube
You may have problems that give you the surface area of a cube. So, you are asked to find the side.
Example: The surface area of a cube is 60 cm². Find the side.

First: Set up the equation to set apart the side length.
So, $60 = 6s^2$ becomes $\frac{60}{6} = \frac{6s^2}{6}$. Then, you are left with $10 = s^2$

Second: Take the square root of both sides to set apart the s.
So, $10 = s^2$ becomes $\sqrt{10} = \sqrt{s^2}$.
Then, you are left with $3.16 = s$

> **Review Video:** Volume and Surface Area of a Rectangular Solid
> *Visit* ***mometrix.com/academy*** *and enter* ***Code:*** **386780**

Cylinder

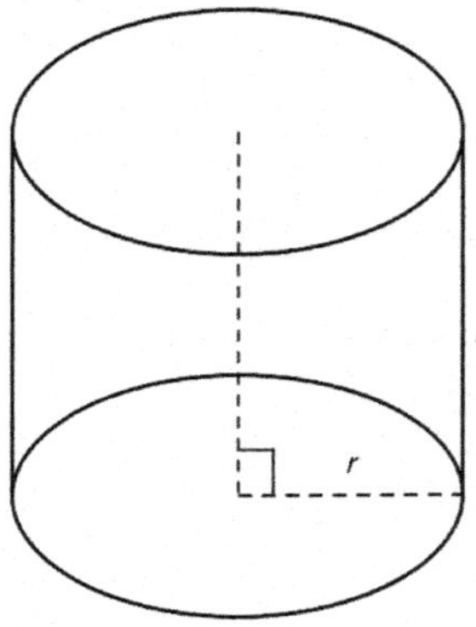

The volume of a cylinder can be calculated by the formula $V = \pi r^2 h$, where r is the radius, and h is the height.

Find the height of a cylinder
You may have problems that give you the volume of a cylinder. So, you are asked to find the height.
Example: The volume of a cylinder is 300 cm³ and the radius is 10 cm. Find the height.

First: Set up the equation and put in the known numbers.
You begin with $300 = \pi 5^2 h$. Now, $\pi 5^2 h = 78.5h$.
So, you have $300 = 78.5h$

Second: Set apart h to solve for the height.
$\frac{300}{78.5} = \frac{78.5h}{78.5}$. So, you are left with: $\frac{300}{78.5} = h$

Solve: $\frac{300}{78.5} = 3.82$cm is the height.

Find the radius of a cylinder

You may have problems that give you the volume of a cylinder. So, you are asked to find the radius. Example: The volume of a cylinder is 200 cm³ and the radius is 15cm. Find the radius.

First: Set up the equation to set apart the radius.

You begin with $200 = \pi(15)r^2$. Now, you move π and (15) to both sides of the equation: $\frac{200}{\pi(15)} = \frac{\pi(15)r^2}{\pi(15)}$. Then, you are left with: $\frac{200}{\pi(15)} = r^2$.

Second: Take the square root of both sides to solve for the radius: $\sqrt{\frac{200}{\pi(15)}} = \sqrt{r^2}$.

Then, you have $\sqrt{4.25} = r$. So, the radius is equal to 2.06.

The surface area of a cylinder can be found by the formula $SA = 2\pi r^2 + 2\pi rh$. The first term is the base area multiplied by two, and the second term is the perimeter of the base multiplied by the height.

Find the height of a cylinder

You may have problems that give you the surface area of a cylinder. So, you are asked to find the height. Example: The surface area of a cylinder is 150 cm² and the radius is 2 cm. Find the height.

First: Set up the equation and put in the known numbers.

You begin with $150 = 2\pi 2^2 + 2\pi(2)h$.

So, you have $150 = 25.12 + 12.56h$.

Second: Subtract 25.12 from both sides of the equation.

So, $150 - 25.12 = 25.12 + 12.56h - 25.12$ becomes $124.85 = 12.56h$.

Then, divide both sides by 12.56.

Now, you are left with $9.94 = h$.

Find the radius of a cylinder

You may have problems that give you the surface area of a cylinder. So, you are asked to find the radius. Example: The surface area of a cylinder is 327 cm², and the height is 12cm. Find the radius.

First: Set up the equation and put in the known numbers.

You begin with $327 = 2\pi r^2 + 2\pi 12(r)$. So, you have $327 = 2\pi r^2 + 75.36r$.

Second: Set up the quadratic formula.

So, you now have $6.28r^2 + 75.36r - 327 = 0$

Third: Solve the equation using the quadratic formula steps.

Now, radius $= \frac{-75.36 \pm \sqrt{(75.36)^2 - 4(6.28)(-327)}}{2(6.28)}$

So, the radius equals a positive 3.39.

- **Review Video: Volume and Surface Area of a Right Circular Cylinder**
  *Visit **mometrix.com/academy** and enter **Code:** **226463***

Statistics and Probability

Statistics

Statistics is the branch of mathematics that deals with collecting, recording, interpreting, illustrating, and analyzing large amounts of data. The following terms are often used in the discussion of data and statistics:

Data – the collective name for pieces of information (singular is datum).

Quantitative data – measurements (such as length, mass, and speed) that provide information about quantities in numbers

Qualitative data – information (such as colors, scents, tastes, and shapes) that cannot be measured using numbers

Discrete data – information that can be expressed only by a specific value, such as whole or half numbers; For example, since people can be counted only in whole numbers, a population count would be discrete data.

Continuous data – information (such as time and temperature) that can be expressed by any value within a given range

Primary data – information that has been collected directly from a survey, investigation, or experiment, such as a questionnaire or the recording of daily temperatures; Primary data that has not yet been organized or analyzed is called raw data.

Secondary data – information that has been collected, sorted, and processed by the researcher

Ordinal data – information that can be placed in numerical order, such as age or weight

Nominal data – information that cannot be placed in numerical order, such as names or places

Measures of Central Tendency

The quantities of mean, median, and mode are all referred to as measures of central tendency. They can each give a picture of what the whole set of data looks like with just a single number. Knowing what each of these values represents is vital to making use of the information they provide.

The mean, also known as the arithmetic mean or average, of a data set is calculated by summing all of the values in the set and dividing that sum by the number of values. For example, if a data set has 6 numbers and the sum of those 6 numbers is 30, the mean is calculated as 30/6 = 5.

The median is the middle value of a data set. The median can be found by putting the data set in numerical order, and locating the middle value. In the data set (1, 2, 3, 4, 5), the median is 3. If there is an even number of values in the set, the median is calculated by taking the average of the two middle values. In the data set, (1, 2, 3, 4, 5, 6), the median would be (3 + 4)/2 = 3.5.

The mode is the value that appears most frequently in the data set. In the data set (1, 2, 3, 4, 5, 5, 5), the mode would be 5 since the value 5 appears three times. If multiple values appear the same number of times, there are multiple values for the mode. If the data set were (1, 2, 2, 3, 4, 4, 5, 5), the modes would be 2, 4, and 5. If no value appears more than any other value in the data set, then there is no mode.

Measures of Dispersion

The standard deviation expresses how spread out the values of a distribution are from the mean. Standard deviation is given in the same units as the original data and is represented by a lower case sigma (σ). A high standard deviation means that the values are very spread out. A low standard deviation means that the values are close together.

If every value in a distribution is increased or decreased by the same amount, the mean, median, and mode are increased or decreased by that amount, but the standard deviation stays the same. If every value in a distribution is multiplied or divided by the same number, the mean, median, mode, and standard deviation will all be multiplied or divided by that number.

The range of a distribution is the difference between the highest and lowest values in the distribution. For example, in the data set (1, 3, 5, 7, 9, 11), the highest and lowest values are 11 and 1, respectively. The range then would be calculated as $11 - 1 = 10$.

The three quartiles are the three values that divide a data set into four equal parts. Quartiles are generally only calculated for data sets with a large number of values. As a simple example, for the data set consisting of the numbers 1 through 99, the first quartile (Q1) would be 25, the second quartile (Q2), always equal to the median, would be 50, and the third quartile (Q3) would be 75. The difference between Q1 and Q3 is known as the interquartile range.

Probability

Probability is a branch of statistics that deals with the likelihood of something taking place. One classic example is a coin toss. There are only two possible results: heads or tails. The likelihood, or probability, that the coin will land as heads is 1 out of 2 (1/2, 0.5, 50%). Tails has the same probability. Another common example is a 6-sided die roll. There are six possible results from rolling a single die, each with an equal chance of happening, so the probability of any given number coming up is 1 out of 6.

➢ **Review Video: Simple Probability**
*Visit **mometrix.com/academy** and enter **Code:*** **212374**

Terms frequently used in probability:
Event – a situation that produces results of some sort (a coin toss)

Compound event – event that involves two or more items (rolling a pair of dice; taking the sum)

Outcome – a possible result in an experiment or event (heads, tails)

Desired outcome (or success) – an outcome that meets a particular set of criteria (a roll of 1 or 2 if we are looking for numbers less than 3)

Independent events – two or more events whose outcomes do not affect one another (two coins tossed at the same time)

Dependent events – two or more events whose outcomes affect one another (two cards drawn consecutively from the same deck)

Certain outcome – probability of outcome is 100% or 1

Impossible outcome – probability of outcome is 0% or 0

Mutually exclusive outcomes – two or more outcomes whose criteria cannot all be satisfied in a single outcome (a coin coming up heads and tails on the same toss)

Theoretical probability is the likelihood of a certain outcome occurring for a given event. It can be determined without actually performing the event. It is calculated as P (probability of success) = (desired outcomes)/(total outcomes).
Example:
There are 20 marbles in a bag and 5 are red. The theoretical probability of randomly selecting a red marble is 5 out of 20, (5/20 = 1/4, 0.25, or 25%).

Most of the time, when we talk about probability, we mean theoretical probability. Experimental probability, or relative frequency, is the number of times an outcome occurs in a particular experiment or a certain number of observed events.

While theoretical probability is based on what *should* happen, experimental probability is based on what *has* happened. Experimental probability is calculated in the same way as theoretical, except that actual outcomes are used instead of possible outcomes.

Theoretical and experimental probability do not always line up with one another. Theoretical probability says that out of 20 coin tosses, 10 should be heads. However, if we were actually to toss 20 coins, we might record just 5 heads. This doesn't mean that our theoretical probability is incorrect; it just means that this particular experiment had results that were different from what was predicted.

> ➢ **Review Video: Theoretical and Experimental Probability**
> *Visit* ***mometrix.com/academy*** *and enter* ***Code:*** **444349**

Expected Value

Expected value is a method of determining expected outcome in a random situation. It is really a sum of the weighted probabilities of the possible outcomes. Multiply the probability of an event occurring by the weight assigned to that probability (such as the amount of money won or lost). A practical application of the expected value is to determine whether a game of chance is really fair. If the sum of the weighted probabilities is greater than or equal to zero, the game is generally considered fair because the player has a fair chance to win, or at least to break even. If the expected value is less than one, then players lose more than they win. For example, a lottery drawing allows the player to choose any three-digit number, 000–999. The probability of choosing the winning number is 1:1000. If it costs $1 to play, and a winning number receives $500, the expected value is $\left(-\$1 \cdot \frac{999}{1{,}000}\right) + \left(\$500 \cdot \frac{1}{1{,}000}\right) = -0.499$ or $-\ \$0.50$. You can expect to lose on average 50 cents for every dollar you spend.

Common Charts and Graphs

Charts and *Tables* are ways of organizing information into separate rows and columns. These rows and columns are labeled to find and to explain the information in them. Some charts and tables are organized horizontally with rows giving the details about the labeled information. Other charts and tables are organized vertically with columns giving the details about the labeled information.

Frequency Tables show how many times each value comes up within the set. A *Relative Frequency Table* shows the proportions of each value compared to the entire set. Relative frequencies are given as percents. However, the total percent for a relative frequency table may not equal 100 percent because of rounding.

This is an example of a frequency table with relative frequencies:

Favorite Color	Frequency	Relative Frequency
Blue	4	13%
Red	7	22%
Purple	3	9%
Green	6	19%
Cyan	12	38%

A *Bar Graph* is one of the few graphs that can be drawn correctly in two ways: horizontally and vertically. A bar graph is similar to a line plot because of how the data is organized on the graph. Both axes must have their categories defined for the graph to be useful. A thick line is drawn from zero to the exact value of the data. This line can be used for a number, a percentage, or other numerical value. Longer bar lengths point to greater data values. To understand a bar graph, read the labels for the axes to know the units being reported. Then look where the bars end and match this to the scale on the other axis. This will show you the connection between the axes. This bar graph shows the responses from a survey about the favorite colors of a group.

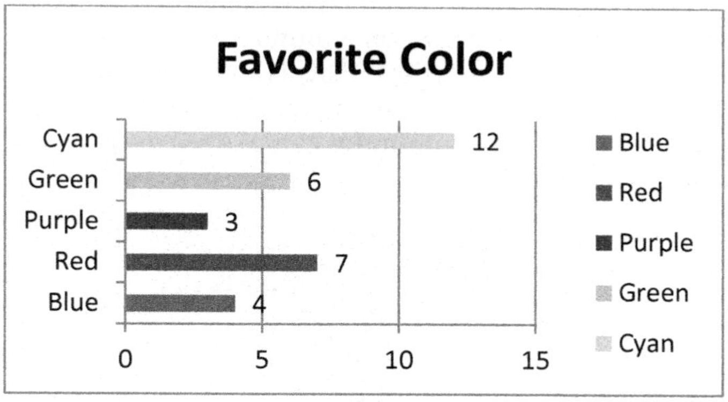

Line Graphs have one or more lines of different styles (e.g., solid or broken). These lines show the different values for a data set. Each point on the graph is shown as an ordered pair. This is similar to a Cartesian plane. In this case, the *x*- and *y*- axes are given certain units (e.g., dollars or time). Each point that is for one measurement is joined by line segments. Then, these lines show what the values are doing.

The lines may be increasing (i.e., line sloping upward), decreasing (i.e., line sloping downward), or staying the same (i.e., horizontal line). More than one set of data can be put on the same line graph. This is done to compare more than one piece of data. An example of this would be graphing test scores for different groups of students over the same stretch of time. This allows you to see which group had the greatest increase or decrease in performance over a certain amount of years. This example is shown in the graph below.

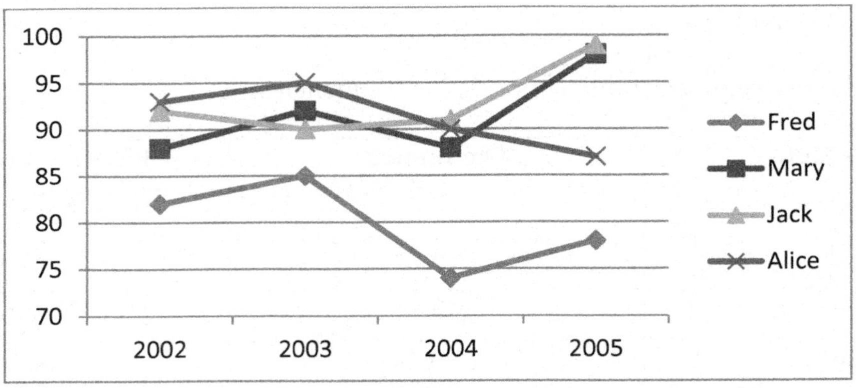

A *Line Plot*, or a *Dot Plot*, has plotted points that are NOT connected by line segments. In this graph, the horizontal axis lists the different possible values for the data. The vertical axis lists how many times one value happens. A single dot is graphed for each value. The dots in a line plot are connected. If the dots are connected, then this will not correctly represent the data.

The *5-Number Summary* of a set of data gives a very informative picture of the set. The five numbers in the summary are the minimum value, maximum value, and the three quartiles. This information gives you the range and the median of the set. Also, this information hints at how the data is spread across the median.

A *Box-and-Whiskers Plot* shows the 5-number summary on a graph. To draw a box-and-whiskers plot, place the points of the 5-number summary on a number line. Draw a box whose ends come through the points for the first and third quartiles. This is called the interquartile range. Draw a vertical line in the box that comes through the median and divides the box in half. Then, draw a line segment from the first quartile point to the minimum value. Also, draw a point from the third quartile point to the maximum value.

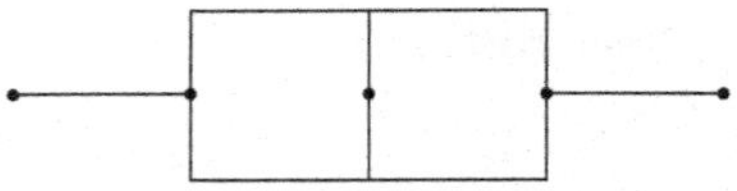

A *Pictograph* is a graph that is given in the horizontal format. This graph uses pictures or symbols to show the data. Each pictograph must have a key that defines the picture or symbol. Also, this key should give the number that stands for each picture or symbol. The pictures or symbols on a pictograph are not always shown as whole elements.

In this case, the fraction of the picture or symbol stands for the same fraction of the quantity that a whole picture or symbol represents. For example, there is a row in the pictograph with $3\frac{1}{2}$ ears of corn. Each ear of corn represents 100 stalks of corn in a field. So, this would equal $3\frac{1}{2} \times 100 = 350$ stalks of corn in the field.

Circle Graphs, or *Pie Charts*, show the relationship of each type of data compared to the whole set of data. The circle graph is divided into sections by drawing radii (i.e., plural for radius) to make central angles. These angles stand for a percentage of the circle. Each 1% of data is equal to 3.6° in the graph. So, data that stands for a 90° section of the circle graph makes up 25% of the whole. The pie chart below shows the data from the frequency table where people were asked about their favorite color.

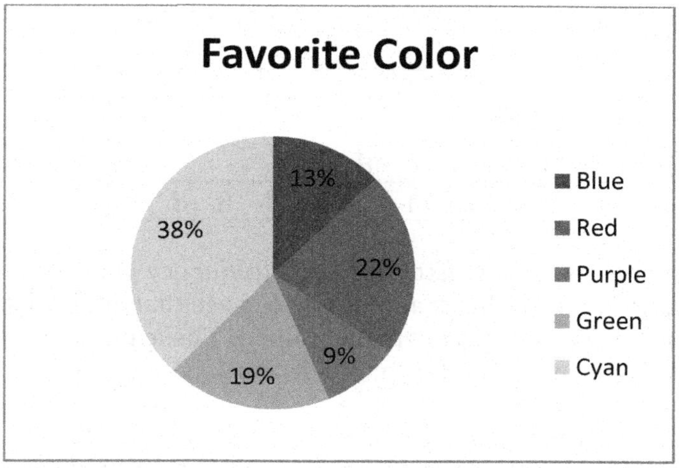

At first glance, a *Histogram* looks like a vertical bar graph. The difference is that a bar graph has a separate bar for each piece of data. A histogram has one bar for each stretch of data. For example, a histogram may have one bar for the stretch of 0–9 and one bar for the stretch of 10–19. A bar graph has numerical values on one axis.

A histogram has numbers on both axes. Each range is of equal size, and they are ordered left to right from lowest to highest. The height of each column on a histogram stands for the number of data values within that range. Like a stem and leaf plot, a histogram makes it easy to look at the graph and find which range has the greatest number of values. Below is an example of a histogram.

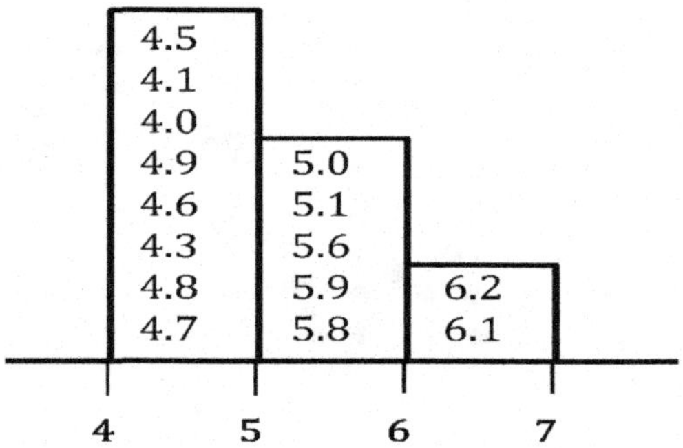

A *Stem and Leaf Plot* can outline groups of data that fall into a range of values. Each piece of data is split into two parts: the first, or left, part is called the stem. The second, or right, part is called the leaf. Each stem is listed in a column from smallest to largest. Each leaf that has the common stem is listed in that stem's row from smallest to largest.

For example, in a set of two-digit numbers, the digit in the tens place is the stem. So, the digit in the ones place is the leaf. With a stem and leaf plot, you can see which subset of numbers (10s, 20s, 30s, etc.) is the largest. This information can be found by looking at a histogram. However, a stem and leaf plot also lets you look closer and see which values fall in that range. Using all of the test scores from the line graph, we can put together a stem and leaf plot:

Test Scores									
7	4	8							
8	2	5	7	8	8				
9	0	0	1	2	2	3	5	8	9

Again, a stem-and-leaf plot is similar to histograms and frequency plots. However, a stem-and-leaf plot keeps all of the original data. In this example, you can see that almost half of the students scored in the 80s. Also, all of the data has been maintained. These plots can be used for larger numbers as well. However, they work better for small sets of data.

Bivariate Data is data from two different variables. The prefix *bi-* means *two*. In a *Scatter Plot*, each value in the set of data is put on a grid. This is similar to the Cartesian plane where each axis represents one of the two variables. When you look at the pattern made by the points on the grid, you may know if there is a relationship between the two variables. Also, you may know what that relationship is and if it exists.

The variables may be directly proportionate, inversely proportionate, or show no proportion. Also, you may be able to see if the data is linear. If the data is linear, you can find an equation to show the two variables. The following scatter plot shows the relationship between preference for brand "A" and the age of the consumers surveyed.

Scatter Plots are useful for knowing the types of functions that are given with the data. Also, they are helpful for finding the simple regression. A simple regression is a regression that uses an independent variable.

A regression is a chart that is used to predict future events. Linear scatter plots may be positive or negative. Many nonlinear scatter plots are exponential or quadratic. Below are some common types of scatter plots:

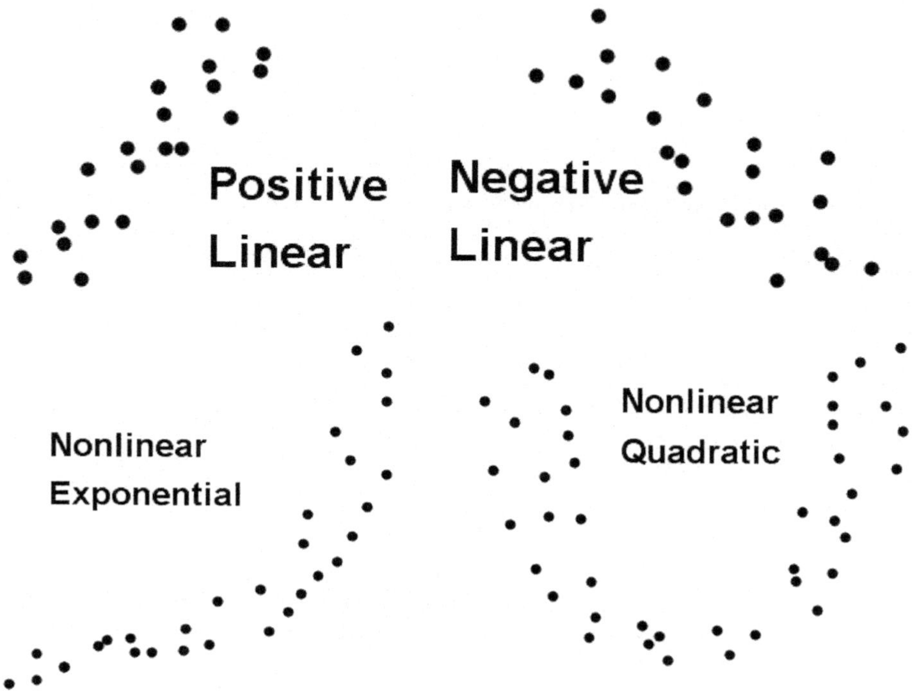

Practice Test

Verbal

1. Enliven means the opposite of
    a. Depress
    b. Imagine
    c. Accost
    d. Refrain

2. Which word does not belong with the others?
    a. Artificial
    b. Synthetic
    c. Natural
    d. Man-made

3. Frog is to amphibian as hydrogen is to:
    a. Aerospace
    b. Element
    c. Galaxy
    d. Instrumental

4. Bernie arrived late for the performance. Tom arrived before Darius. Tom arrived after Bernie. If the first two statements are true, then the third is:
    a. True
    b. False
    c. Unknown
    d. Unimportant

5. Aural most nearly means
    a. Hearing
    b. Language
    c. Circular
    d. Drill

6. Which word does not belong with the others?
    a. Painter
    b. Artist
    c. Musician
    d. Dancer

7. Shun means the *opposite* of
    a. Return
    b. Embrace
    c. Manipulate
    d. Retract

8. Apple is to seed as person is to
   a. Parent
   b. Embryo
   c. Nourishment
   d. Cell

9. Ellie was born one minute after Dean. Dean was born before Rob. Rob was born after Ellie. If the first two statements are true, then the third is:
   a. True
   b. False
   c. Unknown
   d. A contradiction

10. Punishment is to reprimand as impetuous is to
   a. Cautious
   b. Considerate
   c. Hasty
   d. Meticulous

11. Mediocre means the *opposite* of
   a. Stunted
   b. Forgiven
   c. Median
   d. Excellent

12. Which word does not belong with the others?
   a. Toaster
   b. Oven
   c. Appliance
   d. Coffee maker

13. Intricate most nearly means
   a. Woven
   b. Complex
   c. Unified
   d. Simple

14. Temperature is to heat as pound is to
   a. Weight
   b. Height
   c. Measurement
   d. Heavy

15. Furrow means the *opposite* of
   a. Sculpt
   b. Extension
   c. Replace
   d. Mound

16. Counsel most nearly means
   a. Doctor
   b. Committee
   c. Judge
   d. Advise

17. Mackenzie left the daycare right after Austin. Nora left right before Austin. Mackenzie left before Austin. If the first two statements are true, then the third is:
   a. True
   b. False
   c. Unknown
   d. An opinion

18. Light is to hologram as film is to
   a. Aesthetic
   b. Panoramic
   c. Photographer
   d. Video camera

19. Passive means the *opposite* of
   a. Active
   b. Attend
   c. Lassitude
   d. Forlorn

20. Index is to book as elegy is to
   a. Artifact
   b. Audition
   c. Equinox
   d. Funeral

21. Underdog is to audacious as conspirator is to
   a. Altruistic
   b. Elusive
   c. Illegible
   d. Passive

22. Secede means the *opposite* of
   a. Accessible
   b. Recall
   c. Merge
   d. Bail

23. Which word does not belong with the others?
   a. Gasoline
   b. Inflammable
   c. Ignitable
   d. Combustible

24. Samuel invented more patents than his brother James. Horace had twice as many patents as James. Samuel and Horace had the same number of patents. If the first two statements are true, then the third is:
  a. True
  b. False
  c. Unknown
  d. Unimportant

25. Coarse most nearly means
  a. Soft
  b. Polite
  c. Harsh
  d. Direction

26. Impartial means the *opposite* of
  a. Interested
  b. Objective
  c. Passionate
  d. Unfair

27. Intermission is to drama as plant is to
  a. Compliment
  b. Constellation
  c. Habitat
  d. Memorabilia

28. Which word does not belong with the others?
  a. Brick
  b. Bottleneck
  c. Burden
  d. Benchmark

29. Jog is to marathon as hypothesis is to
  a. Discovery
  b. Forgery
  c. Irate
  d. Surreal

30. Deter most nearly means
  a. Stop
  b. Assist
  c. Grind
  d. Sway

31. Esther drove the same distance as Marcus. Lee drove twice as far as Marcus. Esther drove farther than Lee. If the first two statements are true, then the third is:
  a. True
  b. False
  c. Unknown
  d. An opinion

32. Which word does not belong with the others?
   a. Aptitude
   b. Inability
   c. Readiness
   d. Prowess

33. Alleviate means the *opposite* of
   a. Hover
   b. Worsen
   c. Intend
   d. Large

34. Antipathy is to sympathy as convivial is to
   a. Avarice
   b. Gloomy
   c. Harmonious
   d. Sociable

35. Refined most nearly means
   a. Aromatic
   b. Blatant
   c. Cultured
   d. Frightened

36. University Press received more submissions than Institutes Press. Institutes Press received fewer submissions than Academy Press. Academy Press received more submissions than University Press. If the first two statements are true, then the third is:
   a. True
   b. False
   c. Unknown
   d. Redundant

37. Espionage is to discreet as kindling is to
   a. Grotesque
   b. Majestic
   c. Novelty
   d. Ominous

38. Pallid most nearly means
   a. Healthy
   b. Sickly
   c. Rosy
   d. Deep

39. Jovial means the *opposite* of
   a. Revive
   b. Depressed
   c. Obscure
   d. Pretend

40. Otis caught more beads than Steve at Mardi Gras. Steve got as many beads as Carrie. Carrie got fewer beads than Otis. If the first two statements are true, then the third is:

a. True
b. False
c. Unknown
d. Redundant

41. Insufficient means the *opposite* of

a. Deaden
b. Distract
c. Suction
d. Adequate

42. Novice most nearly means

a. Beginner
b. Expert
c. Naught
d. Veteran

43. Foster most nearly means

a. Nurture
b. Woods
c. Home
d. Retain

44. Metal Leather sold far fewer records than The Animal Instincts. The Gang Mentality sold ten times the records the Animal Instincts sold. The Gang Mentality sold fewer records than Metal Leather. If the first two statements are true, then the third is:

a. True
b. False
c. Unknown
d. Incomplete

45. Initiate means the *opposite* of

a. Stop
b. Headlong
c. Internal
d. Sequence

46. Marry most nearly means

a. Jolly
b. Resolve
c. Divorce
d. Join

47. Which word does not belong with the others?
   a. Independence
   b. Irresponsibility
   c. Duty
   d. Maturity

48. General means the *opposite* of
   a. Military
   b. Decisive
   c. Abstract
   d. Particular

49. Paltry most nearly means
   a. Cheap
   b. Valuable
   c. Peaceful
   d. Plenty

50. Optimum most nearly means
   a. Ideal
   b. Visual
   c. Silent
   d. Temporal

51. Pledge means the *opposite* of
   a. Breach
   b. Compromise
   c. Vivid
   d. Sanction

52. Which word does not belong with the others?
   a. Counselor
   b. Nurse
   c. Lawyer
   d. Novelist

53. Reece was married the month before Lee. Darren got married after Lee. Reece got married after Darren. If the first two statements are true, then the third is:
   a. True
   b. False
   c. Unknown
   d. Incomplete

54. Attest means the *opposite* of
   a. Disprove
   b. Abstain
   c. Extract
   d. Vouch

55. Outspoken most nearly means
   a. Demure
   b. Introverted
   c. Candid
   d. Precise

56. Kevin watched fewer television shows than Allen. John watched more television shows than Allen. John watched the greatest amount of television shows of the three. If the first two statements are true, then the third is:
   a. True
   b. False
   c. Unknown
   d. A contradiction

57. Pantomime most nearly means
   a. Mimic
   b. Clothes
   c. Jester
   d. Book

58. Serendipity means the *opposite* of
   a. Ambivalence
   b. Misfortune
   c. Providence
   d. Fluke

59. Pandemonium most nearly means
   a. Chaos
   b. Animal
   c. Monetary
   d. Masculine

60. Which word does not belong with the others?
   a. Restaurant
   b. Airport
   c. Cape Cod
   d. Hotel

Quantitative

1. Which of the following numbers is greatest?
   a. 1/3
   b. 0.25
   c. 0.099
   d. 2/7

2. Determine the number of diagonals of a dodecagon.
   a. 12
   b. 24
   c. 54
   d. 108

3. Which number should come next in the series: 4, 13, 22, 31, ...?
   a. 40
   b. 39
   c. 34
   d. 42

4. Jonas jogs three times faster than he walks. Which graph BEST represents the situation?

a.

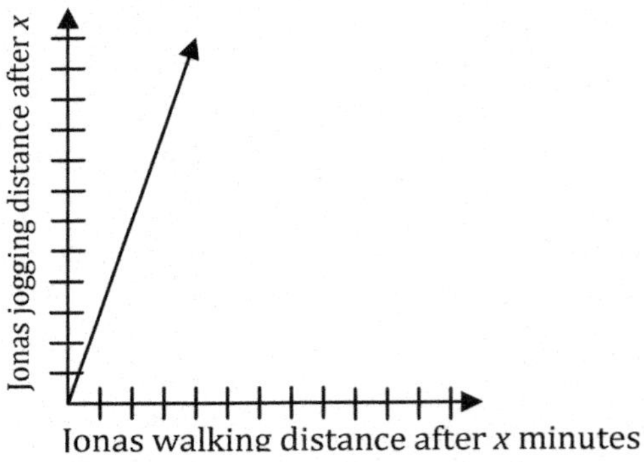

c.

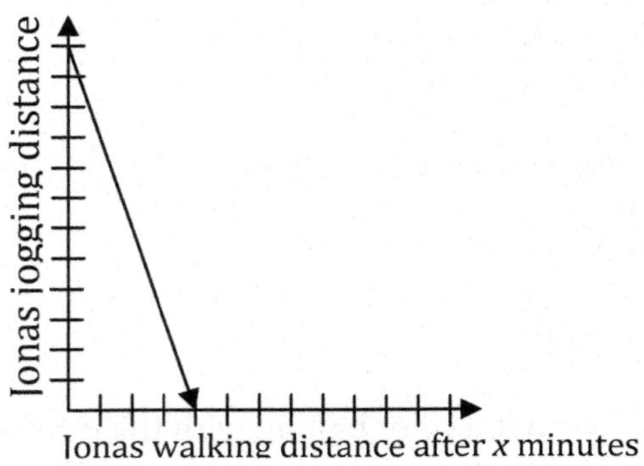

b.

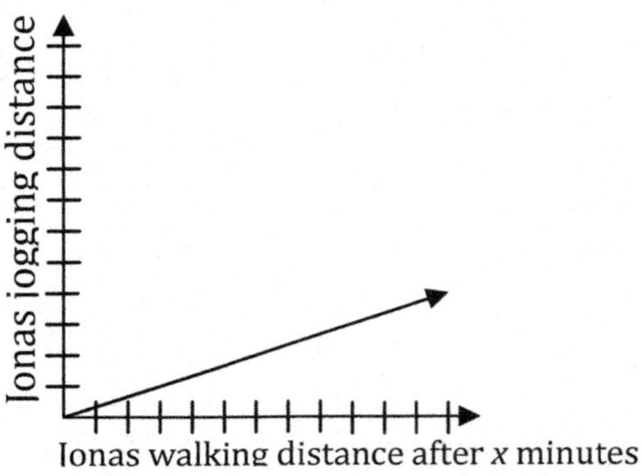

d.

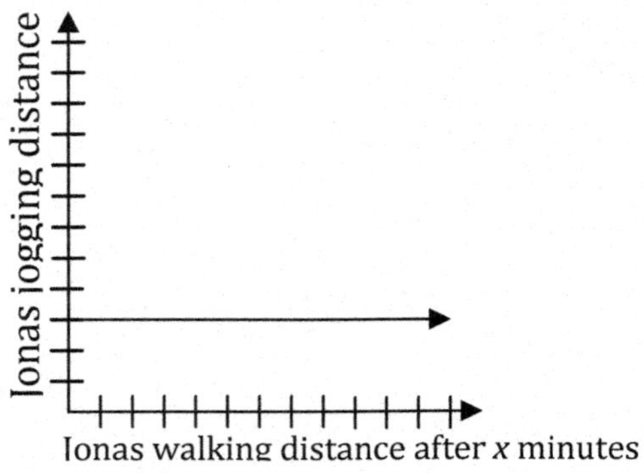

5. Jerry needs to load four pieces of equipment onto a factory elevator that has weight limit of 800 pounds. Jerry weighs 200 pounds. What would the average weight of each item have to be so that the elevator's weight limit is not exceeded?

a. 128 pounds
b. 150 pounds
c. 175 pounds
d. 180 pounds

6. Examine the figure below, which shows two lines passing through the center O of a circle, and select the best answer.

a. AO is greater than OC but less than CD
b. AB is greater than CD and greater than DO
c. AB is greater than OC but less than CD
d. AO is the same length as OC but less than CD

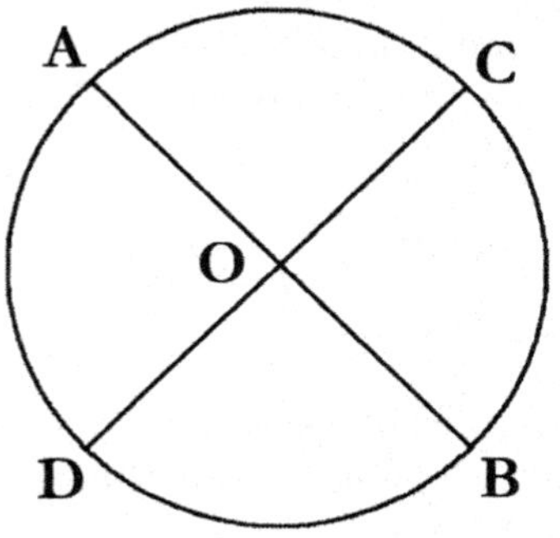

7. A rectangle is twice as long as it is wide. If the width is 3 meters, what is the area in m^2?

a. 12 m^2
b. 6 m^2
c. 9 m^2
d. 18 m^2

8. Chan receives a bonus from his job. He pays 30% in taxes, gives 20% to charity, uses another 20% to pay off an old debt, and sets aside 10% in a savings account. He has $600 remaining from his bonus. What was the total amount of Chan's bonus?

a. $2400
b. $2800
c. $3000
d. $3600

9. An airplane travels at 300 mph relative to the air. It moves against a headwind of 15 mph. what is its speed relative to the ground?

a. 300 mph
b. 315 mph
c. 270 mph
d. 285 mph

10. A jar contains pennies and nickels. The ratio of nickels to pennies is 6:2. What percent of the coins are pennies?

a. 25%
b. 33.3%
c. 40%
d. 50%

11. Given the equation, $ax + b = c$, what is the value of x?

a. $\frac{c+b}{a}$

b. $\frac{ca}{b}$

c. $c - ba$

d. $\frac{c-b}{a}$

12. For the number set {7, 12, 5, 16, 23, 44, 18, 9, Z}, which of the following values could be equal to Z if Z is the median of the set?

a. 10
b. 11
c. 14
d. 17

13. The sides of a triangle are equal to integral numbers of units. Two sides are 4 and 6 units long, respectively; what is the minimum value for the triangle's perimeter?

a. 10 units
b. 11 units
c. 12 units
d. 13 units

14. Which of the following choices is the missing number from this series: 1, 2, 4, __, 16?

a. 6
b. 8
c. 10
d. 12

15. If $x = 2y - 3$ and $2x + \frac{1}{2}y = 3$, then $y = ?$

a. $-\frac{2}{3}$

b. 1

c. 2

d. $\frac{18}{7}$

16. Which of the following numbers is the smallest?

a. 2^8
b. 3^3
c. 16^1
d. 24

17. There are 64 squares on a checkerboard. Bobby puts one penny on the first square, two on the second square, four on the third, eight on the fourth. He continues to double the number of coins at each square until he has covered all 64 squares. How many coins must he place on the last square?

a. 2^{63}
b. $2^{63} + 1$
c. $2^{64} - 1$
d. 2^{64}

18. Which number comes next in the series: 12, 7, 8, 13, 4, 19, 0, ... ?

a. 25
b. 0
c. 19
d. -2

19. Examine i, ii, and iii, and find the best answer.

i. 20% of 80 ii. 50% of 70 iii. 40% of 90

a. (ii)>(iii)
b. (ii)>(i)
c. (i)<(ii) and (ii)=(iii)
d. (i)=(ii)=(iii)

20. A commuter survey counts the people riding in cars on a highway in the morning. Each car contains only one man, only one woman, or both one man and one woman. Out of 25 cars, 13 contain a woman and 20 contain a man. How many contain both a man and a woman?

a. 4
b. 7
c. 8
d. 13

21. The length of Square A is 3 feet longer than the length of Square B. If the difference between their areas is 75 ft^2, what is the length of Square B?

a. 11 feet
b. 12 feet
c. 13 feet
d. 14 feet

22. Given points A and B on a number line, where $A = -3$ and $B = 7$, find point C, located between A and B, such that C is four times farther from A than it is from B.

a. −1
b. 1
c. 3
d. 5

23. Which number comes next in the series: 1, 4, 9, 16, ...?

a. 20
b. 24
c. 25
d. 32

24. Which of the following sums is the greatest?

a. 3 + 4 + 16
b. 6 + 4 + 5 + 7
c. 4 + 5 + 9
d. 10 + 4 + 8

25. Examine i, ii, and iii, and find the best answer.

i. $\frac{1}{3}$ of 24   ii. $\frac{1}{5}$ of 30   iii. $\frac{3}{4}$ of 20

a. (ii)<(iii)
b. (i)<(ii)<(iii)
c. (i)=(ii) and (ii)<(iii)
d. (i)=(ii) and (ii)>(iii)

26. The cost, in dollars, of shipping x computers to California for sale is 3000 + 100x. The amount received when selling these computers is 400x dollars. What is the least number of computers that must be shipped and sold so that the amount received is at least equal to the shipping cost?

a. 10
b. 15
c. 20
d. 25

27. If p and n are positive consecutive integers such that $p > n$, and $p + n = 15$, what is the value of n?

a. 5
b. 6
c. 7
d. 8

28. What number should come next in the series 3, 6, 8, 16, 18, 36, ... ?

a. 38
b. 72
c. 57
d. 44

29. Examine i, ii, and iii, and find the best answer. Consider only the magnitude of each measurement.

i. The perimeter of a rectangle with length of 6 cm and width of 4 cm
ii. The perimeter of a square with sides 4 cm long
iii. The area of a square with sides 4 cm long

a. (ii)>(iii)
b. (i)=(ii)=(iii)
c. (ii)=(iii)
d. (ii)<(iii)

30. On a floor plan drawn at a scale of 1:100, the area of a rectangular room is 30 cm^2. What is the actual area of the room?

a. 30 m^2
b. 300 cm^2
c. 3,000 m^2
d. 30,000 cm^2

31. The repeating pattern shown below uses the same four figures over and over again.

Fig. 1 Fig. 2 Fig. 3 Fig. 4 Fig. 5 Fig. 6 ...

Which of the four figures will the figure in the 31st position look like?

a. Figure 1
b. Figure 2
c. Figure 3
d. Figure 4

32. Examine i, ii, and iii, and find the best answer.

i. $\frac{2}{3}$ ii. $\frac{20}{30}$ iii. $\frac{30}{45}$

a. (ii)>(iii)
b. (i)=(ii)=(iii)
c. (ii)=(iii)
d. (ii)<(iii)

33. Which of the following sums is the least?

a. 4 + 3 + 4 + 5
b. 3 + 6 + 8
c. 9 + 5 + 3
d. 1 + 8 + 7 + 2

34. Examine the diagram of a square and find the best answer.

a. *AD* is equal to *CD*
b. *CE* is equal to *AE*
c. *BD* is equal to *ED*
d. *CB* is equal to *BD*

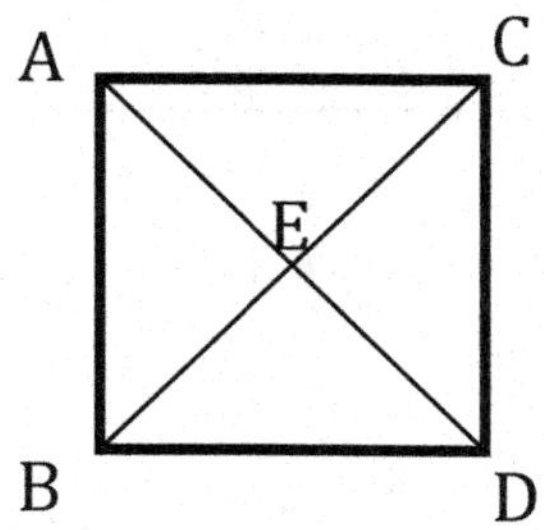

35. Hannah draws two supplementary angles. One angle measures 34°. What is the measure of the other angle?

a. 56°
b. 66°
c. 146°
d. 326°

36. Examine i, ii, and iii, and find the best answer.

i. 0.04 ii. 4% iii. $\frac{2}{50}$

a. (ii)>(iii)
b. (i)=(ii)=(iii)
c. (ii)=(iii)
d. (ii)<(iii)

37. What number should fill the blank in the series 8, 12, 16, ___, 24?

a. 18
b. 20
c. 22
d. 26

38. A long distance runner does a first lap around a track in exactly 50 seconds. As she tires, each subsequent lap takes 20% longer than the previous one. How long does she take to run 3 laps?

a. 72 seconds
b. 160 seconds
c. 180 seconds
d. 182 seconds

39. In Figure 1 (pictured below), the distance from *A* to *D* is 48. The distance from *A* to *B* is equal to the distance from *B* to *C*. If the distance from *C* to *D* is twice the distance of *A* to *B*, how far apart are *B* and *D*?

a. 12
b. 16
c. 24
d. 36

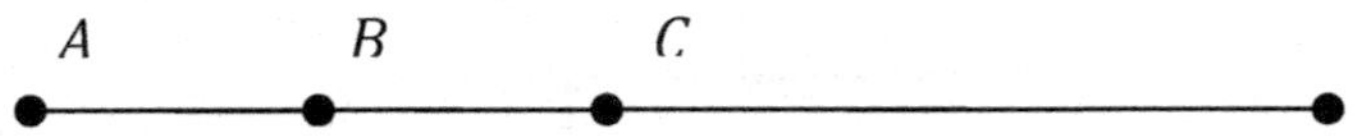

Figure 1

40. Examine i, ii, and iii, and find the best answer.

i. (3 x 4) + 5
ii. (4 + 5) x 6
iii. (3 x 5) + 6

a. (ii) >(iii)
b. (i)=(ii)=(iii)
c. (ii)=(iii)
d. (i)<(ii) and (ii)>(iii)

41. Janice makes *x* phone calls. Elaina makes 23 more phone calls than Janice. June makes 14 more phone calls than Janice. In terms of *x*, what is the sum of their phone calls minus 25 calls?

a. 3x + 37
b. 3x + 12
c. x + 12
d. 3x - 25

42. What number should come next in the series 41, 44, 48, 53, 59, ... ?

a. 64
b. 65
c. 66
d. 67

43. Given the sequence represented in the table below, where n represents the position of the term and a_n represents the value of the term, which of the following describes the relationship between the position number and the value of the term?

n	1	2	3	4	5	6
a_n	5	2	−1	−4	−7	−10

a. Multiply n by 2 and subtract 4
b. Multiply n by 2 and subtract 3
c. Multiply n by −3 and add 8
d. Multiply n by −4 and add 1

44. Jeremy put a heavy chalk mark on the tire of his bicycle. His bike tire is 27 inches in diameter. When he rolled the bike, the chalk left marks on the sidewalk. Which expression can be used to best determine the distance, in inches, the bike rolled from the first mark to the fourth mark?

a. $3(27\pi)$
b. $4\pi(27)$
c. $(27 \div 3)\pi$
d. $(27 \div 4)\pi$

45. A data set has five values: 5, 10, 12, 13, and one unknown value. The average of the data set is 9.6. What is the unknown value?

a. 4
b. 6
c. 7.2
d. 8

46. If a – 16 = 8b + 6, what does a + 3 equal?

a. b + 3
b. 8b + 9
c. 8b + 22
d. 8b + 25

47. What two numbers should come next in the series 1, 1, 2, 3, 5, 8, 13, ... ?

a. 18, 24
b. 20, 28
c. 21, 29
d. 21, 34

48. Examine the diagram of a circle and find the best answer. The chord shown is a diameter of the circle. The shorter line segment is a radius of the circle.

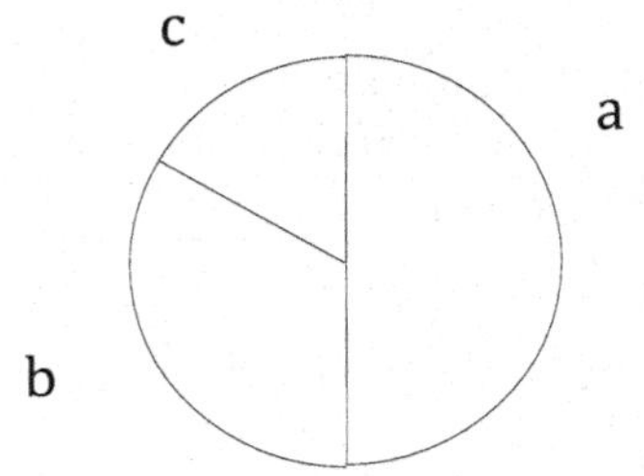

a. a = b = c
b. a > b < c
c. b = a – c
d. a + c = b

49. Examine i, ii, and iii, and find the best answer.

i. 5^2 ii. 2^5 iii. 25

a. (iii)>(ii)
b. (i)=(ii)=(iii)
c. (ii)=(iii)
d. (i)=(iii) and (iii)<(ii)

50. Examine i, ii, and iii, and find the best answer.

i. A number that is 3 less than 2 times 15
ii. A number that is equal to 3 cubed
iii. A number that is 3 more than 80% of 30

a. (ii)>(iii)
b. (i)=(ii)=(iii)
c. (ii)=(iii)
d. (i)<(ii) and (ii)>(iii)

51. Student scores on Mrs. Thompson's last math test are shown below. Which of the following is the best representation of class performance?

76, 39, 87, 85, 91, 93, 86, 90, 77, 89, 74, 82, 68, 86, 79

a. mean
b. median
c. mode
d. range

52. What number should be next in the series 108, 104, 98, 90, 80, ... ?

a. 68
b. 72
c. 76
d. 64

Reading

Comprehension

The Inventions of Technology

Stories have been a part of the world since the beginning of recorded time. For centuries before the invention of the printing press, stories of the world were passed down to generations through oral tradition. With the invention of the printing press, which made written material available to wide ranges of audiences, books were mass-produced and introduced into greater society.

For the last several centuries, books have been at the forefront of education and entertainment. With the invention of the Internet, reliance on books for information quickly changed. Soon, almost everything that anyone needed to know could be accessed through the Internet. Large printed volumes of encyclopedias became unnecessary as all of the information was easily available on the Internet.

Despite the progression of the Internet, printed media was still very popular in the forms of both fiction and non-fiction books. While waiting for an appointment, enduring a several-hour flight, or relaxing before sleep, books have been a reliable and convenient source of entertainment, and one that society has not been willing to give up.

With the progression and extreme convenience of technology, printed books are going to soon become a thing of the past. Inventions such as the iPad from Macintosh and the Kindle have made the need for any kind of printed media unnecessary. With a rechargeable battery, a large screen, and the ability to have several books saved on file, electronic options will soon take over and society will no longer see printed books.

Although some people may say that the act of reading is not complete without turning a page, sliding a finger across the screen or pressing a button to read more onto the next page is just as satisfying to the reader. The iPad and Kindle are devices that have qualities similar to a computer and can be used for so much more than just reading. These devices are therefore better than books because they have multiple uses.

In a cultural society that is part of the world and due to a longstanding tradition, stories will always be an important way to communicate ideas and provide information and entertainment. Centuries ago, stories could only be remembered and retold through speech. Printed media changed the way the world communicated and was connected, and now, as we move forward with technology, it is only a matter of time before we must say goodbye to the printed past and welcome the digital and electronic future.

1. What is the main argument of this essay?
   a. iPad and Kindles are easier to read than books
   b. The printing press was a great invention
   c. The Internet is how people receive information
   d. Technology will soon replace printed material

2. What is the main purpose of paragraph 1?
   a. To explain oral tradition
   b. To explain the importance of the printing press
   c. To explain the progression of stories within society
   d. To introduce the essay

3. In paragraph 3, "enduring" most nearly means:
   a. Quitting
   b. Undergo
   c. Sleeping
   d. Thriving

4. According to the essay, what was the first way that stories were communicated and passed down?
   a. Oral tradition
   b. Printed books
   c. Technology
   d. Hand writing

5. Which of the following statements is an opinion?
   a. Despite the progression of the Internet, printed media was still very popular in the forms of both fiction and non-fiction books
   b. Although some people may say that the act of reading is not complete without turning a page, sliding a finger across the screen or pressing a button to read more onto the next page is just as satisfying to the reader
   c. With the invention of the Internet, reliance on books for information quickly changed
   d. Stories have been a part of the world since the beginning of recorded time

6. What is a secondary argument the author makes?
   a. Devices such as the iPad or Kindle are better than books because they have multiple uses
   b. Books are still important to have while waiting for an appointment or taking a flight
   c. Printed encyclopedias are still used and more convenient that using the Internet
   d. With technology, there will soon be no need for stories

Global Warming

Global warming and the depletion of natural resources are constant threats to the future of our planet. All people have a responsibility to be proactive participants in the fight to save Earth by working now to conserve resources for later. Participation begins with our everyday choices. From what you buy to what you do to how much you use, your decisions affect the planet and everyone around you. Now is the time to take action.

When choosing what to buy, look for sustainable products made from renewable or recycled resources. The packaging of the products you buy is just as important as the products themselves. Is the item minimally packaged in a recycled container? How did the product reach the store? Locally grown food and other products manufactured within your community are the best choices. The fewer miles a product traveled to reach you, the fewer resources it required.

You can continue to make a difference for the planet in how you use what you bought and the resources you have available. Remember the locally grown food you purchased? Don't pile it on your plate at dinner. Food that remains on your plate is a wasted resource, and you can always go back for seconds. You should try to be aware of your consumption of water and energy. Turn off the water when you brush your teeth, and limit your showers to five minutes. Turn off the lights, and don't leave appliances or chargers plugged in when not in use.

Together, we can use less, waste less, recycle more, and make the right choices. It may be the only chance we have.

7. What is the author's primary purpose in writing this article?
    a. The author's purpose is to scare people.
    b. The author's purpose is to warn people.
    c. The author's purpose is to inspire people.
    d. The author's purpose is to inform people.

8. How does the author make a connection between the second and third paragraphs?
    a. The author indicates he will now make suggestions for how to use what you bought.
    b. The author indicates he will continue to give more examples of what you should buy.
    c. The author indicates he will make suggestions for how to keep from buying more items.
    d. The author indicates he will make suggestions for how to tell other people what to buy.

9. What is the main idea of this article?
    a. People should use less water and energy.
    b. People should make responsible choices in what they purchase and how they use their available resources.
    c. People are quickly destroying the earth, and there is no way to stop the destruction.
    d. People should organize everyone they know to join the fight to save the environment.

10. Which organizational pattern did the author use?
    a. Comparison and contrast
    b. Chronological order
    c. Cause and effect
    d. Problem/solution

11. What does the author say is the place to begin saving our planet?
    a. The place to begin is with getting rid of products that are not earth friendly.
    b. The place to begin is with using less water when we take a shower.
    c. The place to begin is with the choices we make every day.
    d. The place to begin is with buying locally-grown food.

12. What does the author imply will happen if people do not follow his suggestions?
    a. The author implies we will run out of resources in the next 10 years.
    b. The author implies water and energy prices will rise sharply in the near future.
    c. The author implies global warming and the depletion of natural resources will continue.
    d. The author implies local farmers will lose their farms.

Close Relationships in the 21st Century

We all know the drill: the consequences of urban sprawl, American's long work hours, and devotion to television and the internet are doing nothing good for American communities.

A new study by sociologists at Duke University and the University of Arizona adds more grist to this mill, noting that Americans in 2004 had smaller networks of people with whom they talk about matters important to them than they did in 1985. (*Social Isolation in America: Changes in Core Discussion Networks Over Two Decades*, American Sociological Review, June 2006.) In 1985, Americans had three confidants, in 2004, we averaged two. The number of Americans who had no one with whom to talk about important matters almost doubled in 2004 to over 25%. Increasingly, most confidants are family: in 2004, 80% of people talked only to family about important matters and about 9% people depended totally on their spouse.

This decrease in confidants is part (a result) of the same trend that's leaving fewer people knowing their neighbors or participating in social clubs or public affairs than in the past (phenomena noted in the book Better Together: Restoring the American Community by Robert Putnam and Lewis Feldstein). We know a lot of people, but not necessarily very well.

Left to our own devices and cultural trends then, we seem to be moving in an unpleasant direction. Communities are formed ad hoc, around specific shared individual interests. This wouldn't be bad, of course, except that those communities seem to exist only within the constraints of those shared interests, and don't develop into close and meaningful relationships. The transient and specific nature of many of our relationships today can keep us socially busy without building the lasting relationships and communities that we want.

So what do we do about it if we want to change things? Harvard University's School of Government put together 150 ways to increase what they call "social capital" (i.e., the value of our social networks). Among their suggestions are: support local merchants; audition for community theater or volunteer to usher; participate in political campaigns; start or join a carpool; eat breakfast at a local gathering spot on Saturdays; and stop and make sure the person on the side of the highway is OK.

13. According to the author, which of the following was true in 2004:
    a. The average American had three confidants and 9% of people depended totally on their spouse for discussion of important matters.
    b. The average American had two confidants, and 80% of people discussed important matters only with their spouses.
    c. The average American had two confidants, and 9% of people discussed important matters only with family members.
    d. The average American had two confidants, and 80% of people discussed important matters only with family members.

14. The author argues that the transient nature of many of today's relationships is problematic because:
    a. we don't share specific interests
    b. we don't know many people
    c. it prevents us building lasting relationships and communities
    d. we have too much social capital

15. Which of the following are some of the causes to which the author attributes problems in American communities:
   a. too much homework and devotion to television
   b. urban sprawl and long work hours
   c. long work hours and growth of exercise
   d. urban sprawl and decline of sports team membership

16. Which of the following is not something the author states was suggested by Harvard University as a way to increase social capital:
   a. eat breakfast at a local gathering spot
   b. join a bowling team
   c. support local merchants
   d. join a carpool

17. How many ways did Harvard University's School of Government suggest to increase social capital?
   a. 25
   b. 50
   c. 80
   d. 150

18. According to the author, "social capital" means which of the following:
   a. the value of our social networks
   b. the number of confidants with whom we share information
   c. the value we place on friendships outside family members
   d. the number of activities in which we engage

Comets

Comets are bodies that orbit the sun. They are distinguishable from asteroids by the presence of coma or tails. In the outer solar system, comets remain frozen and are so small that they are difficult to detect from Earth. As a comet approaches the inner solar system, solar radiation causes the materials within the comet to vaporize and trail off the nuclei. The released dust and gas forms a fuzzy atmosphere called the coma, and the force exerted on the coma causes a tail to form, pointing away from the sun.

Comet nuclei are made of ice, dust, rock and frozen gases and vary widely in size: from 100 meters or so to tens of kilometers across. The comas may be even larger than the Sun. Because of their low mass, they do not become spherical and have irregular shapes.

There are over 3,500 known comets, and the number is steadily increasing. This represents only a small portion of the total comets existing, however. Most comets are too faint to be visible without the aid of a telescope; the number of comets visible to the naked eye is around one a year.

Comets leave a trail of solid debris behind them. If a comet's path crosses the Earth's path, there will likely be meteor showers as Earth passes through the trail of debris.

Many comets and asteroids have collided into Earth. Some scientists believe that comets hitting Earth about 4 billion years ago brought a significant proportion of the water in Earth's oceans. There are still many near-Earth comets.

Most comets have oval shaped orbits that take them close to the Sun for part of their orbit and then out further into the Solar System for the remainder of the orbit. Comets are often classified according to the length of their orbital period: short period comets have orbital periods of less than 200 years, long period comets have orbital periods of more than 200 years, single apparition comets have trajectories which cause them to permanently leave the solar system after passing the Sun once.

19. What does the passage claim distinguishes comets from asteroids?
    a. The make-up of their nuclei
    b. The presence of coma or tails
    c. Their orbital periods
    d. Their irregular shapes

20. According to the passage, which of the following is true?
    a. There are 350 known comets and the number is steadily increasing.
    b. There are 3,500 known comets and the number is staying the same.
    c. There are 3,500 known comets and many more comets that aren't known.
    d. Most comets are visible to the naked eye.

21. According to the passage, why do comets have irregular shapes?
    a. because they are not spherical
    b. because they have orbital periods
    c. because of their low mass
    d. because of their tails

22. What does the passage claim about the size of comets?
    a. Some are tens of kilometers across and can be seen without the use of a telescope
    b. Some are tens of kilometers across and the coma is never larger than the Sun
    c. Some are 100 meters across and the coma is never larger than the Sun
    d. Some are tens of kilometers across and the coma can be larger than the Sun

23. According to the first passage, what does the name "single apparition comets" mean?
    a. They only appear during the part of their orbit that is nearer to the Sun.
    b. They stay in the solar system even though they are only apparent once.
    c. Their orbital periods are so long they only appear once across millennia.
    d. They only remain in the solar system long enough to pass the Sun once.

"The Gettysburg Address" by Abraham Lincoln

Four score and seven years ago our fathers brought forth, upon this continent, a new nation, conceived in Liberty, and dedicated to the proposition that all men are created equal.

Now we are engaged in a great civil war, testing whether that nation, or any nation so conceived, and so dedicated, can long endure. We are met here on a great battlefield of that war. We have come to dedicate a portion of it as a final resting place for those who here gave their lives that that nation might live. It is altogether fitting and proper that we should do this.

But in a larger sense we cannot dedicate - we cannot consecrate - we cannot hallow this ground. The brave men, living and dead, who struggled here, have consecrated it far above our poor power to add or detract. The world will little note, nor long remember, what we say here, but can never forget what they did here.

It is for us, the living, rather to be dedicated here to the unfinished work which they have, thus far, so nobly carried on. It is rather for us to be here dedicated to the great task remaining before us - that from these honored dead we take increased devotion to that cause for which they here gave the last full measure of devotion - that we here highly resolve that these dead shall not have died in; that this nation shall have a new birth of freedom; and that this government of the people, by the people, for the people, shall not perish from the earth.

24. What is the main message of this speech?
   a. Those who died in this battle honor this land we are dedicating today better than anyone else.
   b. As we honor those who died in this battle, we should move forward with renewed dedication to ensuring the nation our founding fathers created continues to function the way they intended.
   c. We need to put the regrets of the past aside, without remembering the sacrifices of those who gave their lives for our country.
   d. The war we are fighting is far from over, as evidenced by the number of lives lost in this battle.

25. The phrase "the world will little note" means what?
   a. The world will not soon forget.
   b. The world will record what we say here.
   c. The world will not spread this information to distant places.
   d. The world will not pay much attention.

26. There were nearly 100 years between the American Revolution and the Civil War. The speech connects ideas about these two conflicts by saying that the ideas of the Civil War
   a. threaten those of the Revolution.
   b. are similar to those of the Revolution.
   c. are newer than those of the Revolution.
   d. are better than those of the Revolution.

27. Why does Lincoln most likely talk about the past before he talks about the present?
   a. to incite listeners of his message to protest
   b. to remember what has been lost in the past
   c. to establish context for his main message
   d. to try to get listeners to side with his position

28. What is the following sentence addressing?

Now we are engaged in a great civil war, testing whether that nation, or any nation so conceived, and so dedicated, can long endure.

   a. whether or not a nation based on ideas of freedom and equality can survive for any significant length of time
   b. whether or not the Union will be able to preserve the existing structure of the United States by preventing the Confederacy from seceding
   c. whether or not the Confederacy will be successful in seceding from the United States and surviving on its own
   d. whether or not Lincoln should continue dedicating troops to the war

29. In paragraph 4, the word "vain" most nearly means:
   a. decisive
   b. frivolous
   c. momentous
   d. practical

Black History Month

Black History Month is still a meaningful observance. Despite the important achievement of the election of our first African American president, the need for knowledge and education about African American history is still unmet to a substantial degree. Black History Month is a powerful tool in working towards meeting that need. There is no reason to give up that tool now, and it can easily coexist with an effort to develop a more comprehensive and inclusive yearly curriculum.

Having a month set aside for the study of African American history doesn't limit its study and celebration to that month; it merely focuses complete attention on it for that month. There is absolutely no contradiction between having a set-aside month and having it be present in the curriculum the rest of the year.

Equally important is that the debate *itself* about the usefulness of Black History Month can, and should, remind parents that they can't necessarily count on schools to teach African American history as thoroughly as many parents would want.

Although Black History Month has, to an extent, become a shallow ritual, it doesn't have to be. Good teachers and good materials could make the February curriculum deeply informative, thought-provoking, and inspiring. The range of material that can be covered is rich, varied, and full of limitless possibilities.

Finally, it is worthwhile to remind ourselves and our children of the key events that happened during the month of February. In 1926, Woodson organized the first Black History Week to honor the birthdays of essential civil rights activists Abraham Lincoln and Frederick Douglass. W. E. B. DuBois was born on February 23, 1868. The 15th Amendment, which granted African Americans the right to vote, was passed on February 3, 1870. The first black U.S. senator, Hiram R. Revels, took his oath of office on February 25, 1870. The National Association for the Advancement of Colored People (NAACP) was founded on February 12, 1909. Malcolm X was shot on February 21, 1965.

30. Based on this passage, what would be the author's argument against the study and celebration of Black History Month being limited to one month of the year?
  a. Black History Month is still a meaningful observance.
  b. Black History Month is a powerful tool in meeting the need for education about African American history.
  c. Having a month set aside for the study of African American history does not limit its study and celebration to that month.
  d. Black History Month does not have to be a shallow ritual.

31. Why does the author believe that the debate itself about Black History Month can be useful?
  a. The people on opposing sides can come to an intelligent resolution about whether to keep it.
  b. African American history is discussed in the media when the debate is ongoing.
  c. The debate is a reminder to parents that they can't count on schools to teach their children about African American history.
  d. Black History Month doesn't have to be a shallow ritual.

32. What does the author say about the range of material that can be taught during Black History Month?
  a. It is rich and varied.
  b. It is important.
  c. It is an unmet need.
  d. It is comprehensive.

33. The author's tone in this passage can be described as:
  a. doubtful
  b. emboldening
  c. jovial
  d. menacing

34. Which of the following can be inferred from the last paragraph?
  a. The most important events in black history happened in the 19th century.
  b. Black history has been influenced by more men than women.
  c. There are several avenues from which to draw on larger lessons of black history.
  d. The most influential black figures served in politics.

<u>Plastics</u>

Plastics have long been considered one of the great conveniences of the modern era, but evidence is mounting to indicate that these conveniences have come at an incredible cost. The chief benefit of plastics is their durability, but this benefit turns out to be the same reason plastic has become a significant problem: It takes between *two and four hundred years* to decompose. All of this plastic has accumulated into a catastrophic mess and has also caused disease in humans.

Between Hawaii and Japan, a giant mass of plastic twice the size of Texas slowly swirls with the currents of the Pacific Ocean. This area has come to be known as the Great Pacific Garbage Patch, and its effects on the ecology of the ocean are unimaginable. According to United Nations researchers, a hundred thousand sea mammals and a million seabirds die each year. They are found with cigarette lighters, syringes, and other plastics that they mistake for food in their stomachs.

Evidence also indicates that the plastic we store our food in poses health risks. For instance, phthalates (pronounced "THEY-lates") have been shown to have detrimental effects on the reproductive system, yet they are found in many plastic products—including baby bottles and water bottles. They have also been linked to various forms of cancer. Additionally, a chemical called bisphenol A that is found in many plastics can mimic the effects of the hormone estrogen, which can also affect the reproductive system.

In short, plastics may turn out to be a lot less convenient than they seem!

35. Which of the following best describes the author's purpose in writing this passage?
   a. To persuade readers to accept the author's point of view.
   b. To explain the benefits of plastic.
   c. To explain the risks of plastic bottles.
   d. To inform the reader of the effects of phthalates in plastics.

36. In the first paragraph, the word "chief" most nearly means:
   a. Main
   b. Least likely
   c. Benefit
   d. Leader of a Native American tribe

37. Which of the following statements can be inferred from paragraph two?
   a. The Great Pacific Garbage Patch is not a significant threat to humans.
   b. No one has determined why sea mammals and seabirds are dying at an alarming rate.
   c. The Great Pacific Garbage Patch is too large to be cleaned up by one country.
   d. Ocean currents carry the plastic to the middle of the ocean.

38. Which of the following statements best summarizes the main idea of this passage?
   a. The benefits of plastics outweigh their risks.
   b. Plastics pose a significant threat to humans and other living creatures.
   c. Phthalates should not be used in baby bottles.
   d. Plastics decompose very slowly.

39. In the third paragraph, the word "mimic" most nearly means:
   a. Reduce
   b. Cancerous
   c. Intensify
   d. Resemble

40. What particular risk does the author say the Great Pacific Garbage Patch poses to marine animals?
   a. It affects yearly temperature averages.
   b. Animals accidentally ingest the plastics and die.
   c. The animals' habitat is poisoned by phthalates.
   d. Seabirds cannot get to the fish below the garbage.

41. Why does this passage not discuss more of plastics' benefits?
   a. Plastics have no benefits.
   b. The passage emphasizes the dangers over the benefits in order to prove that plastics are harmful.
   c. The passage devotes a significant amount of attention to the benefits of plastics.
   d. Discussing the benefits would contradict the author's point that plastics are a necessary evil.

42. In the first paragraph, the word "durability" most nearly means:
   a. Decomposition
   b. Permanence
   c. Coloration
   d. Poisonous

Vocabulary

Choose the appropriate synonym for each underlined word in the following phrases:

43. The <u>peevish</u> instructor
    a. Ill-tempered
    b. Foreign
    c. Unpredictable
    d. Tired

44. The <u>mortified</u> clerk
    a. Cold
    b. Embarrassed
    c. Drowsy
    d. Excited

45. His <u>keen</u> remorse
    a. Relative
    b. Sharp
    c. Long
    d. Large

46. The <u>secluded</u> village
    a. Loud
    b. Remote
    c. Populous
    d. Religious

47. The fortified <u>perimeter</u>
    a. Boundary
    b. Distance
    c. Intimacy
    d. Jewel

48. The painful <u>slight</u>
    a. Daydream
    b. Passive
    c. Formality
    d. Insult

49. Our <u>monetary</u> goals
    a. Financial
    b. Impossible
    c. Particular
    d. Academic

50. The <u>volatile</u> chemical
    a. Harmless
    b. Inert
    c. Small
    d. Explosive

51. <u>Ruddy</u> cheeks
    a. Red
    b. Weary
    c. Swollen
    d. Watery

52. The <u>stellar</u> student
    a. Predictable
    b. Unimpressed
    c. Outstanding
    d. Indifferent

53. The <u>spare</u> tire
    a. Small
    b. Extra
    c. Old
    d. Flat

54. A <u>shrill</u> tone
    a. High-pitched
    b. Low
    c. Punitive
    d. Soft

55. The <u>enthralled</u> audience
    a. Bored
    b. Released
    c. Noisy
    d. Captivated

56. Time for <u>recuperation</u>
    a. Healing
    b. Replacement
    c. Drinking
    d. Discipline

57. <u>Meager</u> wages
    a. Desired
    b. Owed
    c. Insufficient
    d. Exact

58. A <u>severe</u> storm
   a. Relentless
   b. Slight
   c. Cold
   d. Immediate

59. To <u>replicate</u> exactly
   a. Amphibian
   b. Approximate
   c. Apply
   d. Reproduce

60. To <u>repudiate</u> under oath
   a. Lie
   b. Commit
   c. Desist
   d. Renounce

61. To <u>absolve</u> someone's misdeeds
   a. Forgive
   b. Accept
   c. Repeat
   d. Reject

62. The <u>impregnable</u> fortress
   a. Defeated
   b. Indecipherable
   c. Visible
   d. Impenetrable

Mathematics

1. Which number is the least common multiple of 2 and 4?
   a. 2
   b. 4
   c. 8
   d. 12

2. Equation A is $5y - 100x = 25$. What are the slope and y-intercept of the line?
   a. The slope is 100, and the y-intercept is 5.
   b. The slope is 5, and the y-intercept is 100.
   c. The slope is 20, and the y-intercept is 5.
   d. the slope is 25, and the y-intercept is 5.

3. If an odd number is added to an even number, the result must be
   a. odd
   b. even
   c. positive
   d. zero

4. Which of the following is equal to 6.19×10^3?
   a. .00619
   b. .0619
   c. 619
   d. 6,190

5. What is the area of a square with a perimeter of 16 ft?
   a. 4 ft^2
   b. 16 ft^2
   c. 32 ft^2
   d. 256 ft^2

6. The sum of two negative numbers
   a. is always negative.
   b. is always positive.
   c. sometimes is positive and sometimes is negative.
   d. is always zero.

7. Which of the following is equal to $4\sqrt{2^4}$?
   a. 4
   b. 8
   c. 16
   d. 32

8. The Charleston Recycling Company collects 50,000 tons of recyclable material every month. The chart shows the kinds of materials that are collected by the company's five trucks.

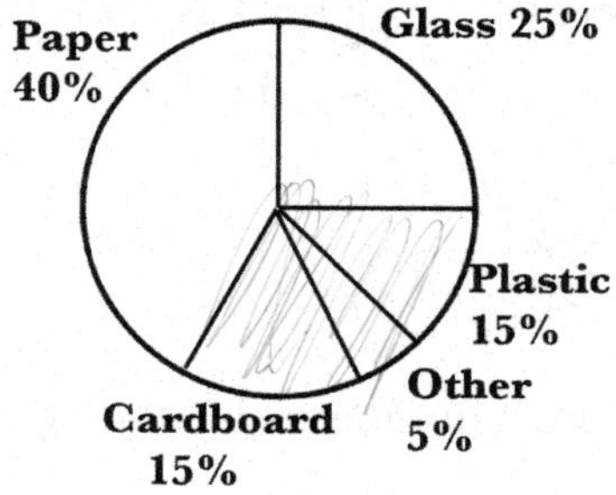

About how much paper is recycled every month?

a. 15,000 tons
b. 20,000 tons
c. 25,000 tons
d. 40,000 tons

9. Which of the following is equal to 12.5%?

a. $\frac{1}{4}$
b. $\frac{1}{8}$
c. $\frac{1}{12}$
d. $\frac{1}{16}$

10. A circle has an area equal to 36π. What is its diameter?

a. 4
b. 6
c. 12
d. 4π

11. Which of the following numerals is not a prime number?

a. 3
b. 6
c. 17
d. 41

12. The number 5 is multiplied by its reciprocal. What is the result?

a. 0
b. 1
c. 1/5
d. 5

13. A dartboard is divided into 8 black and 8 white wedge-shaped sectors, so that when a dart is thrown it has a 50% chance of landing on white, and a 50% chance of landing on black. If a dart is thrown 3 times in a row and lands on black each time, what is the chance that it will land again on black if it is thrown a fourth time?

a. 12.5%
b. 25%
c. 50%
d. 100%

14. How many integers exist between the numbers -4.2 and +6.1?

a. 2
b. 6
c. 10
d. 11

15. Joseph purchased 12 pounds of peaches at 80 cents per pound. He calculated the total amount as 12 x $0.80. = $9.60. Another method Joseph could have used to calculate the total cost of the peaches is:

a. (10 x $0.80) + (2 x $0.80)
b. (12 x $0.40) + (2 x $0.80)
c. (12 x $0.20) + (12 x $0.20)
d. (2 x $0.80) + (10 x $0.40)

16. What is the volume of the cube?

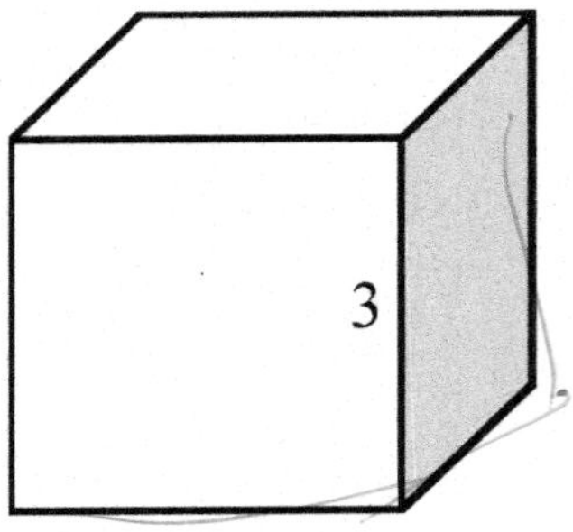

a. 9 cubic units
b. 15 cubic units
c. 27 cubic units
d. 33 cubic units

17. Which of the following expressions represents "five times a number *m* squared"?

a. $\frac{5}{m^2}$
b. $5m^2$
c. $(5m)^2$
d. $5 + m^2$

18. The square root of 6 is between
   a. 0 and 1
   b. 1 and 2
   c. 2 and 3
   d. 3 and 4

19. The radius of a circle with an area of 31 square units is doubled. What is the area of the new circle?
   a. 62 square units
   b. 93 square units
   c. 124 square units
   d. 132 square units

20. Juan got grades of 68 and 73 on his first two math tests. What grade must he get on the third test if all are weighted equally and he wants to raise his grade to a 75 average?
   a. 84
   b. 82
   c. 80
   d. 78

21. The ratio of left-handed to right-handed ballplayers on the girls' softball team is 2:3. If there are 12 left-handed players on the team, how many girls are on the roster in all?
   a. 18
   b. 24
   c. 30
   d. 32

22. Round [illegible]dth.
   a. 1[illegible]
   b. [illegible]
   c. 1[illegible]
   d. 17.19

23. Which function represents the graph?
  a. $y = x + 1$
  b. $y = x - 1$
  c. $y = -x + 1$
  d. $y = -x - 1$

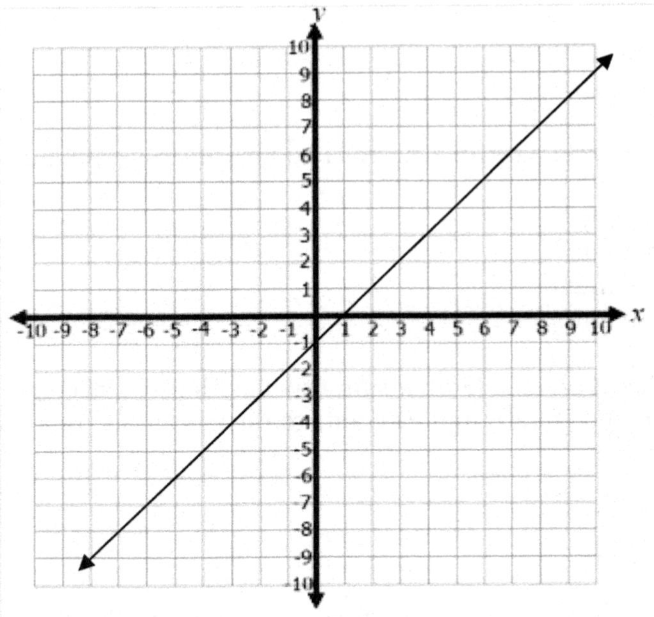

24. Refer to the following chart. Which month shows the greatest increase in rainfall compared to the preceding month?

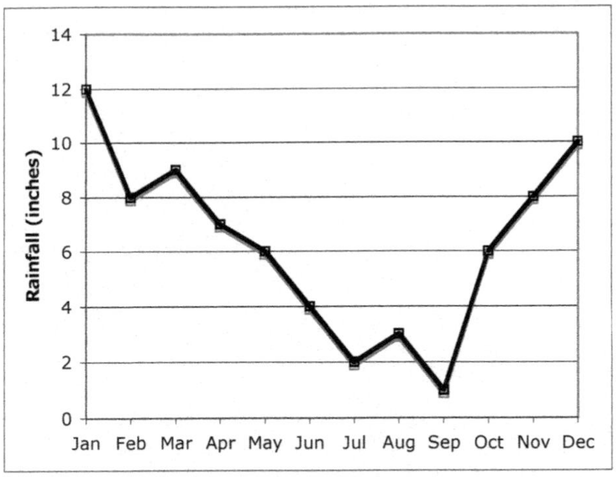

  a. January
  b. March
  c. August
  d. October

25. If $3x + 5 = 11$, then $x = ?$
  a. 6
  b. 3
  c. 2
  d. 1

26. Jamet had $6.50 in his wallet when he left home. He spent $4.25 on drinks and $2.00 on a magazine. Later, his friend repaid him $2.50 that he had borrowed the previous day. How much did Jamet have in his wallet then?

a. $12.25
b. $14.25
c. $3.25
d. $2.75

27. A sailboat is 19 meters long. What is its length in inches?

a. 254
b. 1,094
c. 4,826
d. 748

28. Mrs. Patterson's classroom has sixteen empty chairs in it. All the chairs are occupied when every student is present. If 2/5 of the students are absent, how many students make up her entire class?

a. 16
b. 32
c. 24
d. 40

29. Rachel spent $24.15 on vegetables. She bought 2 pounds of onions, 3 pounds of carrots, and $1\frac{1}{2}$ pounds of mushrooms. If the onions cost $3.69 per pound, and the carrots cost $4.29 per pound, what is the price per pound of mushrooms?

a. $2.60
b. $2.25
c. $2.80
d. $3.10

30. Elijah drove 45 miles to his job in an hour and ten minutes in the morning. On the way home in the evening, however, traffic was much heavier and the same trip took an hour and a half. What was his average speed in miles per hour for the round trip?

a. 30
b. 45
c. $33\frac{3}{4}$
d. $32\frac{1}{2}$

31. Lauren had $80 in her savings account. When she got her paycheck, she made a deposit that brought the total to $120. By what percentage did the total amount in her account increase as a result of this deposit?

a. 50%
b. 40%
c. 35%
d. 80%

32. Which of these is a solution to the inequality $4x - 12 < 4$?

a. x < 2
b. x > 2
c. x > 4
d. x < 4

33. If a = -6 and b = 7, then $4a(3b+5)+2b=?$

a. 638
b. -485
c. 850
d. -610

34. Mark is driving to Phoenix, a distance of 210 miles. He drives the first ten miles in 12 minutes. If he continues at the same rate, how long will it take him to reach his destination?

a. 3 hours 15 minutes
b. 4 hours 12 minutes
c. 3 hours 45 minutes
d. 4 hours 20 minutes

35. An airplane leaves Atlanta at 2 PM and flies north at 250 miles per hour. A second airplane leaves Atlanta 30 minutes later and flies north at 280 miles per hour. At what time will the second airplane overtake the first?

a. 6:00 PM
b. 6:20 PM
c. 6:40 PM
d. 6:50 PM

36. The table shows the cost of renting a bicycle for 1, 2, or 3 hours. Which of the following equations best represents the data, if C represents the cost and h represents the time of the rental?

Hours	1	2	3
Cost	\$3.60	\$7.20	\$10.80

a. $C = 3.60h$
b. $C = h + 3.60$
c. $C = 3.60h + 10.80$
d. $C = 10.80/h$

37. Joshua has to earn more than 92 points on the state test in order to qualify for an academic scholarship. Each question is worth 4 points, and the test has a total of 30 questions. Let x represent the number of test questions.

Which of the following inequalities can be solved to determine the number of questions Joshua must answer correctly?

a. $4x < 30$
b. $4x < 92$
c. $4x > 30$
d. $4x > 92$

38. A tire on a car rotates at 500 RPM (revolutions per minute) when the car is traveling at 50 km/hr (kilometers per hour). What is the circumference of the tire, in meters?

a. $\dfrac{50{,}000}{2\pi}$

b. $\dfrac{50{,}000}{60 \times 2\pi}$

c. $\dfrac{50{,}000}{500 \times 2\pi}$

d. $\dfrac{10}{6}$

39. What is the area of the shaded region? (Each square represents one unit.)

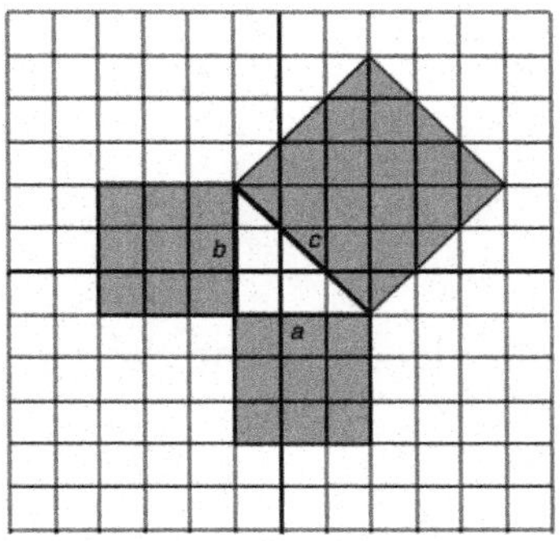

a. 16
b. 18
c. 24
d. 27

40. If $\frac{4}{x-3} - \frac{2}{x} = 1$, then $x = ?$
a. -6
b. -1
c. -6 or -1
d. -1 or 6

41. Richard buys two cups of coffee every day except Saturday and Sunday. On Saturday he buys only one cup, and on Sunday he buys none. If a cup of coffee costs \$2.25, how much does Richard spend on coffee every week?
a. \$25.00
b. \$23.50
c. \$24.75
d. \$25.25

42. Candice is reading a map. She measures a distance along a road as 6.5 inches. If the scale of the map is such that one mile is represented as 2 inches, what is the real distance along the road that Candice has measured?

a. 4 miles
b. 3.25 miles
c. 6.5 miles
d. 13 miles

43. Bob spends $17.90 on sodas and snacks for his study group. The expenses are to be split evenly between five people. How much is each person's share?

a. $3.45
b. $3.58
c. $3.65
d. $3.73

44. What percent of 72 is 9?

a. 16%
b. 12.5%
c. 11%
d. 8%

45. The histogram below represents the overall GRE scores for a sample of college students. Which of the following is a true statement?

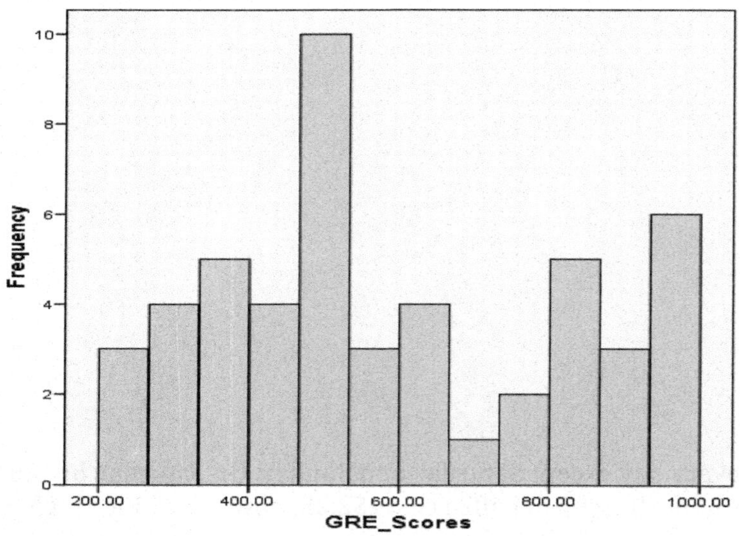

a. The range of GRE scores is approximately 600
b. The average GRE score is 750
c. The median GRE score is approximately 500
d. The fewest number of college students had an approximate score of 800

46. A train takes 40 minutes to go 55 miles. Moving at the same constant speed, how long will the train require to go 220 miles?

a. 4 hours 20 minutes
b. 3 hours 40 minutes
c. 2 hours 40 minutes
d. 2 hours 20 minutes

47. A clothing store offers a red tag sale during which items are offered at 5% off the marked price. Margaret selects a dress with a marked price of $120. How much will she have to pay for it?

a. $115
b. $110
c. $ 96
d. $114

48. Based on the figure below, if $BG = 6x - 4$ and $GD = 2x + 8$, what is the length of $\overline{GD}$?

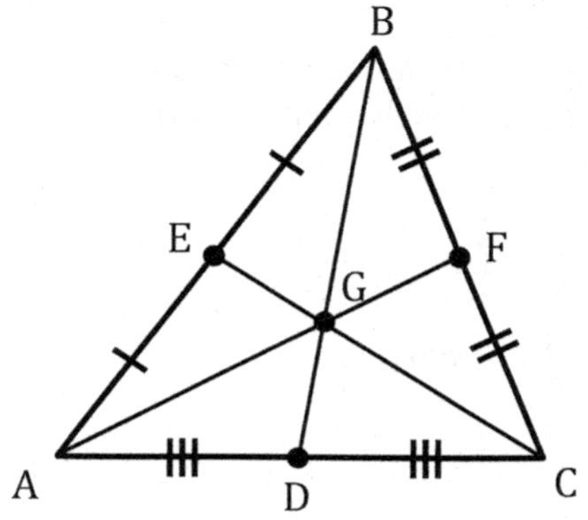

a. 10
b. 14
c. 28
d. 56

49. On his last math test, Sam got 2 questions correct for every 3 questions he missed. If the test had a total of 60 questions, how many questions did Sam answer correctly?

a. 12
b. 24
c. 36
d. 40

50. An automobile gets 34 miles per gallon of gasoline on typical roads. If it gets this fuel efficiency on a drive of 629 miles, how many gallons of gasoline will it burn?

a. 17
b. 18.5
c. 19.25
d. 20.5

51. In the figure below, lines a and b are parallel. Find the value of x.

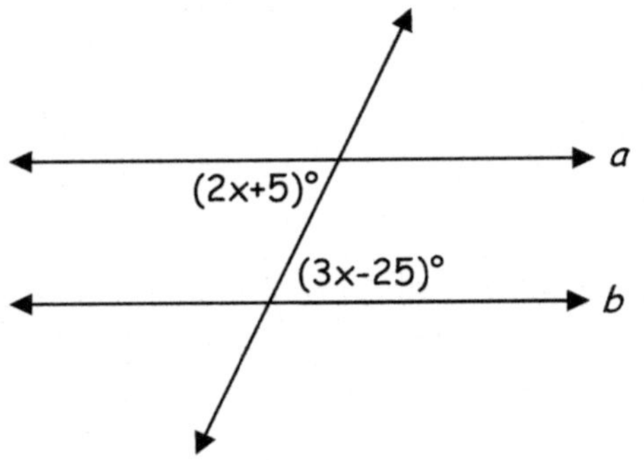

a. x = 22
b. x = 30
c. x = 40
d. x = 55

52. A company is building a track for a local high school. There are two straight sections and two semi-circular turns. Given the dimensions, which of the following most closely measures the perimeter of the entire track?

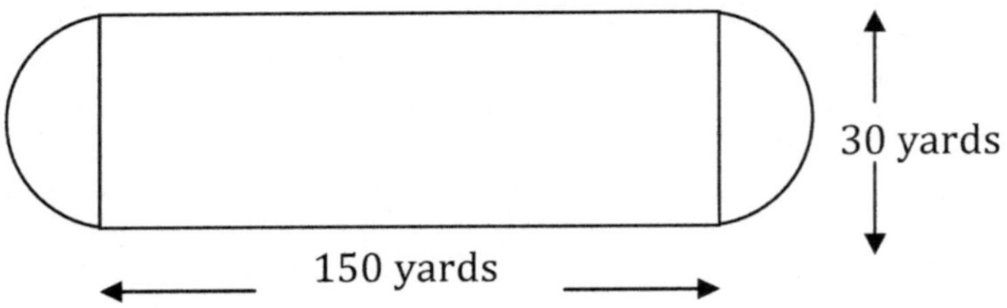

a. 300 yards
b. 180 yards
c. 360 yards
d. 395 yards

53. Rafael has a business selling computers. He buys computers from the manufacturer for $450 each and sells them for $800. Each month, he must also pay fixed costs of $3000 for rent and utilities for his store. If he sells n computers in a month, which of the following equations can be used to find his profit?

a. $P = n(800 - 450)$
b. $P = n(800 - 450 - 3000)$
c. $P = 3000\,n(800 - 450)$
d. $P = n(800 - 450) - 3000$

54. Which of the following statements is true?

a. Perpendicular lines have opposite slopes
b. Perpendicular lines have the same slopes
c. Perpendicular lines have reciprocal slopes
d. Perpendicular lines have opposite reciprocal slopes

55. A bag contains six marbles: two green, two blue, and two red. If two marbles are drawn at random, what is the probability that they are of the same color?

a. 3%
b. 20%
c. 25%
d. 33%

56. Which of the following represents the factors of the expression, $x^2 + 3x - 28$?

a. $(x - 14)(x + 2)$
b. $(x + 6)(x - 3)$
c. $(x + 4)(x - 1)$
d. $(x - 4)(x + 7)$

57. Nancy had $17.25 from her part-time job. She spent $3.15 on a magazine and $6.75 on snacks and drinks. How much does she have left?

a. $7.35
b. $9.15
c. $7.20
d. $7.40

58. A dress is marked down by 20% and placed on a clearance rack, on which is posted a sign reading, "Take an extra 25% off already reduced merchandise." What fraction of the original price is the final sales price of the dress?

a. $\frac{2}{5}$
b. $\frac{9}{20}$
c. $\frac{11}{20}$
d. $\frac{3}{5}$

59. It takes two men 8 hours to paint a wall that is 10 feet high and 18 feet long. How long does it take three men working at the same pace to paint a wall that is 10 feet high and 27 feet long?

a. 6 hours
b. 8 hours
c. 9 hours
d. 10 hours

60. Vivian has $50. She goes to the store and buys a calculator. then she buys a book that costs half what the calculator cost. Then she buys a pen that costs half what the book cost. She has $15 left. How much did she spend on the calculator?

a. $14
b. $15
c. $18
d. $20

61. A rectangular box is twice as long as it is wide. If it were 3 inches shorter and 3 inches wider, it would be square. What is the width in inches of the box?

a. 4
b. 6
c. 8
d. 12

62. In a game of chance, 3 dice are thrown at the same time. What is the probability that all three will land with a 6?

a. 1 in 6
b. 1 in 18
c. 1 in 216
d. 1 in 30

63. Richard sells cell phones. He is paid a commission of 10% for every phone he sells. The phones cost $140 each. How many phones must Richard sell in order to be paid $840?

a. 40
b. 50
c. 60
d. 70

64. What is the value of $2 \times 10^{-2} \times 5 \times 10^{3}$?

a. 1
b. 10
c. 100
d. 1000

Language

Usage, Punctuation, and Grammar

Identify the sentence that contains an error in usage, punctuation or grammar. If there are no errors, choose answer choice "d."

1.
   a. Fear of the number thirteen is called "triskaidekaphobia."
   b. The earwig's name originates in the myth that the insect burrows into the human ear to lay its eggs.
   c. The longest word recorded in an English dictionary are "Pneumonoultramicroscopic-silicovolcanokoniosis."
   d. No mistake.

2.
   a. "Stewardesses," "desegregated," and "reverberated" are the longest words a person can type using only his or her left hand.
   b. The largest catfish ever catch is 646 pounds, the size of an adult brown bear.
   c. A flyswatter has holes in it to reduce air resistance.
   d. No mistake.

3.
   a. The canoe cut a clear swath through the algae.
   b. Though widely ridiculed when first proposed, Alfred Wegener's theory of plate tectonics is now an accepted explanation of how continents are formed.
   c. Though a highly influentially anthropologist, Claude Levi-Strauss often took criticism for spending little time in the field studying real cultures.
   d. No mistake.

4.
   a. Fiction writer David Foster Wallace, author of the influential novel *Infinite Jest*, also authored a book surveying all of the significant theories of infinity in the history of mathematics.
   b. The photograph made the Eiffel Tower look like it was balanced on Oswald's palm.
   c. It is easy to get confused when calculating time differences between time zones a useful way to remember them is that the Atlantic Ocean starts with A, as in A.M., and the Pacific Ocean starts with P, as in P.M.
   d. No mistake.

5.
   a. Arnold was disappointed to discover the model airplane he purchased online was half the size he expected.
   b. Computer storage has come a long way since the days of punched paper tape.
   c. The surrealists were a group of artists who believed that art should reflect the subconscious mind, their images are often very dreamlike, showing businessmen falling like rain over a city and melting clocks.
   d. No mistake.

6.

a. A "moor" is a plot of uncultivated land, similar to prairies in the U.S.
b. "Orange is my favorite color, but not my favorite fruit." said Lisa.
c. Some historians believe that the United States would have been too large for one government to control if the telegraph had not been invented in 1837.
d. No mistake.

7.

a. The largest volcano in our solar system is found on Mars.
b. The deepest canyon, too.
c. The volcano, called the Olympus Mons, is 342 miles in width and 17 miles tall; the canyon, called the Valles Marinaris, is 2,500 miles long.
d. No mistake.

8.

a. Pocahontas spent the last year's of her young life in England under the name Rebecca.
b. Dorine beat me in tennis for three straight matches.
c. Much of the light given off by stars is blocked by cosmic dust before it reaches the Earth's atmosphere.
d. No mistake.

9.

a. The Pima Indians of Arizona have remarkably high rates of diabetes and obesity some scientists believe the gene that causes this present-day health crisis was actually of great value to the Pima's ancestors who had to be able to retain glucose during periods of famine.
b. Recent research has discovered that some types of incense can create effects in the human brain similar to antidepressants.
c. Though debate on the topic has been ongoing, some believe that many amphibian species may be on the brink of extinction.
d. No mistake.

10.

a. The driver's side fender of my car is caved in because the high-speed winds pulled the door open too quickly.
b. While there is some truth to the belief that Eskimos have many words for snow, it is often overlooked that there are quite a few words for snow in English too: snow, slush, flurry, snowflake, and even more if you count the slang of snowboarders.
c. Director Alfred Hitchcock make over 60 films in his career.
d. No mistake.

11.

a. A good pediatrician should try not to laugh at the fears of new parents.
b. Some of the most difficult words to spell include "bureaucracy," "sacrilegious," and "millennium."
c. Sales of digitally downloaded albums have risen from 5.5 million in 2004 to 65.8 million in 2008.
d. No mistake.

12.

a. The earliest recording of a human voice was made by Thomas Edison in 1877, when they recorded himself reciting "Mary Had a Little Lamb."
b. In 2009, *The Simpsons* became the longest running series in television history.
c. Many say that Reunion Tower in downtown Dallas, Texas, resembles a microphone or a golf ball on a tee.
d. No mistake.

13.

a. The *trireme* was a Greek battleship that got its name from the three banks of oars that helped propel the ship into battle.
b. Our basement floods once a yearly.
c. The *novitiate* is the period of time before a monk or priest takes his vows to make sure he is suited for the religious life.
d. No mistake.

14.

a. The trumpet player said, "I played the song right, just not the notes."
b. Woody Allen said, "I don't want to achieve immortality through my work. I want to achieve it through not dying."
c. Samuel Goldwyn is said to have replied to a secretary who asked whether she should destroy files over ten years old, "Yes, but keep copies."
d. No mistake.

15.

a. When asked to take a reduction in pay from $20,000 to $7,500 a year, baseball legend Vernon Gomez replied, "You keep the salary and pay me the cut."
b. The spread of Islam began around 600 A.D. and reached from the Middle East to North Africa, Spain, Central Asia, and India?
c. Hadrian, Emperor of Rome, is credited with halting the expansion of the Roman Empire to concentrate instead on defending its boundaries.
d. No mistake.

16.

a. The Sahara Desert was rarely crossed until the introduction of the camel in 100 A.D.
b. International time standards were not put in place until 1883.
c. The names of the days of the week originate in either Latin or Saxon names for deities Sunday, for instance, is Saxon for "Sun's Day," while Thursday derives from "Thor's Day."
d. No mistake.

17.

a. The origin of the clock is usually traced back to Galileo, who in 1583 reportedly watched a chandelier swinging during a church service and imagined a way to use a pendulum as a time-keeping device.
b. Irvin Hertzel ran a statistical analysis of Monopoly squares and found that players land on some spots more often than others, specifically Illinois Ave., Go, B & O Railroad, and Free Parking.
c. Held in Georgia, the Masters is an annual golf tournament that professional golfers consider the most valuable title in golf.
d. No mistake.

18.

a. Ironically, the namesake of the Nobel Peace Prize, Alfred Nobel, are most noted for his invention of dynamite in the 1860s.
b. The terms of our lease agreement were long and hard to understand.
c. Many terms in our legal system are Latin in origin, such as "nolo contendere" (no contest) and "actus rea" (a wrongful act).
d. No mistake.

19.

a. Loud sounds can causing damage to the hair cells that turn sound waves into electrical signals that the brain perceives as sound.
b. Debate has raged for over 200 years about whether the U.S. should adopt the metric system.
c. The metric system recognizes only seven base units of measurement, including the meter for length, the kilogram for mass, and lesser known units used by specialists like the mole for substance and the candela for light intensity.
d. No mistake.

20.

a. The metric system uses a "base-ten" system of measurement, which means its prefixes indicate multiples of ten.
b. If you ever need to measure something but do not have access to a ruler, these facts can help: The average credit card is $3\frac{3}{8}$ inches by $2\frac{1}{8}$ inches, the diameter of a quarter is around one inch, and the diameter of a penny is about $\frac{3}{4}$ inch.
c. Carbon monoxide Poisoning can cause disorientation and delirium, and it can induce a coma.
d. No mistake.

21.

a. Capgras Syndrome causes the strange delusion that people such as family members and friends are not who they appear to be but are instead imposters.
b. Yvette belonged to three organizations whose schedules constantly conflicted.
c. Owen's shirt was stained pink from his popsicle, purple from jelly, and blue from Kool-Aid.
d. No mistake.

22.

a. They closed the parking deck at midnight, so we could not get no cars out until morning.
b. "Associationism" is the name given to the theory that memories are linked together so that when one is triggered, associated memories are activated as well.
c. Some psychologists believe that many emotional disorders, including depression and anxiety, can be traced back to unrealistic expectations and assumptions.
d. No mistake.

23.

a. Joni designed the grocery stores sign, but Evan painted it.
b. The "figure-ground phenomenon" is a term used to describe the way we perceive some objects to be in the foreground and others to be in the background.
c. The Latin professor called his students "quidnuncs" when they asked too many questions about the course; the term is Latin for "what now?"
d. No mistake.

24.

a. Outside the apartment, the bus stop is a source of constant noise.
b. Few people remembered Sydney's birthday except Jon, whose birthday was the same day.
c. Erin brought cookies and juice on the last day of class.
d. No mistake.

25.

a. In math, the "Goldbach conjecture" states that every even number greater than two is the sum of two primes.
b. Enjil was a complex Sumerian sky god who was at times characterized as wrathful and at others as kind and generous.
c. Twenty-four leaders of the Nazi party was brought to trial at the end of World War II in what became known as the Nuremberg Trials.
d. No mistake.

26.

a. In radio broadcasting, a short jingle called a "bumper" announces the name of the station after commercials.
b. "There weren't any jobs listed in the newspaper this morning," Ed told his father.
c. Water is called "hard water" if it do not quickly create lather upon contact with soap because of mineral compounds dissolved in the water.
d. No mistake.

27.

a. Halley's Comet, which completes its orbit around the sun once every 76 years, was last seen in 1986 and will not be visible again until 2062.
b. Ice crystals in the atmosphere, which can create a halo around the sun or moon.
c. "Abiogenesis" is a term that refers to the discredited belief that living things can be created from nonliving things.
d. No mistake.

28.

a. The term "Algebra" comes from the title of a book written in the ninth century that explains how to balance equations.
b. Atomic clocks keep time by measuring the vibrations of Atoms and molecules.
c. The chemical formula for the caffeine molecule contains calcium, hydrogen, oxygen, and nitrogen.
d. No mistake.

29.

a. Heat was once believes to be a type of fluid called "caloric," which flowed into objects and raised their temperature.
b. Streams of protons and neutrons that escape the sun during solar flares are called "solar wind."
c. The "heat death of the universe" is a theory that predicts the universe will eventually run out of usable energy.
d. No mistake.

30.

a. The epicenter of an earthquake is the point on the Earth's surface that is above the hypocenter, or the point inside the Earth where the earthquake occurs.
b. Apart from a sine wave created by an electronic device, most sounds are not "pure" because they contain many different vibrations at different frequencies pure tones vibrate at only one frequency.
c. Though Chicago is known as the "Windy City" with winds that average 10.4 miles per hour, its winds are far slower than those of Mt. Washington, New Hampshire, where winds average 35.3 miles per hour.
d. No mistake.

31.

a. Arthur, realizing that bugs were turning the roots of his zucchini plants to mush.
b. The Earth moves at different speeds depending on where one stands in relation to the poles; the North Pole spins at about zero miles per hour, while the equator spins at over 1,000 miles per hour.
c. Because maps must distort the size of certain continents to represent a sphere stretched over a two-dimensional plane, Greenland is often depicted as similar in size to South America, even though it is about eight times smaller.
d. No mistake.

32.

a. The Earth is believed to be about 4.6 billion years old.
b. Sequoyah, who created a written script for the Cherokee language, compared the task to "catching a wild animal and taming it."
c. The discovery of gold on Cherokee land in 1828 is considered a significant motivation for the passage of the Indian Removal Act of 1830, which forced Native Americans from their homes.
d. No mistake.

33.

a. In 1803, Robert Livingston and James Monroe, two of Thomas Jefferson's aides, purchased all of the French territories in America.
b. They paid the remarkably low price of $15 million to Napoleon, who wanted to sell the land to finance his military campaigns.
c. This figure amounts to about four cents per acre, or eight dollars per square mile.
d. No mistake.

34.

a. The narwhal is a member of the dolphin family, easily recognized by its long, spiraling tusk, it is often compared to the mythical unicorn.
b. The ocean is saltier in regions where the temperature is higher due to a higher rate of evaporation.
c. The garter snake is often called a "gardener snake" or a "guarder snake" because of the similar sounds of the words.
d. No mistake.

35.

a. Long distance calls were placed by an operator until 1951.
b. The first drive-in movie theater opened in 1933.
c. The first Ferris' Wheel was built in Chicago, Illinois.
d. No mistake.

36.

a. Trees in the Olympic rain forest in northwest Washington State is covered with a thick green moss that is nourished by the 150 annual inches of rainfall.
b. The sand dunes were prettiest at sunset, when the shadows ran across the landscape like dark ribbons.
c. Some of the students were sleeping during reading time.
d. No mistake.

37.

a. Most published writing goes through many drafts and many readers before it is printed.
b. Blogs, however, are rarely edited as carefully.
c. As a result, readers have different expectations of online publications.
d. No mistake.

38.

a. When asked what his songs were about, Bob Dylan replied, "Well, some of them are about five minutes, and some of them are about eleven minutes."
b. I found several fossils of large trilobites on a field trip with my geology class.
c. I was, hoping to avoid the customs official who was yelling at all of the other travelers.
d. No mistake.

39.

a. Reykjavik is the Capitol of Iceland.
b. It is pronounced "Rake-ya-veek."
c. The letter "j" is pronounced like a "y" in English.
d. No mistake.

40.

a. Jen asked the professor for an extension on her first essay.
b. She was asking for more time.
c. The professor added three pages to the required length.
d. No mistake.

Spelling Practice Questions

Choose the sentence that contains a spelling error. If there are no errors, choose answer choice "d."

41.

a. My favorite Beatles' record is Revolver.
b. My favorite Beatles' song is "Strawberry Fields"
c. My favorite Beatle is John Lennon.
d. No mistake.

42.

a. I had to have a tooth pulled after a bike accident.
b. When I received the dentist's bill, I was disgruntled.
c. I was graitful that I couldn't feel a thing.
d. No mistake.

43.

a. Mrs. Albom, the music teacher, financed her summer vacation by bagging groceries at Wal-Mart after school.
b. We put down a tarp and shook the branches to get the mulberries.
c. The citric acid used in Vitamin C tablets makes them taste sower.
d. No mistake.

44.

a. Despite being born a slave, Benjamin Banneker went on to play a pivotal role in the planning of Washington D. C.
b. Andrew Johnson is the only president to serve as a sinator after his time as president, which is ironic because the senate had attempted to impeach him when he was president.
c. The St. Burchardi Church in Halberstadt, Germany, is currently performing a composition by John Cage entitled "As Slow as Possible," a piece that takes 639 years to complete.
d. No mistake.

45.

a. Jan tried to remember her groshery list by turning it into a song that went, "carrots and cashews and rolled toilet tissues."
b. I thought for sure I had killed the basil plant, but it revived with a little water.
c. The washing machine died with a load of wet clothes in it.
d. No mistake.

46.

a. The rock polisher ran all nite and day for months.
b. When the bouquet of flowers started to die, it left a little mound of yellow dust under each flower.
c. Nora wants to become a veterinarian when she grows up.
d. No mistake.

47.

a. Eleanor wove baskets from reeds that she pulled from the bank of the nearby lake.
b. The dog howled whenever the ambulances passed.
c. Gas station coffee alway tastes watered down to me.
d. No mistake.

48.

a. Peter Elbow is famous for his book titled *Writing without Teachers*, in which he promotes "freewriting," or writing for short periods of time without any concern for spelling, grammar, or logic.
b. John Wilkes Booth's intention in assassinating President Lincoln was to avenge the Confederacy, but in effect, his actions hurt the South because Lincoln did not live to oversee his plan for reconstruction.
c. Perspective painting uses techniques to give the two-dimentional surface of a painting the appearance of three-dimentional sprays.
d. No mistake.

49.

a. We entered the church from the south, but the family we were supposed to meet was waiting on the north side of the building.
b. The stained glass cast colorful shadows across the carpet.
c. I filled out the tax forms incorrectly, and that mistake cost me a quadruple-digit figure.
d. No mistake.

50.

a. Enrique loved to sketch copies of the images he found in *National Geographic.*
b. Over 60% of the Netherlands lies below sea level.
c. Jon submitted three poems to the contest and won one thousand dollars.
d. No mistake.

Composition Practice Questions

51. Where should the following sentence be placed in the paragraph below?

Many people have proposed explanations for this drop.

1] Surveys of criminal activity in the United States have shown that the 1990s marked a significant drop in crimes such as vehicle theft, rape, and murder. 2] Economist Rick Nevin argues that one contributing factor is the ban on lead gasoline in the 70s because lead poisoning in children has been linked with criminal behavior later in life. 3] Other theories include the controversial claim that legalizing abortion has led to fewer unwanted children and, as a result, fewer potential criminals. 4] Some politicians, including Rudy Giuliani, even take personal responsibility, identifying their policies as effective deterrents to crime.

a. After sentence 1
b. After sentence 2
c. After sentence 3
d. After sentence 4

52. Where should the following sentence be placed in the paragraph below?

Insects that carry the disease can develop resistance to the chemicals, or insecticides, that are used to kill the mosquitoes.

1] Malaria, a disease spread by insects and parasites, has long proven to be difficult to treat. 2] Part of the explanation has to do with adaptation, or the ability of one generation to pass its strengths on to another. 3] Some insects are simply not affected by these insecticides. 4] Unfortunately, these are the insects that survive and go on to reproduce, creating another generation of insects that are immune to the current insecticides. 5] Many researchers have abandoned hope for insecticides as a cure for malaria, turning their attention instead to other forms of defense, such as protein-blockers that protect humans from the effects of the disease instead of from the carriers.

a. After sentence 1
b. After sentence 2
c. After sentence 3
d. After sentence 4

53. Choose the word or words that best fill the blank.

Disney films often use the same voice actors; _______, Sterling Holloway was the voice for Winnie the Pooh, the stork in *Dumbo*, the snake Kaa in *Jungle Book*, and the Cheshire Cat in *Alice in Wonderland.*

a. but
b. for instance
c. thus
d. so

54. Choose the word or words that best fill the blank.

Many similarities exist between the film *Star Wars IV: A New Hope* and a Japanese film called *The Hidden Fortress*; _______ , *Star Wars* director George Lucas openly acknowledges the film as a significant influence.

a. however
b. or
c. in fact
d. yet

55. Choose the word or words that best fill the blank.

Marty did not realize until he arrived to perform in Philadelphia that he had left his guitar in Pittsburgh; ______, he was fortunate to find a music store that agreed to rent him one for the evening.

a. however
b. because
c. after
d. while

56. Choose the sentence that is correct and most clearly written.

a. The novelist David Markson is known for his experimental works, such as "This Is Not a Novel."
b. Experimental works such as "This Is Not a Novel" have been wrote by David Markson.
c. Novelist David Markson is knew for his experimental works, such as "This Is Not a Novel."
d. David Markson is a novelist who is known for experimentation his works include "This Is Not a Novel."

57. Choose the sentence that is correct and most clearly written.

a. I intended to mow the yard, but I wanted to wait until evening when it are cooler.
b. I intended to mow the yard, but I wanted to wait until evening when it would be cooler.
c. I intended to mow the yard, but not until it getting cooler in the evening.
d. I intended to mow the yard, but I waits until evening when it was cooler.

58. Choose the sentence that is correct and most clearly written.

a. We used to dump our lawn clippings, but now we compost them for the garden.
b. Dumping our lawn clippings used to be something done by us, but now composting is done by us for the garden.
c. We used to dumps our lawn clippings, but now we composts them for the garden.
d. We used to dump our lawn clippings, but now I compost them for the garden.

59. Which sentence does not belong in the following paragraph?

> 1] Though Thomas Jefferson's taste for expensive home furnishings and wine contributed to the substantial debts he faced toward the end of his life, many other factors also contributed. 2] For instance, when Jefferson's father-in-law died, all of his debts were transferred to Jefferson. 3] Additionally, though his holdings in land and slaves were considerable, they were never especially profitable. 4] Jefferson is believed to have fathered children with one of his slaves. 5] Finally, less than a decade before his death, Jefferson unwisely agreed to endorse a $20,000 loan for a friend, and when the friend unexpectedly died a year later, Jefferson inherited yet another large debt. 6] Jefferson's personal experience with debt may have been part of his motivation in criticizing policies that would increase the national debt.

a. Sentence 2
b. Sentence 3
c. Sentence 4
d. Sentence 5

60. Which sentence does not belong in the following paragraph?

> 1] Renowned scientist Richard Feynman once said that the atomic theory is the most profound discoveries scientists have made. 2] Feynman was also an accomplished percussionist who could play nine beats with one hand while playing ten with the other! 3] "All things are made of atoms," explained Feynman, "little particles that...move around in perpetual motion, attracting each other when they are a little distance apart, but repelling upon being squeezed into one another." 4] He then made the claim that this idea is one of the most illuminating ideas in the history of science: "In that one sentence, you will see, there is an enormous amount of information about the world, if just a little imagination and thinking are applied."

a. Sentence 1
b. Sentence 2
c. Sentence 3
d. Sentence 4

Answers and Explanations

Verbal Skills

1. A: To depress is the opposite of enliven, which means to excite or invigorate.

2. C: Natural is the opposite of the other words in the series. Artificial, synthetic, and man-made are all words for non-natural processes.

3. B: The category of amphibians contains frogs. The order of this analogy begins with something that is specific and moves to the general category. Since you are given the specific item of *hydrogen*, then you are looking for the general category which would be choice B: *element*.

4. C: We can diagram this sentence as follows: Tom > Darius, which tells us that Tom arrived before Darius. We do not have enough information to determine when Bernie arrived in relation to the other two people.

5. A: Aural refers to the auditory sense, or hearing.

6. B: "Artist" is the general category that all the other items in the series belong to; painters, musicians, and dancers are all kinds of artists.

7. B: Shun means reject or ignore, the opposite of embrace.

8. B: An apple develops from a seed; a person develops from an embryo.

9. C: We can diagram this sentence as follows: Dean > Ellie; Dean > Rob. In other words, Dean was born before Ellie and before Rob. We do not have enough information to determine whether Ellie > Rob is true.

10. C: This analogy focuses on synonyms. *Reprimand* and *punishment* are close synonyms. *Impetuous* is a sudden or impulsive action with little or no thoughtful planning. So, the best choice is *hasty* which means rapid or very quick.

11. D: Mediocre means unexceptional, which is the opposite of excellent.

12. C: "Appliance" is a general category that the other words in the list belong to. Toasters, ovens, and coffee makers are all appliances.

13. B: Intricate most nearly means complex.

14. A: Temperature is used to measure heat; pounds are used to measure weight.

15. D: Furrow, a word that refers to a line cut into the ground, means the opposite of mound.

16. D: The verb counsel most nearly means to advise.

17. B: We can diagram the first two sentences as follows: Mackenzie > Austin; Nora > Austin. The third sentence, which we could diagram as Mackenzie < Austin, contradicts the first sentence.

18. D: A *hologram* is an image that is made up of beams of *light* from a laser. So, we could say that the order of this analogy is a piece of a whole. The start of the next comparison is *film* which would be a piece of a *video camera*.

19. A: Passive means inactive, or the opposite of active.

20. D: As a reference at the end of a *book*, an *index* may be provided that contains key terms or phrases with page numbers where those terms or phrases can be found. So, we can say that an *index* is a part to the whole of a *book*. The comparison involves an *elegy* which can be a song or a poem that expresses terrible sadness for the death of a person. This *elegy* would then be a part to the whole of a *funeral* service.

21. B: When a strong opponent competes against an unlikely challenger, we sometimes call the unlikely challenger an *underdog* who will face the incredible odds of defeating the strong opponent. An attribute or characteristic of an underdog can be their *audacious* (i.e., confident or bold) attitude. Now, a *conspirator* is a person who is participating in a plan that has some illegal intent. So, a conspirator has the characteristic of being *elusive* (i.e., easily escaping capture).

22. C: To secede is to split apart, the opposite of merge.

23. A: The words inflammable, ignitable, and combustible all describe choice A, gasoline.

24. C: We can diagram the first two sentences as follows: Samuel > James; Horace > James. These sentences do not give us enough information to prove sentence three, Samuel = Horace.

25. C: Coarse, or rough, most nearly means harsh.

26. B: Objective means that something is detached or unbiased, and this is the opposite of impartial.

27. C: An *intermission* is a pause between acts of a play. Two common types of plays are *dramas* and comedies. So, we can determine that an *intermission* is a piece to the whole of a *drama*. Now, the comparison begins with *plant* as in vegetation. So, the best answer choice is *habitat* (i.e., the place where animal and plant life are naturally living) which fills the role of being the whole to the piece of *plant*.

28. C: The other words start with the letter "B" and end with the letter "K." So, the correct answer starts with the letter "B," but it ends with the letter "N."

29. A: This analogy is a matter of degree as starting with something basic and escalating to something more significant. The question begins with *jog* which is basic and general, and this is matched with *marathon* which is a 26.2 mile race that takes several hours to complete. So, the best choice is choice A which starts with a basic *hypothesis* (i.e., educated guess) and escalates to a *discovery*.

30. A: Deter most nearly means stop.

31. B: The first two sentences can be diagrammed as follows: Esther = Marcus; Lee > Marcus. If Lee drove farther than Marcus, he also drove farther than Esther. The third sentence, which we can diagram as Esther > Lee, contradicts sentences one and two, so it is false.

32. B: Inability is an antonym to the other answer choices.

33. B: Alleviate means to ease or lessen, which is the opposite of worsen.

34. B: This analogy focuses on antonyms. *Antipathy* and *sympathy* are opposites as *antipathy* means a strong feeling of opposition, and *sympathy* is the act of understanding another person's feeling or situation. You are given *convivial* which means sociable or cheerful, and you know that you are looking for the antonym of sociable and cheerful. So, *gloomy* means depressed or miserable, and this is the clear opposite to *convivial.*

35. C: To be refined is to be cultured and well-bred.

36. C: We can diagram the first two sentences as follows: University Press > Institutes Press and Institutes Press < Academy Press. , which tells us that University Press and Academy Press received more submissions than Institutes Press. Yet, we cannot be sure which publishing house received the most submissions.

37. D: *Espionage* is the service of spying on opposition in order to gain intelligence. So, the nature (or characteristic) of this task is easily understood to be *discreet* (i.e., tactful and cautious). The analogy continues with *kindling* which are the pieces of material used to start a fire. In many situations, a fire is characteristic of something tragic that is about to happen to someone or something. A name for this foreboding sense of tragedy can be *ominous.* In short, a characteristic of *kindling* is *ominous.*

38. B: A person who is said to be pallid is feeble or sickly.

39. B: Jovial means happy, which is the opposite of depressed.

40. A: We can diagram the first two sentences as follows: Otis > Steve = Carrie. The third sentence claims that Otis > Carrie, which is consistent with the first two sentences.

41. D: Insufficient means inadequate, which is the opposite of adequate.

42. A: A novice is someone who is new to the circumstances, or the person is a beginner.

43. A: Foster most nearly means to care for, or nurture.

44. B: We can diagram the first two sentences as follows: The Gang Mentality > Metal Leather > The Animal Instincts. The third sentence, Gang Mentality < Metal Leather, is inconsistent with the first two.

45. A: Initiate means to start, the opposite of to stop.

46. D: Marry most nearly means join.

47. B: Independence, responsibility, and maturity are positive qualities typically associated with adulthood. Irresponsibility is a negative quality that is often associated with youth.

48. D: General means the opposite of particular.

49. A: Something paltry is cheap, base, or common.

50. A: Optimum most nearly means ideal.

51. A: A pledge is a promise, the opposite of breach, which is the violation or breaking of a promise.

52. D: The work of counselors, nurses, and lawyers call for working with people directly. The work of a novelist may include interviews or research with people, but their work is more solitary than the others.

53. B: The first two sentences can be diagrammed as follows: Reece > Lee > Darren. Sentence three, Darren > Reece, is inconsistent with the first two sentences. It is false.

54. D: To attest is to vouch for or to certify.

55. C: Outspoken most nearly means candid.

56. A: We can diagram the first two sentences as follows: Kevin < Allen and John > Allen. Then, the third sentence claims that, John > Allen > Kevin which is consistent with the first two sentences.

57. A: Pantomime most nearly means mimic.

58. B: Serendipity is the accidental finding of something that is deemed valuable. So, misfortune is an antonym to serendipity.

59. A: Pandemonium most nearly means chaos.

60. C: The other answer choices are general nouns. Choice C is specific noun. Cape Cod is a cape off the coast of Massachusetts

Quantitative Skills

1. A: Convert all the numbers to fractions and compare. The number 0.099 can be rounded to 0.1. Then, the first 3 choices are: a) 1/3; b) 1/4; c) 1/100. Since the numerators are equal, the number with the smallest denominator is greatest, and that is 1/3. To compare that with choice D, note that 1/3 = 2/6 and 2/6 > 2/7.

2. C: Because drawing a dodecagon and counting its diagonals is an arduous task, it is useful to employ a different problem-solving strategy. One such strategy is to draw polygons with fewer sides and look for a pattern in the number of the polygons' diagonals.

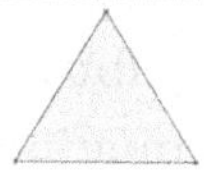	3	0
	4	2
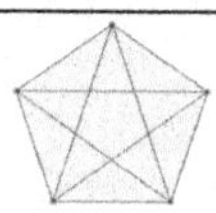	5	5
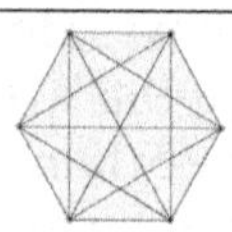	6	9
Heptagon	7	14
Octagon	8	20

A quadrilateral has two more diagonals than a triangle, a pentagon has three more diagonals than a quadrilateral, and a hexagon has four more diagonals than a pentagon. Continue this pattern to find that a dodecagon has 54 diagonals.

3. A: Each element of the series adds 9 to the preceding one. In algebraic terms, $P_n = P_{n-1} + 9$, where P_n is the nth element of the series. Since 31 + 9 = 40, 40 is the correct answer.

4. A: (0.0) is a point because if Jonas doesn't walk, then his running speed is also 0. Another point is (1,3) because if Jonas moves a distance of 1 unit after walking x minutes, then he moves a distance of 3 units after x minutes from jogging.

5. B: To solve, first subtract Jerry's weight from the total permitted: 800-200 = 600. Divide 600 by 4 (the four pieces of equipment) to get 150, the average weight.

6. D: Since the line segments pass through the center of the circle, both $\overline{AB}$ and $\overline{CD}$ are diameters of equal length, and the four line segments radiating outwards from O are all equal-length radii.

7. D: The area of a rectangle is calculated as the product of the width and length. If the length is twice the width of 3 m, it must be 6 m long. Then, 3 x 6 = 18 m^2.

8. C: The correct answer is $3000. Besides the $600 he has remaining, Chan has paid out a total of 80% (30% + 20% +20%+10%) of his bonus for the expenses described in the question. Therefore, the $600 represents the remaining 20%. To determine his total bonus, solve $\frac{100}{20} \times 600 = 3000$.

9. D: Since the airplane is moving against a headwind, it will be slowed relative to the ground. Therefore its final speed will be 300 mph – 15 mph = 285 mph.

10. A: If the ratio of pennies to nickels is 2:6, the ratio of the pennies to the combined coins is 2:2+6, or 2:8. This is $\frac{1}{4}$ or, expressed as a percentage, 25%.

11. D: The literal equation may be solved for *x* by first subtracting *b* from both sides of the equation. Doing so gives $ax = c - b$. Dividing both sides of the equation by *a* gives $x = \frac{c-b}{a}$.

12. C: The median of a set of numbers is one for which the set contains an equal number of greater and lesser values. Besides *Z*, there are 8 numbers in the set, so that 4 must be greater and 4 lesser than *Z*. The 4 smallest values are 5, 7, 9, and 12. The 4 largest are 16, 18, 23, and 44. So *Z* must fall between 12 and 16.

13. D: The sides of a triangle must all be greater than zero. The sum of the lengths of the two shorter sides must be greater than the length of the third side. Since we are looking for the minimum value of the perimeter, assume the longer of the two given sides, which is 6, is the longest side of the triangle. Then the third side must be greater than 6 – 4 = 2. Since we are told the sides are all integral numbers, the last side must be 3 units in length. Thus, the minimum length for the perimeter is 4+6+3 = 13 units.

14. B: The series consists of numbers each of which is double the number preceding. The number prior to the blank is 4: 2 x 4 = 8. The number following the blank is 16: 2 x 8 = 16.

15. C: The given equations form a system of linear equations. Since the first equation is already given in terms of *x*, it will be easier to solve it using the substitution method. Start by substituting 2*y* – 3 for *x* in the second equation:

$$2x + \frac{1}{2}y = 3$$

$$2(2y - 3) + \frac{1}{2}y = 3$$

Next, solve the resulting equation for *y*. Distribute the 2 and then combine like *y*-terms in the result:

$$4y - 6 + \frac{1}{2}y = 3$$

$$\frac{9}{2}y - 6 = 3$$

Finally, isolate the variable *y* by adding 6 to both sides and then dividing both sides by the coefficient of *y*, which is $\frac{9}{2}$ (or, equivalently, multiply by 2 and divide by 9):

$$\frac{9}{2}y = 9$$

$$y = 2$$

16. C: A number raised to the first power is multiplied by itself only once, so 16^1=16. 2^8 is 2 multiplied by itself eight times, so 2^8 = 256. Similarly, 3^3 = 27.

17. A: This table shows the numbers of coins added to the first few squares and the equivalent powers of 2:

Square	1	2	3	4
Coins	1	2	4	8
Power of 2	2^0	2^1	2^2	2^3

In this series, the number of coins on each is the consecutive powers of 2. The reason is that the number doubles with each consecutive square. However, the series of powers begins with 0 for the first square. For the 64th square, the number of coins will be 2^{63}.

18. A: The series alternates between subtracting 4 from the number occurring two positions earlier (12, 8, 4, 0) and adding 6 to the number occurring two positions earlier (7, 13, 19, 25). Therefore, 25 is the next number.

19. B: 20% of 80 = 16; 50% of 70 = 35; and 40% of 90 = 36. Since 36 > 35 > 16, B is correct.

20. C: The correct answer is 8. The total 20 + 13 = 33, but only 25 cars have been scored. Therefore, 33 – 25, or 8 cars must have had both a man and a woman inside.

21. A: First establish a variable, s, for the length of the smaller square. Since the larger square is 3 feet longer than the smaller one, its length is $s + 3$. Given that the difference between the areas of the two squares is 75, and the area of any square is equal to its side lengths squared, the following equation can be established:

$$(s+3)^2 - s^2 = 75$$

Simplify the left side of the equation:

$$(s+3)^2 - s^2 = 75$$

$$(s+3)(s+3) - s^2 = 75$$

$$s^2 + 6s + 9 - s^2 = 75$$

$$6s + 9 = 75$$

Isolate the variable and divide both sides by its coefficient to solve for s:

$$6s = 66$$

$$s = 11$$

Therefore, the length of the smaller square is 11 feet.

22. D: If point C is four times farther from A than from B, it means that the ratio of distances from C to A and B is 4:1, respectively. Therefore, the line segment can be broken up into 4 + 1 = 5 equal

segments. The total distance between points A and B is $7 - (-3) = 10$ units. If we divide 10 by 5, each equal segment is 2 units in length. We can then multiply the ratio by 2 to get the actual distances of C from A and B, $4(2):1(2) = 8:2$. So, C is located 8 units from A and 2 units from B. Since A is located at -3, it means that $-3 + 8 = 5$. Answer A is the location if C is four times farther from B than it is from A. Answer B is just four units from point A. Answer C is just four units from point B.

23. C: The series consists of the squares of consecutive integers, beginning with 1: $1^2 = 1$, $2^2 = 4$, and so on. In the fifth position, $5^2 = 25$, so that choice C is correct.

24. A: The sum $3 + 4 + 16 = 23$. The other choices are less. In particular, although it has more terms, choice B, $6 + 4 + 5 + 7 = 22$, which is less than choice A.

25. A: The numbers defined by (i), (ii), and (iii) are (i) 8; (ii) 6; and (iii) 15, respectively, so that choice A is correct.

26. A: Setting the cost of shipping equal to the amount received gives us the equation $3{,}000 + 100x = 400x$. Subtract 100x from both sides to get $3{,}000 = 300x$, then divide both sides by 300 to see that $x = 10$.

27. C: This can be solved as two equations with two unknowns. Since the integers are consecutive with $p > n$, we have $p - n = 1$, so that $p = 1 + n$. Substituting this value into $p + n = 15$ gives $1 + 2n = 15$, or $n = \frac{14}{2} = 7$.

28. A: In this series, each number is either double the preceding number, or 2 more than the preceding number, and these procedures alternate. Since $36 = 2 \times 18$, the next element of the series will be determined by adding 2. Since $36 + 2 = 38$, the correct answer is A.

29. C: The perimeter of a rectangle of length 6 and width 4 equals $2(6 + 4) = 20$. The perimeter of a square of side 4 equals $4 + 4 + 4 + 4 = 16$. And the area of a square of side 4 equals $4 \times 4 = 16$. Although the units for the measurement of area differ from those of the perimeters, the magnitude of the measurements for (b) and (c) are the same.

30. A: Since there are 100 cm in a meter, on a 1:100 scale drawing, each centimeter represents one meter. Therefore, an area of one square centimeter on the drawing represents one square meter in actuality. Since the area of the room in the scale drawing is 30 cm^2, the room's actual area is 30 m^2.

Another way to determine the area of the room is to write and solve an equation, such as this one: $\frac{l}{100} \cdot \frac{w}{100} = 30\ \text{cm}^2$, where l and w are the dimensions of the actual room

$$\frac{lw}{1000} = 30\ \text{cm}^2$$
$$lw = 300{,}000\ \text{cm}^2$$
$$\text{Area} = 300{,}000\ \text{cm}^2$$

Since this is not one of the answer choices, convert cm^2 to m^2: $300{,}000\ \text{cm}^2 \cdot \frac{1\ \text{m}}{100\ \text{cm}} \cdot \frac{1\ \text{m}}{100\ \text{cm}} = 30\ \text{m}^2$.

31. C: Since the pattern repeats the same 4 figures, each multiple of 4 looks like Fig. 4 (4, 8, 12, ..., 28, 32, ...). The figure in the 31st position is one less than 32, so it should look like the figure left of Fig. 4. That figure is Fig. 3.

32. B: Fractions can be simplified by dividing both numerator and denominator by the same number. Divide the numerator and denominator of item (ii) by 10, and the result is 2/3. Divide the numerator and denominator of (iii) by 15, and the result is 2/3. Therefore, all three fractions are equal.

33. A: The totals of each set of numbers are: A: 16; B: 17; C: 17; and D: 18.

34. B: Since *AB, BD, CD,* and *AC* are sides of the square, they are all equal. They are shorter than the diagonals *AD* and *CB.* These diagonals have the same length and bisect one another at the point *E*, which means that *AE* = *BE* = *CE* = *DE*, and are equal to half the length of the full diagonals.

35. C: Supplementary angles add to 180 degrees. Therefore, the other angle is equal to the difference between 180 degrees and 34 degrees: $180 - 34 = 146$. Thus, the other angle measures 146°.

36. B: A percent is a number divided by 100, so 4% = $\frac{4}{100}$. The decimal 0.04 is also equal to $\frac{4}{100}$. Multiplying both numerator and denominator of the fraction $\frac{2}{50}$ by 2 shows that it, too, is equal to $\frac{4}{100}$.

37. B: Each item in the series is 4 greater than the preceding item. Since 16 + 4 = 20, 20 is the number that belongs in the blank position.

38. D: We know that the first lap takes 50 seconds, and the second one takes 20% more time to complete. This can be written as an equation: $T_2 = 1.2 \times T_1$. In the equation, T_1 is the time required for the first lap, and T_2 is the time required for the second lap. So, you can put in the known information and have: $1.2 \times 50 = 60$ seconds. For the third lap, you would start with the equation: $T_3 = 1.2 \times T_2$. When you put in the numbers, you have: $1.2 \times 60 = 72$ seconds. Now, you can add the times for the three laps: $50 + 60 + 72 = 182$.

39. D: Segment *AD* = 48. Because the length of *CD* is 2 times the length of *AB*, let *AB* = *x* and let *CD* = 2*x*. Since *AB* = *BC*, let *BC* = *x* also. The total length of *AD* = *AB* + *BC* + *CD* = *x* + *x* + 2*x* = 4*x* = 48. Thus, *x* = 12 and *BC* + *CD* = *x* + 2*x* = 3*x* = 3 x 12 = 36.

40. D: Following normal order of operations, the expressions within the parentheses must be evaluated first. Expression (i), $(3\times4)+5=12+5=17$. Expression (ii), $(4+5)\times6=9\times6=54$. Expression (iii), $(3\times5)+6=15+6=21$.

41. B: Translate this word problem into a mathematical equation. Let the number of Janice's phone calls = x. Let the number of Elaina's phone calls = $x + 23$. Let the number June's phone calls = $x + 14$. Add their calls together and subtract 25calls:

$= x + x + 23 + x + 14 - 25$

$= 3x + 37 - 25$

$= 3x + 12$.

42. C: In this series, the number added to the preceding term goes up by one for each term: 41 + 3 = 44; 44 + 4 = 48; 48 + 5 = 53; 53 + 6 = 59. Since 59 + 7 = 66, that is the value of the next term.

43. C: The equation that represents the relationship between the position number, n, and the value of the term, a_n, is $a_n = -3n + 8$. Notice each n is multiplied by −3, with 8 added to that value. Substituting position number 1 for n gives $a_n = -3(1) + 8$, which equals 5. Substitution of the remaining position numbers does not provide a counterexample to this procedure.

44. A: The distance given from the top to the bottom of the tire through the center is the diameter. Finding the distance the bike traveled in one complete roll of the tire is the same as finding the circumference. Using the formula, $C = \pi d$, we multiply 27 by π. From the first mark to the fourth, the tire rolls three times. Then, you would multiply by 3, and the equation would be $3(27\pi)$.

45. D: First: Add the known values together: $5 + 10 + 12 + 13 = 40$. Now, set up an equation with the sum of the known values in the divisor. Then, put the number of values in the dividend.

46. D: Isolate a: $a = 8b + 6 + 16$. Thus, $a = 8b + 22$. Next add 3 to both side of the equation: $a + 3 = 8b + 22 + 3 = 8b + 25$.

47. D: In this series, each number is the sum of the two preceding numbers. For example, 3 = 1 + 2, and 5 = 3 + 2. Therefore, the number following 13 must be 13 + 8 = 21, and the next number must be 21 + 13 = 34.

48. C: The straight line separating section (a) from sections (b) and (c) is a diameter. Therefore, section (a) is equal to one half of the circle. Since (b) and (c) together make up the remaining half of the circle, their sum is equal to section (a). Since b + c = a, it follows that b = a – c.

49. D: 5 squared is equal to 5 x 5 = 25, so that (i) is equal to (iii). However, 2^5 = 2 x 2 x 2 x 2 x 2 = 32, so that (ii) is greater than (i) or (iii).

50. B: (i) 2 x 15 = 30 and 30 – 3 = 27; (ii) 3^3 = 3 x 3 x 3 = 27; (iii) $\frac{80 \times 30}{100} = 24$, and 24 + 3 = 27. Therefore, all three expressions are equal to 27.

51. B: Whenever the data includes an extreme outlier, such as 39, the median is the best representation of the data. The mean would include that score and heavily skew the data.

52. A: In this series, the number subtracted from the preceding term increases by two for each term: 108 – 4 = 104; 104 – 6 = 98; 98 – 8 = 90; 90 – 10 = 80. For the next term, subtract 12: 80 – 12 = 68. Choice A is correct.

Reading Comprehension Skills

1. D: The main argument is stated in paragraph 4: "With the progression and extreme convenience of technology, printed books are going to soon become a thing of the past."

2. C: Paragraph 1 explains how stories have progressed, beginning with oral tradition and past the invention of the printing press. In context with the rest of the essay, this paragraph is important in explaining how stories progress and are provided within society.

3. B: Enduring means to put up with something unpleasant. Within the sentence, the phrase, "enduring a several hour flight," the word enduring, means to undergo.

4. A: In paragraph 1, it is stated that oral tradition was the main medium for storytelling before the invention of the printing press.

5. B: It is not a fact that "sliding a finger across the screen or pressing a button to move onto the next page is just as satisfying to the reader." Satisfaction is not something universal that can be proven for every reader. This statement is an opinion.

6. A: The author makes the argument in paragraph 5 that devices such as the iPad and Kindle are "therefore better than books because they have multiple uses."

7. D: Various parts of the article are intended to scare (choice A), warn (choice B), and inspire (choice C) people, but the primary purpose of the article is to offer practical advice about what products people should buy and how to use their available resources to make responsible decisions for the future of our planet.

8. A: The author begins the third paragraph with, "You can continue to make a difference for the planet in how you use what you bought and the resources you have available." This sentence makes the connection between the second paragraph which deals with what people should buy and the third paragraph which makes suggestions for how to use what they have.

9. B: The author does suggest that people should use less water and energy (choice A), but these are only two suggestions among many and not the main idea of the article. The article does not say that people are destroying the earth (choice C) or make a suggestion that people organize their acquaintances (choice D).

10. D: The author presents the problems of global warming and the rapid depletion of the planet's natural resources and offers several practical suggestions for how to stop global warming and use remaining resources judiciously.

11. C: The author makes suggestions to use less water (choice B) and buy locally grown food (choice D), but they are not suggested as the place to begin saving the planet. The author does not suggest getting rid of products that are not earth friendly (choice A). The author states: "Participation begins with our everyday choices."

12. C: The author does not mention running out of resources in a specific time period (choice A), the cost of water and energy (choice B), or the possibility of hardship for local farmers (choice D).

13. D: This information is all given in the second paragraph.

14. C: In the fourth paragraph, the author states that the transient nature of relationships based solely on shared interests is keeping us "socially busy without building the lasting relationships and communities that we want."

15. B: The author lists urban sprawl, long work hours, and devotion to television and the internet as causes of problems for American communities.

16. B: This is the only one of the answer choices that is not listed in the fourth paragraph as suggestions put forth by the Harvard University study.

17. D: The author states in the fourth paragraph that Harvard University School of Government put forth 150 suggestions for increasing social capital.

18. A: The author puts this definition in parentheses immediately following his first use of the phrase "social capital."

19. B: The second sentence in the passage notes that comets are distinguishable from asteroids by the presence of comas or tails.

20. C: The third paragraph notes that there are over 3,500 known comets. It also notes that this represents only a small portion of those in existence.

21. C: The second paragraph notes that because they have low mass, they don't become spherical and have irregular shapes.

22. D: The second paragraph notes that some comets may be tens of kilometers across. It also notes that comas may be larger than the sun.

23. D: The passage defines single apparition comets as those whose trajectories make them pass the Sun once and then exit our solar system permanently. It also describes most comets as having oval orbits wherein they are nearer to the Sun during part of their orbit, and then move farther away from the Sun *within the solar system* for the rest of the orbit; hence (a) is incorrect. While single apparition comets are only apparent once, they are NOT still in the solar system (b). The passage defines short and long orbital periods, but does not include long orbital periods in that definition (c).

24. B: Lincoln begins this speech by discussing the founding of the U.S. and what the original purpose of the U.S. was. Then, he goes on to talk about how the U.S. is currently engaged in a war intended to fracture the nation, and he states that the battle being discussed was one large tragedy that came out of the war. Next, Lincoln says that his speech and even the memorial itself can't truly honor those who died, and that it's up to those who survived to continue the fight to ensure the nation does not break apart. Answer B best communicates this message.

25. D: The sentence in which this phrase is found is: The world will little note, nor long remember, what we say here, but can never forget what they did here. In this context, the phrase "the world will little note" means that no one outside of those in attendance or possibly those outside the country will pay attention to the speech or the ceremony. This eliminates all of the answer choices except D.

26. A: The ideals of the revolution are addressed in the first paragraph: Four score and seven years ago our fathers brought forth, upon this continent, a new nation, conceived in Liberty, and dedicated to the proposition that all men are created equal. This introduces the point that Lincoln is trying to make about the battle at hand and the war as a whole: the Civil War is threatening the ideas upon which the nation was created.

27. C: There is a comparison between the ideas of the Revolution and the Civil War in this speech. To facilitate understanding of this comparison, Lincoln has to set the stage by telling his audience about the past event he is referencing. This establishes the context of his message.

28. A: This line directly references the idea in the previous paragraph, which is that the U.S. is a nation that was created to ensure liberty and equality. This sentence talks about how the Civil War is testing whether or not a nation that was created to ensure liberty and equality can really survive.

29. B: When President Lincoln argues that the people who died at Gettysburg did not die in vain, he asserts that their passing was not frivolous or unimportant or meaningless.

30. C: The author points out that just because there is a month focused on African American history, this doesn't mean that African American history must be ignored for the rest of the year.

31. C: The author points out in paragraph 3 that the debate about how to meet the need to teach children about African American history can remind parents that this need is not yet fully met.

32. A: In paragraph 4, the author states that the material available is rich and varied.

33. B: Throughout the passage, the author continues to instill hope and encouragement that Black History Month still has a vital role to play in American culture despite opposing attitudes. Therefore, the best choice is emboldening.

34. C: Choice A and D cannot be correct because the paragraph contains only a handful of moments that are important to black history which are narrowed further by occurring in February. While the final paragraph contains only men, you should not make the conclusion of choice B. Nowhere in the passage does the author make a distinction between male and female influence in black history. Many women have made a remarkable difference in black history. Rosa Parks, Barbara Jordan, Diane Nash, and Septima Poinsette Clark are only a few. The number of men or women to make a significant impact on black history is not the author's point. Instead, you should conclude that regardless of a person's background, ethnicity, or position in society, there are many vital moments and people that connect to black history and those should be known by every individual.

35. A: This passage attempts to persuade readers to accept its point of view. While some of the other choices are true of particular statements found in the passage, only choice A is true of the passage as a whole.

36. A: Choice A is best. The chief benefit, in this context, means the main benefit.

37. D: Only choice D can be correctly inferred from the second paragraph.

38. B: Choice B best represents the passage as a whole.

39. D: To mimic is to resemble. Choice D is best.

40. B: The passage mentions the plastics found in the stomachs of dead birds, so choice B is best.

41. B: Choice B best answers the question: The author excludes discussion of plastics' benefits in order to focus on their dangers.

42. B: Durability in this sense means permanence.

Reading Vocabulary

43. A: Peevish means ill-tempered.

44. B: Mortified means embarrassed.

45. B: Keen is another word for sharp.

46. B: The word with the nearest meaning to the word secluded is remote.

47. A: A perimeter is a boundary.

48. D: Slight can mean insult when used as a noun.

49. A: Monetary means financial.

50. D: Volatile means explosive.

51. A: Ruddy means red.

52. C: In this context, stellar means exceptional or outstanding.

53. B: Spare means extra.

54. A: Shrill suggests that something is high-pitched.

55. D: Enthralled means captivated.

56. A: To recuperate is to heal.

57. C: Meager means insufficient.

58. A: The word with the closest meaning to severe in this context is relentless.

59. D: To replicate is to reproduce.

60. D: To repudiate is to renounce.

61. A: To absolve is to forgive.

62. D: In this context, impregnable means impenetrable.

Mathematics Skills

1. B: The least common multiple, or LCM, is the smallest number that is a multiple of two numbers. Since 2 x 2 = 4, and 1 x 4 = 4, 4 is the LCM of the two numbers given.

2. C: First write Equation A in slope-intercept form: $y = mx + b$ where m is the slope and b is the y-intercept.

$5y - 100x = 25$

$5y = 100x + 25$

$y = 20x + 5$

Based on the slope-intercept form of Equation A, the slope, m = 20 and the y-intercept, b = 5.

3. A: An odd number can be considered as an even number *N* plus 1. Two even numbers added together produce an even number, so the result of adding an odd and an even number must be an even number plus 1, which is odd. For example, 4 + 3 = 7.

4. D. In scientific notation, the exponent indicates the number of places that the decimal must be moved to the right. For example, $2.3 \times 10^1 = 2.1 \times 10 = 21$. Moving the decimal three places to the right in this problem is equivalent to multiplying by 1,000, so the result is 6,190.

5. B: The perimeter of a square is 4 times the length of a side. Therefore, in this case, the side *s* must equal $s = \frac{16}{4} = 4$. The area *A* is found by squaring the length a, or $A = s^2 = 4^2 = 16$. Since the area is 16 ft^2, choice B is correct.

6. A: Negative numbers represent segments extending to the left of zero on the number line. Adding a negative number to another negative number extends the segment even further to the left, or into "negative territory". To add two negative numbers, add the magnitudes and retain the negative sign. For example (-3) + (-5) = -8.

7. C: The square root of a number which is raised to the 4th power is the same number raised to the 2nd power. That is, $\sqrt{2^4} = 2^2 = 4$. Since 4 x 4 = 16, C is correct.

8. D: The chart indicates that 40% of the total recycled material is paper. Since 50,000 tons of material are recycled every month, the total amount of paper will be 40% of 50,000 tons, or $\frac{40}{100} \times 50{,}000 = 20{,}000$ tons.

9. B: Percentage is equivalent to dividing by 100, so that $12.5\% = \frac{12.5}{100} = \frac{1}{8}$.

10. C: The area of a circle is equal to πr^2, where *r* is the radius. Therefore, $\pi r^2 = 36\pi$, and $r = \sqrt{36} = 6$. Since the diameter is two times the radius, it is equal to 12.

11. B: A prime number has only two whole integer divisors, 1 and itself. This is true of 3, 17, and 41. However 6 can be divided by 1, 2, 3, and 6. It is therefore not a prime number.

12. B: The reciprocal of 5 is $\frac{1}{5}$. When numbers are multiplied by their reciprocals, the result is always 1. Thus, $5 \times \frac{1}{5} = 1$.

13. C: Each throw of the dart is an independent event, and has no influence on the outcome of any other throw. Every time the dart is thrown, it has a 50% chance of landing on black, irrespective of the results of previous throws.

14. D: The integers are -4, -3, -2, -1, 0, +1, +2, +3, +4, +5, and +6.

15. A: The answer is expanded to simplify the calculations. The total of Choice A is $8.00 + $1.60, which is the same as the total calculated in the problem.

16. C: The volume of a cube of side *a* is given by $Volume = a^3 = a \times a \times a$. In this case, since *a* = 3, the area is 3 x 3 x 3 = 27.

17. B: The verbal description "five times a number *m* squared" means that *m* must be squared, and the resulting number multiplied by 5. Choice C is incorrect because the value within the parentheses is evaluated first, so that both 5 and *m* are squared. This results in a value of $25m^2$, which is incorrect.

18. C: The square root of a number must lie between the square roots of numbers that are larger and smaller than itself. Since $\sqrt{4}$ = 2, and $\sqrt{9}$ = 3, and since 4 < 6 < 9, it follows that $\sqrt{6}$ must lie between 2 and 3.

19. C: The area scales with the square of the radius, so if the radius increases in length by a factor of 2, the area will increase by 2^2, or 4. Since $Area = \pi r^2$, if the radius *r* is replaced with 2*r*, this yields $Area = \pi(2r)^2 = 4\pi r^2$, which is 4 times the original area.

20. A: The average, or arithmetic mean, is computed by totaling all the measurements and dividing by the number of measurements. To obtain an average of 75 from 3 measurements, the measurements must total 3 x 75 = 225. Since 68 + 73 = 141, then 225 – 141 = 84 points are required on the third test.

21. C: The ratio of left- to right-handed players will be the same as the ratio 2:3. Therefore, $\frac{2}{3} = \frac{12}{R}$, so that *R* = 18 right-handed players. The total number on the roster is therefore 12 + 18 = 30.

22. D: To round to 1/100, leave two digits to the right of the decimal. To round digits greater than 5, round up to the next value of the preceding digit.

23. B: The y-intercept of the line is $(0, -1)$. Another point on the line is (1,0). Slope is the vertical change over horizontal change which is $\frac{1}{1} = 1$. Plugging this information into the slope-intercept form $y = mx + b$, the equation is $y = x - 1$.

24. D: Rainfall in October increases to 6 inches, from 1 inch in September. This represents an increase of 5 inches. None of the other month-to-month differences are as great.

25. C: Since 11 – 5 = 6, then 3x = 6, and $x = \frac{6}{3} = 2$.

26. D.: Jamet had $2.75 after all the transactions described. To solve this problem, first subtract $4.25 and then $2.00 from the initial sum of $6.50, leaving $0.25. Then add $2.50, arriving at the final answer of $2.75.

27. D: There are two ways to solve this problem: either convert meters to centimeters and then use the conversion factor in the table to convert centimeters to inches, or else use the table to convert meters to yards, and then convert to inches.

In the first instance, recall that there are 100 centimeters in a meter (*centi* means "hundredth"). Therefore $19m = 1{,}900cm = (\frac{1{,}900}{2.54}) = 748$ inches.

In the second instance, recall that there are 36 inches in a yard, therefore $19m = 19 \times 1.094 = 20.786yd = 20.786 \times 36 = 748$ inches.

28. D: Since 16 chairs are empty, and this represents 2/5 of the total enrollment, then the full class must consist of

$$\text{Class} = \frac{5}{2} \times 16 = 40 \text{ students}$$

29. A: To answer this question, we first determine the total cost of the onions and carrots, since these prices are given. This will equal (2 x $3.69 + 3 x $4.29) = $20.25. Next, this sum is subtracted from the total cost of the vegetables to determine the cost of the mushrooms: $24.15 - $20.25 = $3.90. Finally, the cost of the mushrooms is divided by the quantity in lbs to determine the cost per lb:

$$\text{Cost per lb} = \frac{\$3.90}{1.5} = \$2.60$$

30. C: To determine this, first determine the total distance of the round trip. This is twice the 45 miles of the one-way trip to work in the morning, or 90 miles. Then, to determine the total amount of time Elijah spent on the round trip, first convert his travel times into minutes. One hour and ten minutes equals 70 minutes, and an hour and a half equals 90 minutes. So, Elijah's total travel time was 70 + 90 = 160 minutes. Elijah's average speed can now be determined in miles per minute:

$$Speed = \frac{90 miles}{160 \min} = 0.5625 \text{ miles per minute}$$

Finally, to convert this average speed to miles per hour, multiply by 60, since there are 60 minutes in an hour:

Average speed (mph) = 60 x 0.5625 = 33.75 miles per hour

31. A: The percentage of increase equals the change in the account balance divided by the original amount, $80, and multiplied by 100. First, determine the change in the balance by subtracting the original amount from the new balance: $Change = \$120 - \$80 = \$40$. Now, determine the percentage of increase as described above: $Percent = \frac{\$40}{\$80} \times 100 = 50\%$.

32. D: Adding a constant to each side of the inequality does not change the sense of the inequality, so begin by adding 12: $4x < 4 + 12$, or $4x < 16$. Dividing each side of an inequality by a positive number does not change the sense of the inequality either, so now divide both sides by 4 in order to isolate the variable, *x*: $x < \frac{16}{4}$, or $x < 4$.

33. D: First, compute the value enclosed by the parentheses, $3b + 5 = 3 \times 7 + 5 = 26$. Next, compute $4a = -24$. Note that *a* is negative, so that this product is negative as well. The product $4a(3b + 5)$ will therefore be negative as well, and equals -624. Finally, add the value of 2*b*, or 2 x 7 =14, to -624, to get the final answer $-624 + 14 = -610$.

34. B: Since the rate, miles per minute, is constant, this can be solved by setting up a proportion: $\frac{miles}{\min} = \frac{10}{12} = \frac{210}{t}$. Now, solve for $t = \frac{210 \times 12}{10} = 252$ minutes. Finally, convert to hours by dividing this total by 60, since there are 60 minutes in an hour: $t = \frac{252}{60} = 4$ hours and 12 minutes.

35. C: Define a variable *t* as the elapsed time in minutes from the time the first airplane takes off. Then at any time the distance traveled by the first plane is $d_1 = 250t$. The second plane takes off 30 minutes later, so at any time the distance that it has traveled is $d_2 = 280(t - 30)$. This plane will overtake the first when the two distances are equal, that is when $d_1 = d_2$, or when 250t = 280(t-30). Solve this last equation for *t*. First use the distributive property:
$250t = 280t - 30 \times 280 = 280t - 8{,}400$.

Next, add 8,400 to each side of the equation: $250t + 8{,}400 = 280t$.
Next, subtract 250*t* from each side of the equation: $8{,}400 = 30t$.
Next, divide both sides by 30: 280 = *t*.
This gives the value of *t* in minutes. Convert to hours by dividing 280 by 60 minutes per hour, which yields an elapsed time of 4 hours and 40 minutes. Since the first plane left at 2 PM, 4 hours and 40 minutes later is 6:40 PM.

36. A: This equation represents a linear relationship of slope 3.60 that passes through the origin, or zero point. The table shows that for each hour of rental, the cost increases by an amount equal to $3.60. This corresponds to the slope of the equation. Of course, if the bicycle is not rented at all (0 hours) there will be no charge ($0), so the line must pass through the origin. Relationship *A* is the only one that satisfies these criteria.

37. D: In order to determine the number of questions Joshua must answer correctly, consider the number of points he must earn. Joshua will receive 4 points for each question he answers correctly, and x represents the number of questions. Therefore, Joshua will receive a total of 4x points for all the questions he answers correctly. Joshua must earn more than 92 points. Therefore, to determine the number of questions he must answer correctly, solve the inequality $4x > 92$.

38. D: The formula for the circumference of a circle of radius R is 2πR, but it is not necessary to use this formula to solve the problem. Rather, note first that 50 km/hr corresponds to 50,000 meters per hour. This corresponds to a speed of $\frac{50{,}000}{60}$ meters per minute, as there are 60 minutes in an hour. Since the tire revolves 500 times per minute, you can set up this proportion, where C is the

circumference of the tire, $\frac{50{,}000}{60} = \frac{500C}{1}$. Solving for C, $C = \frac{50{,}000}{60 \times 500} = \frac{10}{6}$ meters per revolution, which is the circumference of the tire.

39. B: The area of the squares, whose side lengths are the legs of the triangles, are a^2 and b^2, or in this example, 9 squares and 9 squares. The area of the square whose side lengths are equal to the hypotenuse of the right triangle is c^2. If the whole squares, and half squares, in the grid are summed, the area of the square with side length c is 18 squares. The area of the squares whose side lengths are the legs of the triangles, summed, equals the area of the square whose side lengths are the hypotenuse of the triangle.
9 squares + 9 squares = 18 squares, or $a^2 + b^2 = c^2$

40. D: To solve the equation, first get rid of the denominators by multiplying both sides of the equation by $x(x - 3)$ and simplifying the result:

$$\frac{4}{x-3} - \frac{2}{x} = 1$$

$$x(x-3)\left[\frac{4}{x-3} - \frac{2}{x}\right] = x(x-3)\cdot 1$$

$$4x - 2(x-3) = x(x-3)$$

$$4x - 2x + 6 = x^2 - 3x$$

$$2x + 6 = x^2 - 3x$$

The result is a quadratic equation. Move everything to one side and then solve for x by factoring the left side and applying the zero-product rule:

$$x^2 - 5x - 6 = 0$$

$$(x + 1)(x - 6) = 0$$

$$x + 1 = 0 \quad \text{or} \quad x - 6 = 0$$

$$x = -1 \qquad x = 6$$

Therefore, the possible solutions are $x = -1$ and $x = 6$. Since neither of these values will cause division by zero when substituted back into the original equation, they are both valid solutions.

41. C: Since he buys two cups per day for five days, and one cup on Saturday, the total number of cups that Richard buys each week is (2 x 5) + 1 = 11 cups. Since each cup costs $2.25, the amount he spends is 11 x $2.25 = $24.75.

42. B: Since each mile is equivalent to 2 inches, then 6.5 inches is equivalent to $\frac{6.5}{2} = 3.25$ miles.

43. B: Since five people are dividing $17.90, each person's share is calculated as $\frac{17.90}{5} = 3.58$.

44. B: Since percentage means parts per 100, calculate $\frac{x}{100} = \frac{9}{72}$. Solving for x yields $x = 12.5\%$.

45. C: The score that has approximately 50% above and 50% below is approximately 500 (517 to be exact). The scores can be manually written by choosing either the lower or upper end of each interval and using the frequency to determine the number of times to record each score, i.e., using the lower end of each interval shows an approximate value of 465 for the median; using the upper end of each interval shows an approximate value of 530 for the median. A score of 500 (and the exact median of 517) is found between 465 and 530.

46. C: Since 220 = 4 x 55 miles, the train will require 4 x 40 = 160 minutes to travel 220 miles. Since 1 hour = 60 minutes, the time required is $\frac{160}{60} = 2$ hours with 40 minutes left over.

47. D: The price is reduced by an amount equal to 5% of the original price, or $\frac{5 \times \$120}{100} = \$6$, so subtract \$6 from the original price of \$120 to calculate the sale price: \$114.

48. C: In ΔABC, the midpoints are marked as D, E, and F. The medians of the triangle are then drawn in as $\overline{AF}$, $\overline{BD}$ and $\overline{CE}$. The medians intersect at a point called the centroid. Based on this intersection, it is the case that $AG = 2GF$, $BG = 2GD$, and $CG = 2GE$. Since we are given that $BG = 6x - 4$ and $GD = 2x + 8$, we can set up the equation as $6x - 4 = 2(2x + 8)$. Simplifying that equation, it becomes $6x - 4 = 4x + 16$. After subtracting $4x$ from both sides and adding 4 to both sides, the equation becomes $2x = 20$. Divide both sides by 2 to get $x = 10$. Then, the length of $\overline{GD}$ is calculated as $2(10) + 8 = 20 + 8 = 28$.

49. B: The ratio of correct to incorrect answers is 2:3, giving a whole of 5. It takes 12 sets of 5 questions to total 60 questions. To determine how many correct answers Sam gave, multiply 2 by 12, for a total of 24.

50. B: Determine the number of gallons used by dividing the distance in miles by the fuel efficiency in miles per gallon: $\frac{629}{34} = 18.5$ gallons of gasoline.

51. B: The listed angles are located in the alternate interior angles position. According to the Alternate Interior Angle Theorem, when a transversal cuts across parallel lines, the alternate interior angles are congruent. Since lines a and b are parallel, it means that $2x + 5 = 3x - 25$. After subtracting $2x$ from both sides and adding 25 to both sides, the equation simplifies as $30 = x$.

52. D: First, add the two straight 150 yard portions. Also, note that the distance for the two semi-circles put together is the circumference of a circle. The radius (r) of that circle is half of the dimension given as the width of the track. In other words, it is 15 yards. Now, use the formula for the circumference of a circle: $2\pi r$. Then, add it to the length of the two straight portions of the track. So, you have:
$Length = (2\pi \times 15) + (2 \times 150) = 394.25$
Choice D is the closest to this calculated answer.

53. D: Rafael's profit on each computer is the difference between the price he pays and the price he charges his customer: \$800-\$450. If he sells n computers in a month, his total profit will be n times

this difference: $n(800 - 450)$. However, it is necessary to subtract his fixed costs of $3000 from $n(800 - 450)$ to find his final profit per month.

54. D: The slopes of perpendicular lines are reciprocals and have the opposite sign. In the figure below, line A has a slope of -1/2, and line B has a slope of 2.

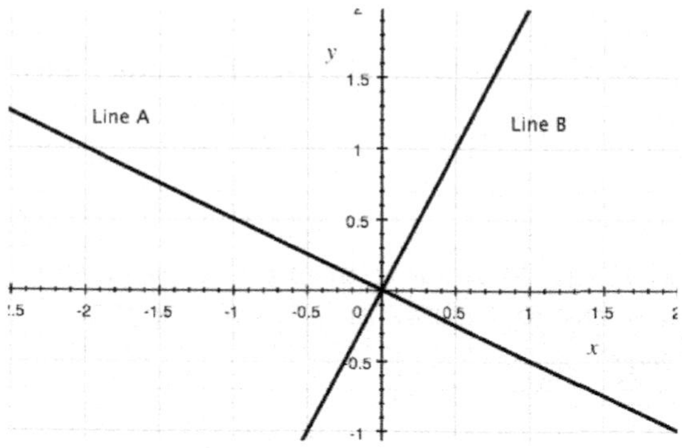

55. B: Any color can be drawn the first time, leaving five marbles. At this point, only one of the five is the same color as the one that was drawn the first time. The odds of selecting this marble are one chance in five, or 20%.

56. D: When the factors, $(x - 4)$ and $(x + 7)$ are multiplied, the x-terms sum to $3x$ and the constants produce a product of -28.

57. A: Nancy spent a total of $3.15 + $6.75 = $9.90. Subtracting $9.90 from $17.25 yields $7.35.

58. D: When the dress is marked down by 20%, the cost of the dress is 80% of its original price; thus, the reduced price of the dress can be written as $\frac{80}{100}x$, or $\frac{4}{5}x$, where x is the original price. When discounted an extra 25%, the dress costs 75% of the reduced price, or $\frac{75}{100}\left(\frac{4}{5}x\right)$, or $\frac{3}{4}\left(\frac{4}{5}x\right)$, which simplifies to $\frac{3}{5}x$. So the final price of the dress is three-fifths of the original price.

59. B: The first wall has an area of 10 x 18 = 180 square feet. Two men working for 8 hours is equivalent to 16 man-hours of work. Thus, each man paints $\frac{180}{16} = \frac{90}{8}$ square foot per hour. The new wall is 27 x 10 = 270 square feet. It will require $\frac{270}{\frac{90}{8}} = 270\frac{8}{90} = 24$ man-hours to paint. Since there are three men, each is responsible for $\frac{24}{3} = 8$ man-hours.

60. D: If x is the cost of the pen, then, $2x$ is the cost of the book and $4x$ is the cost of the calculator. Vivian has spent x + 2x + 4x, or 7x. She started with $50 and had $15 left, so 50 – $7x$ = 15. Solving for x, $x = \frac{35}{7} = 5$, and the cost of the calculator was $4x$ = $20.

61. B: If x represents the width of the box, its length is equal to $2x$. Since the sides of a square are equal, $2x - 3 = x + 3$, and x = 6. So the box is 6 inches wide.

62. C: For each die there is 1 in 6 chance that a 6 will be on top. The reason is that the die has 6 sides. The probability that a 6 will show for each die is not affected by the results from another roll of the die. In other words, these probabilities are independent. So, the overall probability of throwing 3 sixes is the product of the individual probabilities: $P = \frac{1}{6} \times \frac{1}{6} \times \frac{1}{6} = \frac{1}{6^3} = \frac{1}{216}$

63. C: At 10%, Richard is paid $\$140 \times 10\% = \frac{10(140)}{100} = \$14$ for every phone he sells. To make $840, he must sell $\frac{840}{14} = 60$ phones.

64. C: In scientific notation, the negative exponent means that the decimal point must be moved to the left. Therefore, $2 \times 10^{-2} = 0.02$. The positive exponent moves the decimal point to the right. Therefore $5 \times 10^3 = 5{,}000$. Sine $0.02 \times 5{,}000 = 100$, C is correct.

Language

Usage, Punctuation, and Grammar

1. C: The longest word recorded in an English dictionary are "Pneumonoultramicroscopicsilicovolcanokoniosis."

   Error: *Subject-verb disagreement*

   The subject of this sentence is the singular noun "word," so the plural verb "are" disagrees with the subject. The verb used here should be the singular "is."

2. B: The largest catfish ever catch is 646 pounds, the size of an adult brown bear.

   Error: *Incorrect verb tense*

   The verb "catch" is not in the appropriate tense. It should be written in the past tense, "caught."

3. C: Though a highly influentially anthropologist, Claude Levi-Strauss often took criticism for spending little time in the field studying real cultures.

   Error: *Adverb / adjective error*

   The adverb "influentially" is being used to modify the noun "anthropologist." Since adverbs cannot modify nouns, "influentially" should be written in adjective form: "influential."

4. C: It is easy to get confused when calculating time differences between time zones a useful way to remember them is that the Atlantic Ocean starts with A, as in A.M., and the Pacific Ocean starts with P, as in P.M.

   Error: *Run-on sentence*

   Choice C contains two complete thoughts, each with its own subject and predicate. The second complete thought begins, "a useful way to remember them...." A sentence composed of two complete thoughts joined together without appropriate punctuation is called a "run-on." A period or semicolon should appear between the phrases "time zones" and "a useful way."

5. C: The surrealists were a group of artists who believed that art should reflect the subconscious mind, their images are often very dreamlike, showing businessmen falling like rain over a city and melting clocks.

   Error: *Comma splice*

   There are two complete sentences here joined by only a comma. A period or semicolon should replace the comma after "mind."

6. B: "Orange is my favorite color, but not my favorite fruit." said Lisa.

   Error: *Punctuation*

   The period that appears at the end of the quote should be a comma.

7. B: The deepest canyon, too.

   Error: *Fragment*

   This phrase contains a subject, but it does not contain a predicate, which makes it a sentence fragment.

8. A: Pocahontas spent the last year's of her young life in England under the name Rebecca.

   Error: *Apostrophe*

   The apostrophe in the word "year's" is unnecessary. The sentence should read, "Pocahontas spent the last years...."

9. A: The Pima Indians of Arizona have remarkably high rates of diabetes and obesity some scientists believe the gene that causes this present-day health crisis was actually of great value to the Pima's ancestors who had to be able to retain glucose during periods of famine.

Error: *Run-on sentence*

A sentence composed of two complete thoughts joined together without appropriate punctuation is called a "run-on." A period or semicolon should appear between "obesity" and "some scientists."

10. C: Director Alfred Hitchcock make over 60 films in his career.

Error: *Subject-verb disagreement*

The subject "Alfred Hitchcock" is a singular subject, which requires a singular verb. "Make" should be "makes."

11. D: No error.

12. A: The earliest recording of a human voice was made by Thomas Edison in 1877, when they recorded himself reciting "Mary Had a Little Lamb."

Error: *Pronoun-antecedent agreement*

Thomas Edison is singular, so the plural pronoun "they" is incorrect. It should read "he."

13. B: Our basement floods once a yearly.

Error: *Adjective/adverb*

Here the adverb "yearly" is incorrectly used. It should be replaced with the noun "year."

14. D: No error.

15. B: The spread of Islam began around 600 AD and reached from the Middle East to North Africa, Spain, Central Asia, and India?

Error: *Punctuation*

Since this is a declarative sentence and not a question, the question mark should be a period.

16. C: The names of the days of the week originate in either Latin or Saxon names for deities, Sunday, for instance, is Saxon for "Sun's Day," while Thursday derives from "Thor's Day."

Error: *Comma Splice*

There are two complete sentences here joined by only a comma. A period or semicolon should replace the comma after "deities."

17. D: No error.

18. A: Ironically, the namesake of the Nobel Peace Prize, Alfred Nobel, are most noted for his invention of dynamite in the 1860s.

Error: *Subject-verb disagreement*

The subject of this sentence is the singular noun "namesake." The plural verb "are" is incorrect. It should be replaced with the singular verb "is."

19. A: Loud sounds can causing damage to the hair cells that turn sound waves into electrical signals, which the brain perceives as sound.

Error: *Verb tense*

The verb "causing" is the progressive tense, which is the incorrect tense for this sentence. The sentence should read, "Loud sounds can cause...."

20. C: Carbon monoxide Poisoning can cause disorientation and delirium, and it can induce a coma.
Error: *Capitalization*
The word "poisoning" does not need to be capitalized because it is not a proper noun.

21. D: No error.

22. A: They closed the parking deck at midnight, so we could not get no cars out until morning.
Error: *Double negative*
The phrase "could not get no" is an example of a double negative. The phrase should read, "could not get any ...."

23. A: Joni designed the grocery stores sign, but Evan painted it.
Error: *Apostrophe*
Since the sign belongs to the grocery store, an apostrophe should be used to indicate possession. The sentence should read, "...the grocery store's sign...."

24. D: No error.

25. C: Twenty-four leaders of the Nazi party was brought to trial at the end of World War II in what became known as the Nuremberg Trials.
Error: *Subject-verb disagreement*
The subject of this sentence is the plural noun "leaders," which requires a plural verb. "Was" is a singular verb. The sentence should use the plural verb "*were*."

26. C: Water is called "hard water" if it do not quickly create lather upon contact with soap because of mineral compounds dissolved in the water.
Error: *Subject-verb disagreement*
The pronoun "it" is singular, and the verb "do" is plural. The sentence should read, "if it does not quickly create...."

27. B: Ice crystals in the atmosphere, which can create a halo around the sun or moon.
Error: *Sentence fragment*
This sentence contains a subject, but it does not contain a predicate, which makes it a fragment. *Rule of thumb*: Watch out for words such as "which" or "that" in a sentence because the verb that comes afterward *oftentimes does not function* as the main verb of the sentence. One way to correct this sentence would be to delete the comma and the word "which." "Ice crystals in the atmosphere can create a halo around the sun or moon" is a complete thought because it contains a subject, "Ice crystals," and a main verb, "can create."

28. B: Atomic clocks keep time by measuring the vibrations of Atoms and molecules.
Error: *Capitalization*
The word "Atoms" should not be capitalized because it is not a proper noun.

29. A: Heat was once believes to be a type of fluid called "caloric," which flowed into objects and raised their temperature.
Error: *Verb tense*
The verb phrase "was once believes" uses two different tenses: past and present. It should read, "Heat was once *believed*...."

30. B: Apart from a sine wave created by an electronic device, most sounds are not "pure" because they contain many different vibrations at different frequencies pure tones vibrate at only one frequency.

Error: *Run-on sentence*

This sentence contains two complete thoughts without punctuation separating them. The second one begins with the words "pure tones vibrate...." A period or semicolon should be inserted before these words.

31. A: Arthur, realizing that bugs were turning the roots of his zucchini plants to mush.

Error: *Sentence fragment*

These words form an incomplete thought; it does not contain a subject and verb. *Rule of thumb*: Watch out for verbs ending in –ing. These verbs *cannot* be the main verb of a sentence *on their own*. They need another verb (called a "helping verb"), such as "was." The following sentence is a complete thought because the –ing verb is not alone: "Arthur *was realizing* that bugs were turning the roots of his zucchini plants to mush."

32. D: No error.

33. D: No error.

34. A: The narwhal is a member of the dolphin family, easily recognized by its long, spiraling tusk, it is often compared to the mythical unicorn.

Error: *Comma splice*

There are two complete thoughts here, joined together with a comma. The second complete thought begins with the words "it is often...." To correct this sentence, replace the comma after "tusk" with a period or semicolon.

35. C: The first Ferris' Wheel was built in Chicago, Illinois.

Error: *Apostrophe*

The apostrophe at the end of "Ferris" is incorrect because it is not a possessive noun.

36. A: Trees in the Olympic rain forest in northwest Washington State is covered with a thick green moss that is nourished by the 150 annual inches of rainfall.

Error: *Subject-verb agreement*

The subject of the sentence is "trees," which is a plural form; the verb "is" does not agree with the subject because it is singular. The main verb in this sentence should be "are." *Rule of thumb:* Watch out for sentences that have a lot of words between the subject and verb. Often, these sentences contain subject-verb verb errors.

37. D: No error.

38. C: I was, hoping to avoid the customs official who was yelling at all of the other travelers.

Error: *Comma*

The comma between "was" and "hoping" is incorrect. A single comma should not come between a helping verb and an –ing verb.

39. A: Reykjavik is the Capitol of Iceland.
Error: Capitalization
The word "Capitol" does not need to be capitalized because it is not a proper noun.

40. D: No error.

Spelling

41. D: No error.

42. C: "Graitful" should be spelled "grateful."

43. C: "Sower" should be spelled "sour."

44. B: "Sinator" should be spelled "senator."

45. A: "Groshery" should be spelled "grocery."

46. A: Though "nite" has become a common informal spelling, the formal spelling of the word is "night."

47. C: "Alway" should be spelled "always."

48. C: "Spays" should be spelled "space."

49. D: No error.

50. D: No error.

Composition

51. A: The sentence, "Many people have proposed explanations for this drop," provides an introduction to the short explanations that follow. It should come after the first sentence.

52. B: The third sentence of this passage refers to "these insecticides," but there is no earlier reference to any insecticides in the paragraph. The sentence, "Insects that carry the disease can develop resistance to the chemicals, or insecticides, that are used to kill the mosquitoes," needs to be placed after sentence 2 for sentence 3 to make sense.

53. B: Since the second part of this sentence goes on to list examples that help support the point made in the first sentence, "for instance" is the best transitional phrase.

54. C: The second part of the sentence adds additional evidence to prove the claim made in the first part. "In fact" is the best transition to introduce supporting evidence.

55. A: The second part of the sentence contrasts with the first. "However" is the most appropriate transition to use to help create that sense of contrast.

56. A: All of the sentences except sentence A contain errors. Sentences B and C contain verb errors; sentence D is a run-on sentence.

57. B: All of the sentences except sentence B contain verb errors.

58. A: Sentence A contains no errors. Sentence B is less clear than sentence A because it is awkwardly written in the passive voice. Sentence C contains a subject-verb agreement error. Sentence C switches pronouns from "We" to "I" in mid-sentence.

59. C: Sentence 4, regarding Jefferson's affair with one of his slaves, is not directly relevant to the main topic at hand, which is Jefferson's debts.

60. B: Sentence 2, regarding Feynman's musicianship, is of little relevance to the discussion of the atomic theory.

Secret Key #1 – Time is Your Greatest Enemy

To succeed on the HSPT, you must use your time wisely. Most students do not finish at least one section. The time limits are presented in the table below:

As you can see, the time constraints are brutal. To succeed, you must ration your time properly.

SECTION	Total amount of time allotted	Number of questions	Time to answer each question
Verbal Skills	16 min	60	.27 min
Quantitative	30 min	52	.58 min
Reading Comprehension	25 min	62	.40 min
Mathematics	45 min	64	.70 min
Language	25 min	60	.42 min

The reason that time is so critical is that every question counts the same toward your final score. If you run out of time on any section, the questions that you do not answer will hurt your score far more than earlier questions that you spent extra time on and feel certain are correct.

Success Strategy #1

Pace Yourself

Wear a watch to the HSPT Test. At the beginning of the test, check the time (or start a chronometer on your watch to count the minutes), and check the time after each passage or every few questions to make sure you are "on schedule."

If you find that you are falling behind time during the test, you must speed up. Even though a rushed answer is more likely to be incorrect, it is better to miss a couple of questions by being rushed, than to completely miss later questions by not having enough time. It is better to end with more time than you need than to run out of time.

If you are forced to speed up, do it efficiently. Usually one or more answer choices can be eliminated without too much difficulty. Above all, don't panic. Don't speed up and just begin guessing at random choices. By pacing yourself, and continually monitoring your progress against your watch, you will always know exactly how far ahead or behind you are with your available time. If you find that you are a few minutes behind on a section, don't skip questions without spending any time on it, just to catch back up. Begin spending a little less time per question and after a few questions, you will have caught back up more gradually. Once you catch back up, you can continue working each problem at your normal pace. If you have time at the end, go back then and finish the questions that you left behind.

Furthermore, don't dwell on the problems that you were rushed on. If a problem was taking up too much time and you made a hurried guess, it must have been difficult. The difficult questions are the ones you are most likely to miss anyway, so it isn't a big loss. If you have time left over, as you review the skipped questions, start at the earliest skipped question, spend at most another minute, and then move on to the next skipped question.

Always mark skipped questions in your workbook, NOT on the Scantron. Last minute guessing will be covered in the next chapter.

Lastly, sometimes it is beneficial to slow down if you are constantly getting ahead of time. You are always more likely to catch a careless mistake by working more slowly than quickly, and among very high-scoring students (those who are likely to have lots of time left over), careless errors affect the score more than mastery of material.

Estimation

For some math questions, estimate. Calculation takes time, and you should avoid it whenever possible. You can usually eliminate three obviously wrong choices quite easily. For example, suppose a graph shows that an object has traveled 48 meters in 11 seconds, and you are asked to find its speed. You are given these choices:

a. 250 m/s
b. 42 m/s
c. 4.4 m/s
d. 1.2 m/s

You know that 48 divided by 11 will be a little over 4, so you can pick out C as the answer without ever doing the calculation.

Scanning

Don't waste time reading, enjoying, and completely understanding passages. Simply scan the passage to get a rough idea of what it is about. You will return to the passage for each question, so there is no need to memorize it. Only spend as much time scanning as is necessary to get a vague impression of its overall subject content.

Secret Key #2 – Guessing is not Guesswork

Most students do not understand the impact that proper guessing can have on their score. Unless you score extremely high, guessing will contribute a significant amount of points to your score.

Monkeys Take the HSPT

What most students don't realize is that to insure that random 25% chance, you have to guess randomly. If you put 20 monkeys in a room to take the HSPT, assuming they answered once per question and behaved themselves, on average they would get 25% of the questions correct. Put 20 students in the room, and the average will be much lower among guessed questions. Why?

1. HSPT intentionally writes deceptive answer choices that "look" right. A student has no idea about a question, so picks the "best looking" answer, which is often wrong. The monkey has no idea what looks good and what doesn't, so will consistently be lucky about 25% of the time.
2. Students will eliminate answer choices from the guessing pool based on a hunch or intuition. Simple but correct answers often get excluded, leaving a 0% chance of being correct. The monkey has no clue, and often gets lucky with the best choice.

This is why the process of elimination endorsed by most test courses is flawed and detrimental to your performance- students don't guess, they make an ignorant stab in the dark that is usually worse than random.

Success Strategy #2

Let me introduce one of the most valuable ideas of this course- the $5 challenge:

You only mark your "best guess" if you are willing to bet $5 on it.
You only eliminate choices from guessing if you are willing to bet $5 on it.

Why $5? Five dollars is an amount of money that is small yet not insignificant, and can really add up fast (20 questions could cost you $100). Likewise, each answer choice on one question of the HSPT will have a small impact on your overall score, but it can really add up to a lot of points in the end.

The process of elimination IS valuable. The following shows your chance of guessing it right:

If you eliminate this many choices:	0	1	2	3	4
Chance of getting it correct (4 choice)	25%	33%	50%	100%	N/A
Chance of getting it correct (5 choice)	20%	25%	33%	50%	100%

However, if you accidentally eliminate the right answer or go on a hunch for an incorrect answer, your chances drop dramatically: to 0%. By guessing among all the answer choices, you are GUARANTEED to have a shot at the right answer.

That's why the $5 test is so valuable- if you give up the advantage and safety of a pure guess, it had better be worth the risk.

What we still haven't covered is how to be sure that whatever guess you make is truly random. Here's the easiest way:

Always pick the first answer choice among those remaining.

Such a technique means that you have decided, **before you see a single test question**, exactly how you are going to guess- and since the order of choices tells you nothing about which one is correct, this guessing technique is perfectly random.

Let's try an example.

A student encounters the following problem on the Mathematics test:

What is the cosine of an angle in a right triangle that is 3 meters on the adjacent side, 5 meters on the hypotenuse, and 4 meters on the opposite side?

a. 1
b. 0.6
c. 0.8
d. 1.25

The student has a small idea about this question- he is pretty sure that cosine is opposite over hypotenuse, but he wouldn't bet $5 on it. He knows that cosine is "something" over hypotenuse, and since the hypotenuse is the largest number, he is willing to bet $5 on both choices A and D not being correct. So he is down to B and C. At this point, he guesses B, since B is the first choice remaining.

The student is correct by choosing B, since cosine is adjacent over hypotenuse. He only eliminated those choices he was willing to bet money on, AND he did not let his stale memories (often things not known definitely will get mixed up in the exact opposite arrangement in one's head) about the formula for cosine influence his guess. He blindly chose the first remaining choice, and was rewarded with the fruits of a random guess.

This section is not meant to scare you away from making educated guesses or eliminating choices- you just need to define when a choice is worth eliminating. The $5 test, along with a pre-defined random guessing strategy, is the best way to make sure you reap all of the benefits of guessing.

Specific Guessing Techniques

<u>Similar Answer Choices</u>
When you have two answer choices that are direct opposites, one of them is usually the correct answer.
Example:

a. forward
b. backward

These two answer choices are very similar and fall into the same family of answer choices. A family of answer choices is when two or three answer choices are very similar. Often two will be opposites and one may show an equality.
Example:

a. excited
b. overjoyed
c. thrilled
d. upset

Note how the first three choices are all related. They all ask describe a state of happiness. However, choice D is not in the same family of questions. Being upset is the direct opposite of happiness.

Summary

1. Eliminate as many choices as you can by using the $5 test. Use the common guessing strategies to help in the elimination process, but only eliminate choices that pass the $5 test.
2. Among the remaining choices, only pick your "best guess" if it passes the $5 test.
3. Otherwise, guess randomly by picking the first remaining choice that was not eliminated.

Secret Key #3 – Practice Smarter, Not Harder

Many students delay the test preparation process because they dread the awful amounts of practice time they think necessary to succeed on the test. We have refined an effective method that will take you only a fraction of the time.

There are a number of "obstacles" in your way on the HSPT. Among these are answering questions, finishing in time, and mastering test-taking strategies. All must be executed on the day of the test at peak performance, or your score will suffer. The HSPT is a mental marathon that has a large impact on your future.

Just like a marathon runner, it is important to work your way up to the full challenge. So first you just worry about questions, and then time, and finally strategy:

Success Strategy #3

1. Find a good source for HSPT practice tests.
2. If you are willing to make a larger time investment, consider using more than one study guide- often the different approaches of multiple authors will help you "get" difficult concepts.
3. Take a practice test with no time constraints, with all study helps "open book." Take your time with questions and focus on applying the strategies.
4. Take another test, this time with time constraints, with all study helps "open book."
5. Take a final practice test with no open material and time limits.

If you have time to take more practice tests, just repeat step 5. By gradually exposing yourself to the full rigors of the test environment, you will condition your mind to the stress of test day and maximize your success.

Secret Key #4 – Prepare, Don't Procrastinate

Let me state an obvious fact: if you take the HSPT three times, you will get three different scores. This is due to the way you feel on test day, the level of preparedness you have, and, despite HSPT's claims to the contrary, some tests WILL be easier for you than others.

Since your acceptance will largely depend on your score, you should maximize your chances of success. In order to maximize the likelihood of success, you've got to prepare in advance. This means taking practice tests and spending time learning the information and test taking strategies you will need to succeed.

Since you have to pay a registration fee each time you take the HSPT, don't take it as a "practice" test. Feel free to take sample tests on your own, but when you go to take the HSPT, be prepared, be focused, and do your best the first time!

Secret Key #5 – Test Yourself

Everyone knows that time is money. There is no need to spend too much of your time or too little of your time preparing for the HSPT. You should only spend as much of your precious time preparing as is necessary for you to pass it.

Success Strategy #5

Once you have taken a practice test under real conditions of time constraints, then you will know if you are ready for the test or not.

If you have scored extremely high the first time that you take the practice test, then there is not much point in spending countless hours studying. You are already there.

Benchmark your abilities by retaking practice tests and seeing how much you have improved. Once you score high enough to get accepted into the school of your choice, then you are ready.

If you have scored well below where you need, then knuckle down and begin studying in earnest. Check your improvement regularly through the use of practice tests under real conditions. Above all, don't worry, panic, or give up. The key is perseverance!

Then, when you go to take the HSPT, remain confident and remember how well you did on the practice tests. If you can score a passing score on a practice test, then you can do the same on the real thing.

General Strategies

The most important thing you can do is to ignore your fears and jump into the test immediately- do not be overwhelmed by any strange-sounding terms. You have to jump into the test like jumping into a pool- all at once is the easiest way.

Make Predictions
As you read and understand the question, try to guess what the answer will be. Remember that several of the answer choices are wrong, and once you begin reading them, your mind will immediately become cluttered with answer choices designed to throw you off. Your mind is typically the most focused immediately after you have read the question and digested its contents. If you can, try to predict what the correct answer will be. You may be surprised at what you can predict.

Quickly scan the choices and see if your prediction is in the listed answer choices. If it is, then you can be quite confident that you have the right answer. It still won't hurt to check the other answer choices, but most of the time, you've got it!

Answer the Question
It may seem obvious to only pick answer choices that answer the question, but the test writers can create some excellent answer choices that are wrong. Don't pick an answer just because it sounds right, or you believe it to be true. It MUST answer the question. Once you've made your selection, always go back and check it against the question and make sure that you didn't misread the question, and the answer choice does answer the question posed.

Benchmark
After you read the first answer choice, decide if you think it sounds correct or not. If it doesn't, move on to the next answer choice. If it does, mentally mark that answer choice. This doesn't mean that you've definitely selected it as your answer choice, it just means that it's the best you've seen thus far. Go ahead and read the next choice. If the next choice is worse than the one you've already selected, keep going to the next answer choice. If the next choice is better than the choice you've already selected, mentally mark the new answer choice as your best guess.

The first answer choice that you select becomes your standard. Every other answer choice must be benchmarked against that standard. That choice is correct until proven otherwise by another answer choice beating it out. Once you've decided that no other answer choice seems as good, do one final check to ensure that your answer choice answers the question posed.

Valid Information
Don't discount any of the information provided in the question. Every piece of information may be necessary to determine the correct answer. None of the information in the question is there to throw you off (while the answer choices will certainly have information to throw you off). If two seemingly unrelated topics are discussed, don't ignore either. You can be confident there is a relationship, or it wouldn't be included in the question, and you are probably going to have to determine what is that relationship to find the answer.

Avoid "Fact Traps"

Don't get distracted by a choice that is factually true. Your search is for the answer that answers the question. Stay focused and don't fall for an answer that is true but incorrect. Always go back to the question and make sure you're choosing an answer that actually answers the question and is not just a true statement. An answer can be factually correct, but it MUST answer the question asked. Additionally, two answers can both be seemingly correct, so be sure to read all of the answer choices, and make sure that you get the one that BEST answers the question.

Milk the Question

Some of the questions may throw you completely off. They might deal with a subject you have not been exposed to, or one that you haven't reviewed in years. While your lack of knowledge about the subject will be a hindrance, the question itself can give you many clues that will help you find the correct answer. Read the question carefully and look for clues. Watch particularly for adjectives and nouns describing difficult terms or words that you don't recognize. Regardless of if you completely understand a word or not, replacing it with a synonym either provided or one you more familiar with may help you to understand what the questions are asking. Rather than wracking your mind about specific detailed information concerning a difficult term or word, try to use mental substitutes that are easier to understand.

The Trap of Familiarity

Don't just choose a word because you recognize it. On difficult questions, you may not recognize a number of words in the answer choices. The test writers don't put "make-believe" words on the test; so don't think that just because you only recognize all the words in one answer choice means that answer choice must be correct. If you only recognize words in one answer choice, then focus on that one. Is it correct? Try your best to determine if it is correct. If it is, that is great, but if it doesn't, eliminate it. Each word and answer choice you eliminate increases your chances of getting the question correct, even if you then have to guess among the unfamiliar choices.

Eliminate Answers

Eliminate choices as soon as you realize they are wrong. But be careful! Make sure you consider all of the possible answer choices. Just because one appears right, doesn't mean that the next one won't be even better! The test writers will usually put more than one good answer choice for every question, so read all of them. Don't worry if you are stuck between two that seem right. By getting down to just two remaining possible choices, your odds are now 50/50. Rather than wasting too much time, play the odds. You are guessing, but guessing wisely, because you've been able to knock out some of the answer choices that you know are wrong. If you are eliminating choices and realize that the last answer choice you are left with is also obviously wrong, don't panic. Start over and consider each choice again. There may easily be something that you missed the first time and will realize on the second pass.

Tough Questions

If you are stumped on a problem or it appears too hard or too difficult, don't waste time. Move on! Remember though, if you can quickly check for obviously incorrect answer choices, your chances of guessing correctly are greatly improved. Before you completely give up, at least try to knock out a couple of possible answers. Eliminate what you can and then guess at the remaining answer choices before moving on.

Brainstorm

If you get stuck on a difficult question, spend a few seconds quickly brainstorming. Run through the complete list of possible answer choices. Look at each choice and ask yourself, "Could this answer the question satisfactorily?" Go through each answer choice and consider it independently of the other. By systematically going through all possibilities, you may find something that you would otherwise overlook. Remember that when you get stuck, it's important to try to keep moving.

Read Carefully

Understand the problem. Read the question and answer choices carefully. Don't miss the question because you misread the terms. You have plenty of time to read each question thoroughly and make sure you understand what is being asked. Yet a happy medium must be attained, so don't waste too much time. You must read carefully, but efficiently.

Face Value

When in doubt, use common sense. Always accept the situation in the problem at face value. Don't read too much into it. These problems will not require you to make huge leaps of logic. The test writers aren't trying to throw you off with a cheap trick. If you have to go beyond creativity and make a leap of logic in order to have an answer choice answer the question, then you should look at the other answer choices. Don't overcomplicate the problem by creating theoretical relationships or explanations that will warp time or space. These are normal problems rooted in reality. It's just that the applicable relationship or explanation may not be readily apparent and you have to figure things out. Use your common sense to interpret anything that isn't clear.

Prefixes

If you're having trouble with a word in the question or answer choices, try dissecting it. Take advantage of every clue that the word might include. Prefixes and suffixes can be a huge help. Usually they allow you to determine a basic meaning. Pre- means before, post- means after, pro - is positive, de- is negative. From these prefixes and suffixes, you can get an idea of the general meaning of the word and try to put it into context. Beware though of any traps. Just because con is the opposite of pro, doesn't necessarily mean congress is the opposite of progress!

Hedge Phrases

Watch out for critical "hedge" phrases, such as likely, may, can, will often, sometimes, often, almost, mostly, usually, generally, rarely, sometimes. Question writers insert these hedge phrases to cover every possibility. Often an answer choice will be wrong simply because it leaves no room for exception. Avoid answer choices that have definitive words like "exactly," and "always".

Switchback Words

Stay alert for "switchbacks". These are the words and phrases frequently used to alert you to shifts in thought. The most common switchback word is "but". Others include although, however, nevertheless, on the other hand, even though, while, in spite of, despite, regardless of.

New Information

Correct answer choices will rarely have completely new information included. Answer choices typically are straightforward reflections of the material asked about and will directly relate to the question. If a new piece of information is included in an answer choice that doesn't even seem to relate to the topic being asked about, then that answer choice is likely incorrect. All of the information needed to answer the question is usually provided for you, and so you should not have to make guesses that are unsupported or choose answer choices that require unknown information that cannot be reasoned on its own.

Time Management
On technical questions, don't get lost on the technical terms. Don't spend too much time on any one question. If you don't know what a term means, then since you don't have a dictionary, odds are you aren't going to get much further. You should immediately recognize terms as whether or not you know them. If you don't, work with the other clues that you have, the other answer choices and terms provided, but don't waste too much time trying to figure out a difficult term.

Contextual Clues
Look for contextual clues. An answer can be right but not correct. The contextual clues will help you find the answer that is most right and is correct. Understand the context in which a phrase or statement is made. This will help you make important distinctions.

Don't Panic
Panicking will not answer any questions for you. Therefore, it isn't helpful. When you first see the question, if your mind goes blank, take a deep breath. Force yourself to mechanically go through the steps of solving the problem and using the strategies you've learned.

Pace Yourself
Don't get clock fever. It's easy to be overwhelmed when you're looking at a page full of questions, your mind is full of random thoughts and feeling confused, and the clock is ticking down faster than you would like. Calm down and maintain the pace that you have set for yourself. As long as you are on track by monitoring your pace, you are guaranteed to have enough time for yourself. When you get to the last few minutes of the test, it may seem like you won't have enough time left, but if you only have as many questions as you should have left at that point, then you're right on track!

Answer Selection
The best way to pick an answer choice is to eliminate all of those that are wrong, until only one is left and confirm that is the correct answer. Sometimes though, an answer choice may immediately look right. Be careful! Take a second to make sure that the other choices are not equally obvious. Don't make a hasty mistake. There are only two times that you should stop before checking other answers. First is when you are positive that the answer choice you have selected is correct. Second is when time is almost out and you have to make a quick guess!

Check Your Work
Since you will probably not know every term listed and the answer to every question, it is important that you get credit for the ones that you do know. Don't miss any questions through careless mistakes. If at all possible, try to take a second to look back over your answer selection and make sure you've selected the correct answer choice and haven't made a costly careless mistake (such as marking an answer choice that you didn't mean to mark). This quick double check should more than pay for itself in caught mistakes for the time it costs.

Beware of Directly Quoted Answers
Sometimes an answer choice will repeat word for word a portion of the question or reference section. However, beware of such exact duplication – it may be a trap! More than likely, the correct choice will paraphrase or summarize a point, rather than being exactly the same wording.

Slang
Scientific sounding answers are better than slang ones. An answer choice that begins "To compare the outcomes…" is much more likely to be correct than one that begins "Because some people insisted…"

Extreme Statements
Avoid wild answers that throw out highly controversial ideas that are proclaimed as established fact. An answer choice that states the "process should be used in certain situations, if..." is much more likely to be correct than one that states the "process should be discontinued completely." The first is a calm rational statement and doesn't even make a definitive, uncompromising stance, using a hedge word "if" to provide wiggle room, whereas the second choice is a radical idea and far more extreme.

Answer Choice Families
When you have two or more answer choices that are direct opposites or parallels, one of them is usually the correct answer. For instance, if one answer choice states "x increases" and another answer choice states "x decreases" or "y increases," then those two or three answer choices are very similar in construction and fall into the same family of answer choices. A family of answer choices is when two or three answer choices are very similar in construction, and yet often have a directly opposite meaning. Usually the correct answer choice will be in that family of answer choices. The "odd man out" or answer choice that doesn't seem to fit the parallel construction of the other answer choices is more likely to be incorrect.

Special Report: How to Overcome Test Anxiety

The very nature of tests caters to some level of anxiety, nervousness or tension, just as we feel for any important event that occurs in our lives. A little bit of anxiety or nervousness can be a good thing. It helps us with motivation, and makes achievement just that much sweeter. However, too much anxiety can be a problem; especially if it hinders our ability to function and perform.

"Test anxiety," is the term that refers to the emotional reactions that some test-takers experience when faced with a test or exam. Having a fear of testing and exams is based upon a rational fear, since the test-taker's performance can shape the course of an academic career. Nevertheless, experiencing excessive fear of examinations will only interfere with the test-takers ability to perform, and his/her chances to be successful.

There are a large variety of causes that can contribute to the development and sensation of test anxiety. These include, but are not limited to lack of performance and worrying about issues surrounding the test.

Lack of Preparation

Lack of preparation can be identified by the following behaviors or situations:

- Not scheduling enough time to study, and therefore cramming the night before the test or exam
- Managing time poorly, to create the sensation that there is not enough time to do everything
- Failing to organize the text information in advance, so that the study material consists of the entire text and not simply the pertinent information
- Poor overall studying habits

Worrying, on the other hand, can be related to both the test taker, or many other factors around him/her that will be affected by the results of the test. These include worrying about:

- Previous performances on similar exams, or exams in general
- How friends and other students are achieving
- The negative consequences that will result from a poor grade or failure

There are three primary elements to test anxiety. Physical components, which involve the same typical bodily reactions as those to acute anxiety (to be discussed below). Emotional factors have to do with fear or panic. Mental or cognitive issues concerning attention spans and memory abilities.

Physical Signals

There are many different symptoms of test anxiety, and these are not limited to mental and emotional strain. Frequently there are a range of physical signals that will let a test taker know that he/she is suffering from test anxiety. These bodily changes can include the following:

- Perspiring
- Sweaty palms
- Wet, trembling hands
- Nausea
- Dry mouth
- A knot in the stomach
- Headache
- Faintness
- Muscle tension
- Aching shoulders, back and neck
- Rapid heart beat
- Feeling too hot/cold

To recognize the sensation of test anxiety, a test-taker should monitor him/herself for the following sensations:

- The physical distress symptoms as listed above
- Emotional sensitivity, expressing emotional feelings such as the need to cry or laugh too much, or a sensation of anger or helplessness
- A decreased ability to think, causing the test-taker to blank out or have racing thoughts that are hard to organize or control.

Though most students will feel some level of anxiety when faced with a test or exam, the majority can cope with that anxiety and maintain it at a manageable level. However, those who cannot are faced with a very real and very serious condition, which can and should be controlled for the immeasurable benefit of this sufferer. Naturally, these sensations lead to negative results for the testing experience. The most common effects of test anxiety have to do with nervousness and mental blocking.

Nervousness

Nervousness can appear in several different levels:

- The test-taker's difficulty, or even inability to read and understand the questions on the test
- The difficulty or inability to organize thoughts to a coherent form
- The difficulty or inability to recall key words and concepts relating to the testing questions (especially essays)
- The receipt of poor grades on a test, though the test material was well known by the test taker

Conversely, a person may also experience mental blocking, which involves:

- Blanking out on test questions
- Only remembering the correct answers to the questions when the test has already finished.
- Fortunately for test anxiety sufferers, beating these feelings, to a large degree, has to do with proper preparation. When a test taker has a feeling of preparedness, then anxiety will be dramatically lessened.

The first step to resolving anxiety issues is to distinguish which of the two types of anxiety are being suffered. If the anxiety is a direct result of a lack of preparation, this should be considered a normal reaction, and the anxiety level (as opposed to the test results) shouldn't be anything to worry about. However, if, when adequately prepared, the test-taker still panics, blanks out, or seems to overreact, this is not a fully rational reaction. While this can be considered normal too, there are many ways to combat and overcome these effects.

Remember that anxiety cannot be entirely eliminated, however, there are ways to minimize it, to make the anxiety easier to manage. Preparation is one of the best ways to minimize test anxiety. Therefore the following techniques are wise in order to best fight off any anxiety that may want to build.

To begin with, try to avoid cramming before a test, whenever it is possible. By trying to memorize an entire term's worth of information in one day, you'll be shocking your system, and not giving yourself a very good chance to absorb the information. This is an easy path to anxiety, so for those who suffer from test anxiety, cramming should not even be considered an option.

Instead of cramming, work throughout the semester to combine all of the material which is presented throughout the semester, and work on it gradually as the course goes by, making sure to master the main concepts first, leaving minor details for a week or so before the test.

To study for the upcoming exam, be sure to pose questions that may be on the examination, to gauge the ability to answer them by integrating the ideas from your texts, notes and lectures, as well as any supplementary readings.

If it is truly impossible to cover all of the information that was covered in that particular term, concentrate on the most important portions, that can be covered very well. Learn these concepts as best as possible, so that when the test comes, a goal can be made to use these concepts as presentations of your knowledge.

In addition to study habits, changes in attitude are critical to beating a struggle with test anxiety. In fact, an improvement of the perspective over the entire test-taking experience can actually help a test taker to enjoy studying and therefore improve the overall experience. Be certain not to overemphasize the significance of the grade - know that the result of the test is neither a reflection of self worth, nor is it a measure of intelligence; one grade will not predict a person's future success.

To improve an overall testing outlook, the following steps should be tried:

- Keeping in mind that the most reasonable expectation for taking a test is to expect to try to demonstrate as much of what you know as you possibly can.
- Reminding ourselves that a test is only one test; this is not the only one, and there will be others.

- The thought of thinking of oneself in an irrational, all-or-nothing term should be avoided at all costs.
- A reward should be designated for after the test, so there's something to look forward to. Whether it be going to a movie, going out to eat, or simply visiting friends, schedule it in advance, and do it no matter what result is expected on the exam.

Test-takers should also keep in mind that the basics are some of the most important things, even beyond anti-anxiety techniques and studying. Never neglect the basic social, emotional and biological needs, in order to try to absorb information. In order to best achieve, these three factors must be held as just as important as the studying itself.

Study Steps

Remember the following important steps for studying:

- Maintain healthy nutrition and exercise habits. Continue both your recreational activities and social pass times. These both contribute to your physical and emotional well being.
- Be certain to get a good amount of sleep, especially the night before the test, because when you're overtired you are not able to perform to the best of your best ability.
- Keep the studying pace to a moderate level by taking breaks when they are needed, and varying the work whenever possible, to keep the mind fresh instead of getting bored.
- When enough studying has been done that all the material that can be learned has been learned, and the test taker is prepared for the test, stop studying and do something relaxing such as listening to music, watching a movie, or taking a warm bubble bath.

There are also many other techniques to minimize the uneasiness or apprehension that is experienced along with test anxiety before, during, or even after the examination. In fact, there are a great deal of things that can be done to stop anxiety from interfering with lifestyle and performance. Again, remember that anxiety will not be eliminated entirely, and it shouldn't be. Otherwise that "up" feeling for exams would not exist, and most of us depend on that sensation to perform better than usual. However, this anxiety has to be at a level that is manageable.

Of course, as we have just discussed, being prepared for the exam is half the battle right away. Attending all classes, finding out what knowledge will be expected on the exam, and knowing the exam schedules are easy steps to lowering anxiety. Keeping up with work will remove the need to cram, and efficient study habits will eliminate wasted time. Studying should be done in an ideal location for concentration, so that it is simple to become interested in the material and give it complete attention. A method such as SQ3R (Survey, Question, Read, Recite, Review) is a wonderful key to follow to make sure that the study habits are as effective as possible, especially in the case of learning from a textbook. Flashcards are great techniques for memorization. Learning to take good notes will mean that notes will be full of useful information, so that less sifting will need to be done to seek out what is pertinent for studying. Reviewing notes after class and then again on occasion will keep the information fresh in the mind. From notes that have been taken summary sheets and outlines can be made for simpler reviewing.

A study group can also be a very motivational and helpful place to study, as there will be a sharing of ideas, all of the minds can work together, to make sure that everyone understands, and the studying will be made more interesting because it will be a social occasion.

Basically, though, as long as the test-taker remains organized and self confident, with efficient study habits, less time will need to be spent studying, and higher grades will be achieved.

To become self confident, there are many useful steps. The first of these is "self talk." It has been shown through extensive research, that self-talk for students who suffer from test anxiety, should be well monitored, in order to make sure that it contributes to self confidence as opposed to sinking the student. Frequently the self talk of test-anxious students is negative or self-defeating, thinking that everyone else is smarter and faster, that they always mess up, and that if they don't do well, they'll fail the entire course. It is important to decreasing anxiety that awareness is made of self talk. Try writing any negative self thoughts and then disputing them with a positive statement instead. Begin self-encouragement as though it was a friend speaking. Repeat positive statements to help reprogram the mind to believing in successes instead of failures.

Helpful Techniques

Other extremely helpful techniques include:

- Self-visualization of doing well and reaching goals
- While aiming for an "A" level of understanding, don't try to "overprotect" by setting your expectations lower. This will only convince the mind to stop studying in order to meet the lower expectations.
- Don't make comparisons with the results or habits of other students. These are individual factors, and different things work for different people, causing different results.
- Strive to become an expert in learning what works well, and what can be done in order to improve. Consider collecting this data in a journal.
- Create rewards for after studying instead of doing things before studying that will only turn into avoidance behaviors.
- Make a practice of relaxing - by using methods such as progressive relaxation, self-hypnosis, guided imagery, etc - in order to make relaxation an automatic sensation.
- Work on creating a state of relaxed concentration so that concentrating will take on the focus of the mind, so that none will be wasted on worrying.
- Take good care of the physical self by eating well and getting enough sleep.
- Plan in time for exercise and stick to this plan.

Beyond these techniques, there are other methods to be used before, during and after the test that will help the test-taker perform well in addition to overcoming anxiety.

Before the exam comes the academic preparation. This involves establishing a study schedule and beginning at least one week before the actual date of the test. By doing this, the anxiety of not having enough time to study for the test will be automatically eliminated. Moreover, this will make the studying a much more effective experience, ensuring that the learning will be an easier process. This relieves much undue pressure on the test-taker.

Summary sheets, note cards, and flash cards with the main concepts and examples of these main concepts should be prepared in advance of the actual studying time. A topic should never be eliminated from this process. By omitting a topic because it isn't expected to be on the test is only setting up the test-taker for anxiety should it actually appear on the exam. Utilize the course syllabus for laying out the topics that should be studied. Carefully go over the notes that were made in class, paying special attention to any of the issues that the professor took special care to emphasize while lecturing in class. In the textbooks, use the chapter review, or if possible, the chapter tests, to begin your review.

It may even be possible to ask the instructor what information will be covered on the exam, or what the format of the exam will be (for example, multiple choice, essay, free form, true-false). Additionally, see if it is possible to find out how many questions will be on the test. If a review sheet or sample test has been offered by the professor, make good use of it, above anything else, for the preparation for the test. Another great resource for getting to know the examination is reviewing tests from previous semesters. Use these tests to review, and aim to achieve a 100% score on each of the possible topics. With a few exceptions, the goal that you set for yourself is the highest one that you will reach.

Take all of the questions that were assigned as homework, and rework them to any other possible course material. The more problems reworked, the more skill and confidence will form as a result. When forming the solution to a problem, write out each of the steps. Don't simply do head work. By doing as many steps on paper as possible, much clarification and therefore confidence will be formed. Do this with as many homework problems as possible, before checking the answers. By checking the answer after each problem, a reinforcement will exist, that will not be on the exam. Study situations should be as exam-like as possible, to prime the test-taker's system for the experience. By waiting to check the answers at the end, a psychological advantage will be formed, to decrease the stress factor.

Another fantastic reason for not cramming is the avoidance of confusion in concepts, especially when it comes to mathematics. 8-10 hours of study will become one hundred percent more effective if it is spread out over a week or at least several days, instead of doing it all in one sitting. Recognize that the human brain requires time in order to assimilate new material, so frequent breaks and a span of study time over several days will be much more beneficial.

Additionally, don't study right up until the point of the exam. Studying should stop a minimum of one hour before the exam begins. This allows the brain to rest and put things in their proper order. This will also provide the time to become as relaxed as possible when going into the examination room. The test-taker will also have time to eat well and eat sensibly. Know that the brain needs food as much as the rest of the body. With enough food and enough sleep, as well as a relaxed attitude, the body and the mind are primed for success.

Avoid any anxious classmates who are talking about the exam. These students only spread anxiety, and are not worth sharing the anxious sentimentalities.

Before the test also involves creating a positive attitude, so mental preparation should also be a point of concentration. There are many keys to creating a positive attitude. Should fears become rushing in, make a visualization of taking the exam, doing well, and seeing an A written on the paper. Write out a list of affirmations that will bring a feeling of confidence, such as "I am doing well in my English class," "I studied well and know my material," "I enjoy this class." Even if the affirmations aren't believed at first, it sends a positive message to the subconscious which will result in an alteration of the overall belief system, which is the system that creates reality.

If a sensation of panic begins, work with the fear and imagine the very worst! Work through the entire scenario of not passing the test, failing the entire course, and dropping out of school, followed by not getting a job, and pushing a shopping cart through the dark alley where you'll live. This will place things into perspective! Then, practice deep breathing and create a visualization of the opposite situation - achieving an "A" on the exam, passing the entire course, receiving the degree at a graduation ceremony.

On the day of the test, there are many things to be done to ensure the best results, as well as the most calm outlook. The following stages are suggested in order to maximize test-taking potential:

- Begin the examination day with a moderate breakfast, and avoid any coffee or beverages with caffeine if the test taker is prone to jitters. Even people who are used to managing caffeine can feel jittery or light-headed when it is taken on a test day.
- Attempt to do something that is relaxing before the examination begins. As last minute cramming clouds the mastering of overall concepts, it is better to use this time to create a calming outlook.
- Be certain to arrive at the test location well in advance, in order to provide time to select a location that is away from doors, windows and other distractions, as well as giving enough time to relax before the test begins.
- Keep away from anxiety generating classmates who will upset the sensation of stability and relaxation that is being attempted before the exam.
- Should the waiting period before the exam begins cause anxiety, create a self-distraction by reading a light magazine or something else that is relaxing and simple.

During the exam itself, read the entire exam from beginning to end, and find out how much time should be allotted to each individual problem. Once writing the exam, should more time be taken for a problem, it should be abandoned, in order to begin another problem. If there is time at the end, the unfinished problem can always be returned to and completed.

Read the instructions very carefully - twice - so that unpleasant surprises won't follow during or after the exam has ended.

When writing the exam, pretend that the situation is actually simply the completion of homework within a library, or at home. This will assist in forming a relaxed atmosphere, and will allow the brain extra focus for the complex thinking function.

Begin the exam with all of the questions with which the most confidence is felt. This will build the confidence level regarding the entire exam and will begin a quality momentum. This will also create encouragement for trying the problems where uncertainty resides.

Going with the "gut instinct" is always the way to go when solving a problem. Second guessing should be avoided at all costs. Have confidence in the ability to do well.

For essay questions, create an outline in advance that will keep the mind organized and make certain that all of the points are remembered. For multiple choice, read every answer, even if the correct one has been spotted - a better one may exist.

Continue at a pace that is reasonable and not rushed, in order to be able to work carefully. Provide enough time to go over the answers at the end, to check for small errors that can be corrected.

Should a feeling of panic begin, breathe deeply, and think of the feeling of the body releasing sand through its pores. Visualize a calm, peaceful place, and include all of the sights, sounds and sensations of this image. Continue the deep breathing, and take a few minutes to continue this with closed eyes. When all is well again, return to the test.

If a "blanking" occurs for a certain question, skip it and move on to the next question. There will be time to return to the other question later. Get everything done that can be done, first, to guarantee all the grades that can be compiled, and to build all of the confidence possible. Then return to the weaker questions to build the marks from there.

Remember, one's own reality can be created, so as long as the belief is there, success will follow. And remember: anxiety can happen later, right now, there's an exam to be written!

After the examination is complete, whether there is a feeling for a good grade or a bad grade, don't dwell on the exam, and be certain to follow through on the reward that was promised...and enjoy it! Don't dwell on any mistakes that have been made, as there is nothing that can be done at this point anyway.

Additionally, don't begin to study for the next test right away. Do something relaxing for a while, and let the mind relax and prepare itself to begin absorbing information again.

From the results of the exam - both the grade and the entire experience, be certain to learn from what has gone on. Perfect studying habits and work some more on confidence in order to make the next examination experience even better than the last one.

Learn to avoid places where openings occurred for laziness, procrastination and day dreaming.

Use the time between this exam and the next one to better learn to relax, even learning to relax on cue, so that any anxiety can be controlled during the next exam. Learn how to relax the body. Slouch in your chair if that helps. Tighten and then relax all of the different muscle groups, one group at a time, beginning with the feet and then working all the way up to the neck and face. This will ultimately relax the muscles more than they were to begin with. Learn how to breathe deeply and comfortably, and focus on this breathing going in and out as a relaxing thought. With every exhale, repeat the word "relax."

As common as test anxiety is, it is very possible to overcome it. Make yourself one of the test-takers who overcome this frustrating hindrance.

Additional Bonus Material

Due to our efforts to try to keep this book to a manageable length, we've created a link that will give you access to all of your additional bonus material.

Please visit http://www.mometrix.com/bonus948/hspt to access the information.

CPSIA information can be obtained
at www.ICGtesting.com
Printed in the USA
LVOW06s1532021117
554758LV00006B/407/P

9 781609 718671